Great Crises of Capitalism

Great Crises of capitalism

PD Jonson
(A.K.A. Henry Thornton)

connorcourt
PUBLISHING

Published in 2011 by Connor Court Publishing Pty Ltd.

Copyright © P.D. Jonson.

Connor Court Publishing Pty Ltd.
PO Box 1
Ballan VIC 3342
sales@connorcourt.com
www.connorcourt.com

ISBN: 9781921421891 (pbk.)

National Library of Australia Cataloguing-in-Publication entry

Author: Jonson, P. D.

Title: Great crises of capitalism / Peter D. Jonson.

Notes: Includes bibliographical references and index.

Subjects: Capitalism--History.

Economics--History.

Dewey Number: 330.122

Cover design by Ian James
Printed in Australia.

CONTENTS

Preface	1
Introduction	5
1. The Crash of 2007-08, as it seemed at the time	11
2. Capitalism is Crisis, and Crisis is Opportunity	31
3. War and Peace and Capitalism; a many stranded rope	57
4. Dutch Tulip Mania,of 1636; with brief comments on the modern market for art	79
5. The Twin Bubbles of 1720; France and England gulled by professionals	97
6. The Age of Innovation spreads the Industrial Revolution	121
7. Marvellous Melbourne's Astonishing Property Boom and Bust; and a short subsequent history of Australia	143
8. The Roaring Twenties and the Great Depression	167
9. The Age of Aquarius; oil crisis, inflation and unemployment	191
10. Asian Magic and Western Witchcraft	209
11. How Capitalism Works, and its weaknesses	229
12. The messages of boom and bust	247
13. Future Crises of capitalism	265
Endnotes	287
Bibliography	297
Glossary of terms	305
Data appendix	315
Index	317

Preface

I have written this book because I have serious concerns about how economic policy is being practiced. Too much experimental 'discretion', too little use of stable, well understood rules. Unhelpful actions include near zero interest rates in the USA plus 'quantitative easing' (=printing money). Massive, largely wasteful, fiscal spending in advanced western nations in 2008 in a panicked response to the crisis, followed two years later by angst and hand-wringing about the size of government debt in major nations. Plus willingness to bail out all the major financial institutions in trouble but one, Lehman Brothers. This inconsistency almost created a massive crisis in global finance.

There are important lessons for governments, for central banks and for all of us as investors concerned to build and protect wealth. Karl Marx said that capitalism is crisis, and that capitalism would be destroyed by crisis created by its internal conflicts. He failed to see that crisis brings opportunity, which is my key conclusion about the Great Crises of Capitalism.

Writing Great Crises of Capitalism has helped bring together and integrate a lifetime's interest in economics, economic history and economic policy. The finished product reflects my inherent weaknesses – not keeping track of all the details and working on challenging projects instead of undertaking far more boring money-making activities.

My relative strength is a keen interest in the views of others, especially those masters such as Blainey, Clapham, Ferguson,

Friedman, Galbraith, Hayek, Hume, Keynes, Kindleberger, MacKay, Minsky, Skidelsky and Smith (carefully listed in alphabetical order), as well as other, potential masters, quoted in this book.

I am grateful to many people for help and encouragement. To my wife Elizabeth for unstinting support and trenchant criticism. To my son David for keen criticism of the text, for preparing the glossary of terms and for preparing the index. To family friend Nicholas Malon for collecting the data and drawing the graphs. The cattle farmer and retired Federal politician (long-standing member of the House of Representatives), Stewart McArthur, read the entire manuscript, asked tough questions and made many suggestions designed to improve both the exposition and the content. Stewart is also the person who convinced me that my alternative persona, 'Henry Thornton', should have an independent voice. This character was suggested by the late P.P. (Paddy) McGuinness as a *nom de plume*, the simple way of continuing to write serious economics when I took a job where such an activity was unlikely to be welcomed. 'Henry' provided a lot to live up to, and in an interesting way led me to be bolder, as I struggled to throw off my training as a (very discreet) central banker. 'Henry's' comments are in italics at the head of each chapter and in other places.

The economist Ross Garnaut and historians Geoffrey Blainey and Boris Schedvin also read the manuscript and made many valuable suggestions. These men are lifetime friends and teachers and each caused me to stop and think more than once. I suspect all of them feel that I bit off more than I could chew with the subject, but I hope they are pleasantly surprised. If they are it will be because of the quality of their comments and the seriousness with which I responded to them. I should also acknowledge the work of Bert Kelly, a 'modest member' of the Australian parliament, whose writings on economics showed a whole generation of Australian economists they do not have to write in a boring or overtly technocratic manner, and in so doing prepared the way for the serious economic reforms implemented by the Hawke, Keating and Howard governments of Australia from 1983 to 2007.

To the many authors on whose broad shoulders I stood I also offer sincere thanks. I spent a small fortune on books and a lot of time

reading books and journal articles borrowed from Melbourne and
Monash universities. When all else failed I used Google and Wikipedia,
though I soon learned both about the difficulty of drinking from a
firehose and the need to check carefully the facts from cyberspace. I
had quoted from articles that disappeared between my reading them
and returning to confirm their accuracy – but I have of course omitted
those quotes.

Every author I was able to contact directly immediately gave
permission to quote freely; publishers mostly ignored my letter or
email requesting similar approval, although one or two suggested a
fee per word. I have taken no response as implying that permission
is granted, and if there is any subsequent claim it shall of course be
remedied in following editions. There has been a lot of reprints of
the classic crisis books, and in some cases the reprinters have claimed
copyright. I am no lawyer, but this seems outrageous. I learned
that the original editions, clearly out of copyright, are available with
sufficient effort.

I thank also my publisher, Anthony Cappello of Connor Court
Publishing. He has reacted well to changes of emphasis and showed
a commendable flexibility of response to a set of suggestions from
two high-powered marketing experts.

Naturally, remaining errors of fact or interpretation are my
responsibility entirely. I remain keenly interested in this subject and
anyone wishing to comment on any matter may contact me on
peterdjonson@gmail.com.

I must emphasise that, despite considerable time and effort
studying some of the *Great Crises of Capitalism*, I have not changed
my core belief. Capitalism is far from perfect but, like democracy
in the political domain, it is by far the best organising system so far
invented. The challenge is to improve the regulation of capitalism and
(for individuals) to learn how best to build and protect wealth in the
volatile environment of modern capitalism.

P.D. Jonson (AKA Henry Thornton)
December 2010

Introduction

The Global Financial Crisis of 2007-08 might still produce a Great Depression. Massive monetary and fiscal stimulus has been thrown at the problem. Major financial institutions, with one exception, have been bailed out by taxpayers. The problems created by excessive debt and over-easy monetary policy have been 'solved' by more of the same. The bailout of Wall Street by Main Street entrenches, indeed reinforces, what economists call 'moral hazard'. The previous Chairman of the US Federal Reserve Board, Alan Greenspan, did not believe in opposing asset bubbles but cut interest rates under his control almost to zero when his asset bubble burst. This was a mistake repeated by his successor, Ben Bernanke, in the crash of 2007-08.

To make my position clear at the outset, I come to this work with the belief that capitalism, like democracy, is far from perfect but better than all the alternatives. The questions, however, are many. Are great crises of capitalism inevitable? Can crises be eliminated or modified without damaging capitalism's essence? Might we regulate prosperity into oblivion? I am firmly of the view that better regulatory mechanisms can be devised, but that trying too strenuously to prevent crises would strangle the golden goose that is capitalism.

One can examine the history of capitalism in as much detail as time, ability and available records permit. For the purposes of this book, I have made no study of original sources. Instead I accept the classic studies, starting with Charles MacKay's *Memoirs of Extraordinary Popular Delusions and the Madness of Crowds,* (which later analysis has criticised, unfairly in my view, from a late twentieth century perspective). With the classic accounts of the classic crises described in broad outline – building on the work of the master chroniclers who have led the way – my aim is to distil lessons about the nature and evolution of capitalism and the recurrent pattern of boom and bust and war and peace. The end point is what these great historical patterns mean for governments, central bankers, private individuals and families who wish to accumulate and protect wealth.

I have divided the historical description into several parts. My historical description and analysis comes initially from Europe, starting with war and peace. For my purposes this is mostly about the struggle for Europe which at the time of its climax in the first half of the twentieth century was the struggle for the soul of the world. I am interested here mainly in the relationships between war and peace and economic fluctuations, which can be described as a rope of many strands. Subsequent chapters cover the Dutch Tulip boom and the Twin Bubbles of 1720, the episodes described so colourfully by Charles MacKay. These events were dramatic and raise many issues, although they were fairly limited geographically and there is little or no hard data on their consequences.

Next comes discussion of the nineteenth century's Age of Innovation, 'Marvellous Melbourne's' astounding property boom and bust and Wall Street's roaring twenties and market crash, and subsequent Great Depression. By the time of the latter experience, plentiful data as well as the literary accounts serve to show just how devastating the whole episode was. The fluctuations of the nineteenth century were more regular and less damaging, partly because the gold standard was managed skilfully by the Bank of England and partly because markets were freer than they were to become in the twentieth century.

I then move on to discuss experiences I have lived through, both as a central banker and as a business leader. The Age of Aquarius discusses the great inflation of the 1970s and its aftermath. Asian Magic covers several of the many Asian booms and corrections in the late twentieth century. Western Witchcraft tells the story of the development of the Internet and the associated boom in 'new economy' stocks. This 'new economy' boom (of course) in short order produced a very old economy bust, though the leading new economy stocks are still producing extraordinary returns.

The world is now a two-speed economy, with greatly different culture and outcomes in the 'developed' West and the 'developing' East. Australia is geographically in Asia, culturally in the Anglosphere and, by virtue of its role as a supplier of resources (and some services) to China, Japan and other Asian nations, economically and politically poised somewhat uneasily between East and West. Australia's own two-speed economy has messages for its big brothers and sisters, for sibling resource producing nations such as Canada and the international econocrats. Australia's experience is slotted into the other historical chapters as appropriate, although Melbourne's great land boom and bust of the nineteenth century is in the gold medal category of its class and has its own chapter.

My penultimate two chapters distil the lessons of history, the coded messages from the past. Decoding these messages is my main aim, to learn more about how capitalism works and how this can be improved. We need to recognise of course that economic analysis is still part science and part artistic endeavour and these days I am more of an artist than a scientist. The penultimate chapters draw lessons for governments and central banks, and lessons for individuals and families who wish to create and protect their wealth.

Governments need to make economic policy more responsive both to booms and busts – with rules that raise rates of broad-based taxes in economic booms and cut taxes in the slumps. Central banks should take more account of asset and credit booms (and busts) in their setting of monetary policy but like governments relying more on predictable and well-understood responses than on supposedly inspired acts of discretionary response. Financial system regulators need automatic rules that require larger margins of capital to be locked away as an asset boom hots up. Along with rising cash rates, this approach should aim to provide a more testing environment rather than attempting to stifle booms or to protect capitalism against the consequences of occasional major booms. Like the flooding rains that break a devastating drought, the great booms of capitalism mostly do more good than harm.

Whether the world would benefit from a new version of the nineteenth century gold standard is an issue that I longed to discuss more thoroughly, but ultimately was too big a challenge for this book. The current standard monetary policy regime has as its main objective controlling goods and services inflation by varying official cash rates. A new commodity standard would start with steady growth in a monetary quantity, perhaps a bundle of commodities, and see what that implied for interest rates and other indicators of the state of the economy. This question deserves serious study, as it is perhaps receiving in the world's leading central banks and universities.

This writer also believes that governments and regulators should rely more on education and cultural leadership than on ever more intrusive black letter law. Greed – the self interest of the butcher and baker – is good, but excessive, short-sighted greed is potentially very damaging. Protecting consumers from loan sharks and outright criminals is probably necessary, but teaching and reminding consumers that they are responsible for their actions is better than any approach that might be devised by an 'all-wise' nanny state. Opinion leaders, including school teachers and college instructors, should remind students that, if something looks too good to be true, it almost certainly is. Work is needed on incentive plans, perhaps for bankers with principles enforced by bank regulators to ensure proper account is taken of sustainable outcomes. I also strongly support Paul Volcker's plea for a return of the Glass-Steagall Act in the United States, with equivalent legislation in other capitalist nations, to enforce separation of traditional banking and far more highly speculative financial ventures.

If readers sincerely wish to become rich, and to protect their wealth, they need to devote serious time to that objective. For those of an entrepreneurial bent, fierce concentration on some new invention, new market opportunity or new place for an old activity may generate great wealth. But considerable wealth may also be created by managers of the world's significant corporations as such managers are paid very well and mostly have incentive plans that enable then to accumulate equity in the enterprises they manage.

Protecting and growing wealth despite the vagaries of modern financial markets is a very different activity than building wealth through outstanding personal efforts, whether as an entrepreneur or as a manager of a wealthy corporation. Often the task of protecting and growing wealth is entrusted to specialised managers of money. 'Time in the market beats market timing' is a general refrain among professional fund managers and individuals or families those who like to set and forget a fixed portfolio of well diversified assets. But analysis of the typical, repeated pattern of asset boom and bust suggests ways to do better than setting and forgetting a portfolio of assets no matter how well chosen.

Taking an active approach to managing wealth is often described as 'speculation', which is an activity often criticised. But life itself is a speculation, and in making life choices all people battle both risk – which can sometimes be insured against – as well as uncertainty, which requires a speculative response. 'Speculation' is not something to be treated lightly, and speculation in financial markets is rarely a part-time activity. Families need to take a dynastic approach to this matter, which means that one or more members of a family in each generation may have to devote him or herself to the demanding task of following the great waves of economic development and market fluctuation. My motivation in writing this book is partly to celebrate a rich life as an economist in a variety of roles, but also to distil lessons that I feel happy to pass on to my children, and to other young people also.

My final chapter is more speculative. It peers into the dark glass that is the uncertain future. The only certainty is that there will be future crises of capitalism, one hopes more financial than military. As Lord Rothschild is reputed to have said, however, the time to buy is when the blood is running in the streets, so it pays to be prepared for every eventuality. If I were to wax lyrical, I would conclude that the twenty-first century will see the making or breaking of capitalism and its most frequent political partner, democracy. I suspect that, in the absence of some great catastrophe, the future will be like the past, only more so. There will be the same challenges, the same risks and the same opportunities, but the technology will be more effective.

The capitalist world needs policies to counter geopolitical risk, epidemics and shortages of clean water and other resources as the global population approaches 9 billion people. New technologies, if allied to sensible pricing of some types of risk (which may require co-ordinated action by governments), will solve most of these challenges to capitalism. However, the biggest threat to capitalism is instability caused by policy swings: expansion; recovery; asset inflation; goods inflation; policy-tightening; economy experiences recession; and the whole process repeating itself. The Great Depression of the 1930s was capitalism's greatest crisis. So far, despite accelerating episodes of asset boom and bust from the 1980s on, there has been no experience of devastating depression to provide a similar challenge to modern capitalism.

Karl Marx predicted that capitalism would bring about its own demise through recurrent crisis. But crisis also creates opportunity, a point that Marx was unable to appreciate except in his own political career. This is the greatest lesson of the Great Crises of Capitalism.

Currently, however, interest rates in the USA are close to zero, sowing the seeds of the next inflationary bubble. The developed world is seeking to solve the problems of thirty years of over-lending and over-borrowing by more of the same medicine. China is America's banker and there are deep divisions among these two major powers about monetary policy and how best to solve global economic 'imbalances'. There is plenty of hard thinking and hard work to be done by political leaders and the global econocrats who monitor and advise on the matters covered in this book. Non-governmental readers will use their votes wisely but also keep firmly in mind that recurrent crisis presents opportunity.

1

The Crash of 2007-08, as it seemed at the time

It began, as great events so often do, as a cloud no bigger than a man's hand. Yet within eighteen months the capitalist world was close to panic, with share prices slammed, credit markets gridlocked, bailouts of some of the world's largest banks, and failure of many others, industrial production falling as fast as in the Great Depression of the 1930s and unemployment and underemployment rising sharply. Vast and generally wasteful schemes of fiscal expansion were underway, interest rates were close to zero in many nations and widespread 'quantitative easing' ('printing money' in oldspeak) was underway.

The year 2007 had opened in many countries with consumer confidence high, indeed rising, and the rate of unemployment falling. Australia's mining boom was roaring and what became known as the 'two-speed economy' was emerging. Severe drought was creating misery on the farms of South East Australia and damaging century-old gardens in the cities. Various experts said that modern economic management had eliminated the business cycle, at least in Australia's 'miracle economy'.

2007 was an election year in Australia, but continued strong economic growth was expected to favour the ruling Liberal-National Party coalition – after all, as President Clinton famously said in his successful 1992 presidential campaign against George H. W. Bush: 'It's the economy, stupid'. In the USA in 2007, presidential candidates were beginning to position themselves for the election of 2008. There, the costly occupation of Iraq was beginning to take centre stage and Barack Obama was polishing his campaign slogan of 'Yes we can!' China was working hard to produce a memorable Olympic games to showcase its rapidly developing economy.

Friday April 13, 2007, 'Black Friday' for the superstitious, saw the Australian dollar again hit another high, being traded for just under 83 US cents. The rising dollar was beginning to hurt exporters and help importers. Cheap goods from Asia were pouring into Australia, the United States and indeed most 'developed' nations. Western consumerist culture was about to receive its most serious setback since the Great Depression of the 1930s.

The US dollar had hit a two-year low against the Euro overnight. Sluggish US Labour Department figures, showing a 19,000 jump in jobless benefit claims in the previous week, had helped convince world market participants that they would see two American interest rate cuts in 2007.

In Australia the Howard government's politically unpopular WorkChoices legislation was restraining wage costs despite the pressures of a tight labor market. But inflation fears were gathering strength, creating expectations of interest rate hikes in an election year.[1]

Why were house prices falling in the mighty USA? This was the first question of those Australians who looked at what became known as the 'sub-prime crisis'. This was the small cloud on the far horizon.

It seems US house prices were falling because they had earlier gone up – a standard experience of boom and bust. But the strength of the housing boom was severely exaggerated in the USA in the time from 2003 to 2007 because of the widespread practice of housing lenders making 'sub-prime' loans. These, as we now know, were loans made to people with a sub-par credit rating, often with sub-par documentation or, in some cases, virtually no documentation. In particular, interest on the loans was initially, for a year or two, low or even zero. As Robert Skidelsky put it in his 2009 account of the eventual crisis: '... private mortgage lenders, having exhausted the middle-class demand for mortgages, started vacuuming up *Ninjas* –

borrowers with no income, no job, no assets.[2]

Two more funadamental developments had allowed and fostered these foolish practices. There had been widespread 'deregulation' of American finance. Of particular importance was the cancellation in 1999 of the Glass-Steagall Act of 1933. This Act had enforced a separation of commercial banking and much riskier investment banking. This was like harnessing a thoroughbred racehorse with a draughthorse to pull a buggy – bound to cause trouble.

The American bankers, it seemed, had forgotten the fundamentals of banking. Could this be true?

Wall Streeters became used to making massive profits and rewarding themselves with massive bonuses. The new banking practices involved far greater risks, the results of which justified the risks – at least while the boom continued.

Equally important, American interest rates had been held far below neutral by the central bank Chairman, Alan Greenspan, who feared recession and did not believe in opposing asset inflation. The ultimate consequences of these beliefs were far from totally obvious in early 2007, when Greenspan had been retired for a year after a record 19 years of dominance, stamping his deepest beliefs on the beating heart of American finance.[3]

Australia, like all western nations, had followed the American preference for deregulated finance. Fortunately our bankers were not so driven as their colleagues in New York to be masters of the universe, and may have been regulated more effectively. London financiers were more like the Americans and were also to suffer greatly in the Crash of 2007-08.

Every adult should know that there is no such thing as a free lunch. Whenever one hears, or sees on television, retailers who offer no interest and no repayments on purchases for a year, or even longer, it should tell all adults that the interest is added into the price and that the person getting the 'interest free loan' is either paying way over the odds for the goods or else is headed for a crisis in his or her personal financial situation – or about to experience both unhappy events. That such a practice could be embedded to a significant degree into the US banking system was, at first, literally impossible to believe.

Early reports of a 'sub-prime crisis' were greeted with great skepticism. Surely US bankers could not be so silly? Surely there could only be a few 'sub-prime' loans made by foolish or indeed crooked financiers. But no, this was apparently a big problem, and it became clear that things were worse than the mere existence of a lot of dud house loans. Clever financiers had packaged up the dud loans, sometimes but not always with loans of better quality, and on-sold them to other financial institutions. Being 'housing loans' they were given a strong credit rating by the agencies whose job it was to judge these matters. In reality the packages were bombs waiting to go off.

Bank failures surfaced first in the UK where, in September 2007, the Bank of England was forced to provide emergency support to a British bank, Northern Rock. The third largest home lender in the UK, it had been offering home loans of up to 125% of the value of the property. 60% of this bank's total lending was financed by short-term borrowing, and it was caught out by steep rises in cost of borrowing in credit markets following the onset of the sub-prime crisis.[4]

Now it was the British bankers who had gone bonkers. Could this be true?

In a further early warning of trouble to come, this was in the same month in 2007 that Lehman Brothers closed its sub-prime lender. Thirteen months later, Lehman Brothers filed for bankruptcy in the USA, the British Financial Services regulator having reportedly vetoed a takeover by Barclay's Bank and the American authorities having failed, or declined, to arrange, a rescue. Northern Rock was eventually nationalised on 17 February 2008 at a cost to the British taxpayer of 100 million pounds.

For most of 2007, global share prices continued to boom. Indeed, to many experienced observers, the boom had become a frightening bubble. It is widely understood that asset booms have to end badly. As John Kenneth Galbraith says in his classic book, *The Great Crash 1929*, 'When prices stopped rising – when the supply of people who were buying for an increase was exhausted – then ownership on margin would become meaningless and everyone would want to sell. The market wouldn't level out; it would fall precipitately.'[5]

In late May a prominent resource analyst, the author of Henry

Thornton's Raff Report (a regular report on economies and markets), said he remembered Black Monday in 1987 like it was yesterday. 'Any scientist or other sensible person could see that the trend was completely unsustainable. That picture looked a little like the Shanghai share price indexes today where price earnings multiples are stretched averaging over 100 times. The Shenzhen Composite Index is up 211% on a year ago and the Shanghai SE Composite Index is up 163% on a year ago. Even official comments from Beijing that China is in the midst of the mother of stock exchange bubbles has not dulled the thirst to try and get fabulously wealthy without working'.

'But it is not just China where there is a bit of a bubble, but one is also building in the USA'. An American broker had reported overnight that 3.1% of US stocks are now short-sold. This is supposedly the highest proportion since 1931, 'a truly horrible year for US stocks'. The Raff Report concluded: 'There will be another correction and it will be a beauty – investors leveraged to junior explorers with only moose pasture risk heavy losses'... [6]

In the event, the share price bubble did not burst until mid-October of 2007, when Wall Street fell sharply, led by bank shares. As the graph shows, and as is also typical of movements on equity markets other than Wall Street, there were setbacks – with

There is a saying among market traders: 'The trend is your friend, until the end'.

market falls of varying severity - in the progress to the eventual market peak. Also typical was that the downward trend, once established, was far steeper than the earlier rise.

Dow Jones Industrial Index 1995 to 2010

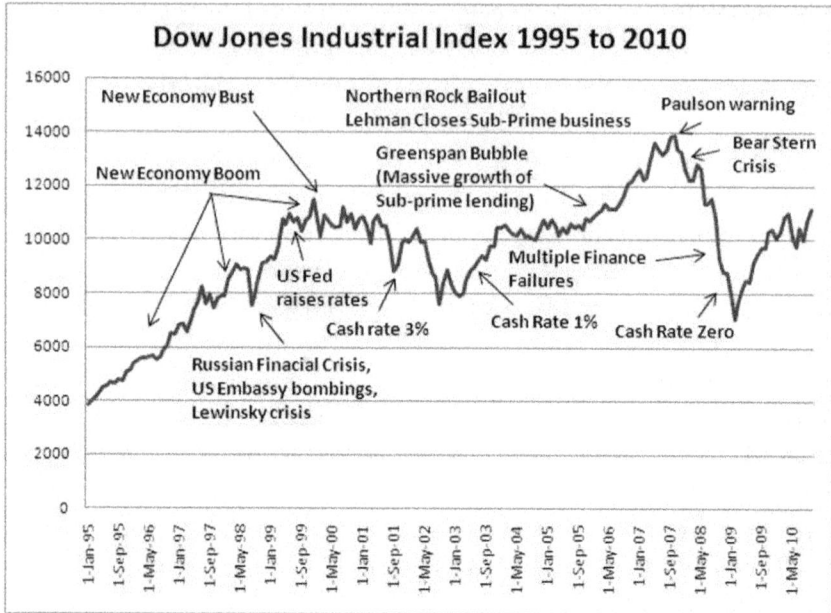

In mid-July share prices were still rising. It was on another Friday 13 in Australia that the morning market report said that the Dow Jones index had risen overnight in New York by more than 2%. This meant it would be a boomer of a day for stock prices in Asia, including Australia. Clearly asset price inflation was alive and well, and it seemed clear that the eventual correction would cause serious heartburn.

The Henry Thornton Blog, in a rare moment of despair, advised: 'But we might just as well enjoy it while it lasts ... The Aussie dollar has reached fresh heights today, and the smarties are beginning to think that parity (with a weak US dollar) is possible. Be ready for the 'parity parties that occasionally embarrass New Zealanders'.[7] For the financial year that had just ended, Australia's equity market had closed up 30% (including dividends) for the year. This marked the fourth year of annual returns above 20%. Two questions were asked: 'Surely it doesn't get any better than this? But could it get much worse?'

There was a complex technical issue that it seemed no-one was getting to grips with. The Nobel Prize winning economist Milton

Friedman famously said: 'Inflation is everywhere and always a monetary phenomenon'. The overlooked issue was what sort of inflation, how precisely does easy money show up? By the middle of 2007 in Australia, house prices had soared, share prices had rocketed, resource company shares were glowing in the dark, but consumer prices were subdued.

The magnitudes involved were startling. By March 2007, compared with June 1986, consumer prices had slightly more than doubled, implying annual goods and services inflation of 3.8%. Over the same 21 years, average Australian house prices had risen by 450%, the share price index had risen by a similar 480% while shares in BHP Billiton had soared by a massive 1150%. While the out-performance of BHP Billiton shares was in part, perhaps large part, due to the 'China boom', other asset prices had risen by an order of magnitude faster than prices of goods and services.

This was a common theme around the world. China share prices had been rising almost vertically. In the mighty USA sensible analysts worried about the next share price correction and the current house price correction and in other nations strong asset inflation co-existed with subdued consumer goods and services inflation. Extreme asset inflation with subdued consumer inflation was in fact a global phenomenon. Was it also a global problem? This was a big question for modern central banks, and my regular Henry Thornton column for 5 June 2007 (published as usual in *The Australian* newspaper on the morning of the meeting of the board of the Reserve Bank of Australia) advised independent directors to ask the Chairman ('Governor') Glenn Stevens and his team for their answer at that day's meeting.

Sensible people felt it was important to be concerned because history tells us that extreme booms in any market are followed by busts. It seemed clear that the inevitable global asset price bust would create substantial misery. But there is a deeper problem. The problem with Friedman's dictum is to define inflation. Friedman focused on goods and services inflation. His implied economic model consisted of one good and one asset, 'money'. It assumed a stable relation between the quantity of money and the price of the single good, on the plausible assumption that the volume of that good was fixed except for short periods of disequilibrium.

For the past two decades, the rapid development of China and India has held down global goods and services inflation. For much of the time, the US Fed created easy money with low nominal rates of interest on short-term cash, sometimes even negative in 'real' (inflation adjusted) terms. Note again the need to define 'inflation' broadly. The moment you include asset inflation you will see the point.

Economic theory, like any theory, has to simplify, to pick the essence of the problem being analysed. For the modern world, there are weaknesses in Friedman's simple monetarist theory.

With goods and services inflation subdued by the rebalancing of global economic activity, excess money had to bubble up somewhere, and it showed up as asset inflation – sharp increases in the prices of shares, houses, commodities, art and other assets. Returns greatly exceeded the cost of borrowing in real (inflation adjusted) terms. Alan Greenspan had opposed acting against asset booms and other central banks followed his lead.

When the asset bubble bursts, the dynamics change, and goods and service inflation is likely to emerge, unless the elimination of excess money was the reason for the asset bust. Typically, central banks have not produced the asset bust, which has occurred because of some scandal or bank in trouble.

In the long boom of the 1980s, 1990s and the 2000s smart people recognised that they could borrow cheaply to buy assets, not-so-smart bankers accommodated them and the credit boom was born. As the world headed inevitably to the great crash of 2007-08, the dramatic growth of China and India as major providers of cheap goods and services constrained the goods and services inflation that was the focus both of Friedman's analysis and central banking practice.

With constrained goods and services inflation, easy money spilled into excess asset prices. It was as if economists and central bankers were blind to the new world economic order and its consequences for markets and monetary policy. My June 2007 article was headed 'Asset inflation conundrum' and attempted to persuade the Reserve Bank of Australia to focus on the vast disconnect between their goods and service theory, and its embodiment in their formal agreement with government.[8]

The third week of July 2007 saw more bad news in US financial markets. Henry Thornton's *Lexington* wrote from his ringside seat in Washington: 'The drivers of the great global stock market rally of 2002-2007 had a bad week. But, characteristic of the equity market mania, the Dow Jones closed over 14,000, an all-time high, while Bear Stearns informed investors in its two hedge funds holding $20 billion in securitization of sub-prime mortgages (Collateralized Debt Obligations) that their $1.5 billion investment was wiped out! Most of the securities were highly rated AA or AAA but Bear discovered now no one believes the ratings or wants to bid on the securities, rendering them near worthless'.[9]

By mid August, market volatility had greatly increased and Martin Wolf of the *Financial Times* said 'Fear makes its welcome return'. Wolf is not totally insensitive, of course, just a student of booms and busts. He said 'It has been a world of confidence, cleverness and too much cheap credit'. Wolf added: 'This is not new. It is as old as financial capitalism itself'.

The 'great bubbles' of recent decades – in Japanese stocks in the late 1980s, in east Asia's stocks and property meltdown in the late-1990s, in the US (and European) stock markets in the late 1990s and, finally, in the housing markets of much of the advanced world in the 2000s – had all been bailed out by accommodating central banks. This introduced systematic 'moral hazard' into financiers' mindsets and makes repeat performances more likely. This time, Wolf argued, the pressure for another bailout 'should be resisted'.

It was not necessary to agree with this controversial opinion. Financial firm failures so far had reintroduced financiers to 'fear'. Most commentators thought bailouts should proceed, in line with the classic advice of the nineteenth century writer Baghot – lend to sound institutions at a penal rate. Then after markets were stabilised, excess liquidity should be soaked up quickly. For the future, central banks should take asset inflation into account in setting monetary policy and 'lean into the wind' of asset inflation the next time it arises.

This would establish new rules of the game in a far less risky way than withholding necessary accommodation at this time.

One could readily agree that Martin Wolf's tougher approach might be required if central bankers do not have the steady purpose needed to implement a less draconian approach. But the costs in lost jobs and economic misery would be great. The coming financial firestorm was to provide evidence for both views and, in the process, create fear in the minds of many people, including presidents, prime ministers and central bankers.[10]

By early August financial markets began to spin out of control. Apart from asset inflation, the US sub-prime lending crisis was the major obvious cause for concern for the global economy. Its ripples were still spreading and included a substantial equity market correction in most markets. When the Australian equity market closed on Friday 16 August the correction was around 8% from the recent peak, but Wall Street's ugly Friday trading was almost certain to increase the size of the correction at the start of the next week.

Another bear point in the global outlook was the price of oil, which had been steadily rising for some time after a welcome drop in the lead up to the Northern summer. The upturn in the price of oil and of many other commodities was a clear manifestation of global commodity inflation on the rise. Equity markets had become inured to the effects of oil prices headed to the stratosphere, but more *I still do not know if Battellino was offering solace, issuing a warning or indeed laying a landmine, as the Reserve bank had done in focussing on Australia's external debt twenty years earlier.* thoughtful investors had quietly factored goods and services inflation and the accompanying increase in global interest rates into their calculations.

Excessive credit growth was an important part of the problem in all the Anglo nations, with cheap money and stable goods and services prices creating the asset inflation that so bedevilled the world from 2003 to 2007. Australia's credit bubble was reported by Reserve Bank deputy-governor Ric Battellino in September, and was written as the financial crisis was building inevitable momentum in Washington.[11]

In mid-September there was a chilling warning by US Treasury Secretary Hank Paulson: 'The crisis of confidence in credit markets is likely to last longer than the previous financial shocks of the past two decades'. In effect, this was the big one. Paulson said the uncertainty in credit markets would last longer than the turmoil that followed the Asian crisis and the Russian default of the 1990s or the Latin American debt crisis of the 1980s. A natural question was whether the crisis would result in a Great Depression.

These comments by US Treasury Secretary Hank Paulson, and also those of Bank of England governor, Mervyn King, led many people to conclude that 'The world's central banks will almost certain err, if at all, on the side of reducing the risk of recession as opposed to playing tough with the authors of risky lending practices. This will add to the current inflationary tendency, itself not great for the prospects for sustainable strong growth. Notwithstanding the predictable bias, the good news is that the various trade-offs are being professionally considered'.[12]

The International Monetary Fund's (IMF) report provided similar comfort on the Australian economy. 'Executive Directors commended the Australian authorities for their exemplary macroeconomic management, which is widely recognized as being at the forefront of international best practice.'[13] This was indeed a fulsome report. This might have been interpreted as 'All's well in the Nirvana economy, and the only puzzle (not canvassed by the IMF) is why the poplace are so down on the government that has delivered such an outcome'.

By late October it was becoming clear that the global share price bubble had run its course. No longer did it seem like a mere 'correction'; now the word 'crash' could be used, but the hope was this would not turn into a full blown catastrophe. As a technical aside, classification of share market moves is an imperfect art. It is generally agreed that a fall of 10 % is a "correction". A "crash" requires a fall of 25% or more over a relatively short period. This becomes a "catastrophe" if the person doing the describing held a lot of shares at the time. It is a "coup" if the writer had short sold stock.

At this time, a visitor from America addressed a select group in an upmarket restaurant in Richmond, *Vlado's Charcoal Grill*. It was crowded, with high levels of happy chatter. No depression here, though many pundits were writing gloomy articles. Our report on the visitor's address was titled: 'US recession certain; China unstoppable'. The expert did not wish to be identified but claimed to be an expert in bubbles, having seen three bubbles, as he put it, 'close up and personal'.

The guru's starting point was simple: 'get used to hearing the "r" word'. 'Slowly, slowly and inexorably the US is headed for recession.' This is not widely agreed since 'market economists are in denial'. After some lurid description of the US housing markets and related matters, the guru moved on: With the audience taking an extra drink to settle their nerves, he moved to discuss China. 'The US has got to keep the capital coming in or there will be a major problem. The deal has been China provides cheap goods to the US in exchange for cheap dollars. But there is a limit'.

'China's Sovereign fund has $300 billion and is buying real assets – oil, gas, minerals – anywhere it can.' When China gets dollars it exchanges them for RMB. This boosts money supply, so China tries to soak up the excess money – sterilization is the technical word, meaning the central bank soaks up the excess liquidity. As seen in many other countries with an undervalued currency, sterilization is impossible and the money sloshing around produces share and real estate bubbles. Eventually the asset bubbles lead to inflation of goods and services – currently well underway in China.

'The leaders in Beijing believe that their predecessors had their political futures ruined by inflation'. The guru noted that in the lead up to the massacre in Tiananmen Square inflation was 15 or 16%. 'So the leaders are worried now. President Hu knows all this. The only solution is to allow the currency to appreciate faster. But the leaders know the risks in this course of action – a massive upvaluation would decimate manufacturing industry and destroy millions of jobs. Thus a total 'unhooking' of the currency is impossible'.

'There is another change that is important. People in the country ("peasants" one well fed fellow interjected helpfully) see on TV the prosperity in the cities and are getting restive. President Hu clearly understands this, and the US Fed is flying blind. We must cross our fingers and pray that the US dollar does not plunge and that China's inflation does not take off'.[14]

It did not take too long for opinion leaders to catch up with the guru's bold views. Australia's nirvana economy kept on rolling along, credit growth too strong, unemployment falling and inflation too high. In early November, urged on by Henry Thornton and other worthies, the Reserve Bank made history by raising interest rates during an election campaign. As widely predicted, Kevin Rudd's Labor Party won government, disproving the conventional wisdom – 'It's the economy stupid' - that a strong economy and global threats invariably favour incumbent governments.

Goods and services inflation was finally recognised as a serious problem, though in retrospect the global crisis plus rate hikes to date had probably put a fix into the pipeline. We learned in a major weekend story that inflation was now regarded by Treasury as a really serious problem. Treasury, of course, is the agency that has been relatively laid back about inflation, reportedly arguing against necessary interest rate hikes at RBA board meetings and briefing journalists against people who predicted the whole sorry state of affairs.[15]

In retrospect, the Crisis of 2007-08 seemed like a train wreck in slow motion. There was a lot going on, and serious financial market participants could sense the coming storm even as they generally could see no way to avoid its effects – it takes great courage to short an equity market when a bubble is still expanding. The Bush administration was in lame duck mode, and presidential candidate Barack Obama was making serious progress, at first against his Democrat opponents and then against Senator McCain.

Australians were also distracted by matters political, in our case the settling in of a new government. The new winners were reviewing all the programs bequeathed by the losers as well as planning how best to implement the new programs promised from opposition. Climate change was an issue Labor had given high priority to, and this received a lot of attention. The new Prime Minister, Kevin Rudd, seemed determined to lead the world into a new, emission-constrained, future.

By April 2008, thoughtful people everywhere were concerned that now goods and services inflation was rising, impacted as ever by global forces. (It was no coincidence that asset inflation had turned to asset deflation.) Shortages of food, oil (and therefore petrol) and home-grown shortages of rental accommodation, all were making life difficult for those citizens whom Australians call 'battlers'.

The International Monetary Fund (IMF) revised down its activity forecasts and revised up its inflation forecasts. There were to be several such adjustments before the year was over, reminding one of the first rule of the professional soothsayer – 'Forecast early and forecast often'.

Yet the Reserve Bank of Australia was still raising interest rates in pursuit of a goods and services inflation target that some analysts were wondering might not be totally appropriate to the circumstances. Henry Thornton was asked to write for *The Australian* on the subject and did so on ANZAC Day, Australia's Remembrance Day. 'For the Reserve Bank governor Glenn Stevens to keep overall inflation "mild" when important particular prices – food, petrol, rents – are rising sharply he must keep monetary policy firm and rely on this to force down sharply the prices of other goods and services or indeed of assets.

'Owners of other goods and services, or assets, resist price falls and complain loudly to their governments. So do – and with greater cause – those people suffering from the direct effect of rising prices of food, petrol and housing.

'All this is why Australian economic policy, and that of other inflation targeting nations, is at risk of causing an unnecessary recession. Or of abandoning inflation targeting, with all the loss of credibility that would entail. Or of explaining the suspension of inflation targeting while conditions normalise'.[17]

Rapid food price inflation had direct and immediate consequences. Many people in developing nations could no longer afford sufficient food, and would starve or become malnourished if generous aid was not quickly available. People in developed nations have their standards of living cut when the price of food rises, and this is compounded by rising petrol prices, in some nations falling house prices, or falling share prices or falling real wages, as money wage increases lag goods and services price inflation.

US interest rates had been falling from late 2007, slightly anticipating the end of the long share price boom, and by early May 2008 had reached 2%. We asked if Ben Bernanke was repeating Alan Greenspan's mistake, a question that became more urgent as US cash rates sunk almost to zero, which occurred in December 2008. By late May, the price of oil was US$133 per barrel, and at this level was beginning to bite, reducing growth while boosting inflation. *The Australian Financial Review* sought the views of Nobel Prize winning economist Joe Stiglitz and learned that, like this author, he was a skeptic about inflation targeting. In early July, the Bank for International Settlements (BIS) also was to say in its *Annual Report 2007-08* that simple inflation targeting was not sensible.[18]

At the time, Wal-Mart in America was reported to be rationing rice to wholesale buyers, a first for the mighty USA. Imagine the panic if food rationing had become common in America? Imagine it anywhere, not so difficult when the evening television news show food riots and starving children in refugee camps in third world countries.

Oil was eventually to reach almost $US150 per barrel, and by June fear of inflation became widespread. Central banks – who had let the anchor of inflation slip – began to question their overly simple understanding of the new economic order. We said 'Inflation fears go global' and this is (so far) our most read Blog – almost 12,000 hits on Henry's site and who knows how many on that of *The Australian*.[19]

But it was not just inflation that was worrying policy makers. *The Economist* said 'The most recent unemployment figures have hit Washington like a brick: the unemployment rate jumped to 5.5% in May, a hefty half-point hike from April. Much of the rise came from young Americans unsuccessfully seeking work for the first time, but the capital is again buzzing with recession worries.[20] US unemployment was eventually to exceed 10%, with as many again underemployed as hours worked plummeted. Elsewhere, unemployment was far worse, close to 20% in Spain, with (I guess) another 20% severely underemployed. Ordinary people, even if still employed, had greater cause for concern than the econocrats who had let them down so obviously.

In June 2009, two American economists, Barry Eichengreen and Kevin O'Rourke, demonstrated that world industrial production, trade and stock markets were diving faster than during 1929-30. This created enormous interest, with the Vox column that presented this alarming picture generating 30,000 views in less than 48 hours, and over 100,000 within a week. Later updates showed a continuation of this trend, although by June 2010, the authors were able to report that 'Global industrial production continues to recover – something for which policy deserves considerable credit ... But before indulging in self-congratulation, policymakers should note that the level of industrial production is still 6% below its previous peak. (At the trough it was 13% below its previous peak.) It follows that considerable excess capacity remains in a number of important economies. Exiting now from policies of stimulus in those countries would therefore be premature.'[21]

Lord Skidelsky was to name his 2009 book on the crisis *Keynes. The Return of the Master*. Governments everywhere began to plan deficit spending on the grand scale, in most cases creating record peacetime deficits. By the time President Obama had worked his first budget the deficits were in the trillions and the red ink stretched 'as far as the eye could see' – and the US seemed headed for a decade of deficits measured in the trillions.

Deficits on this scale, especially combined with very easy monetary policy, make activity higher in their immediate aftermath. Expectations of mountains of debt to repay, coming on top of inflation at worrying levels may douse the "animal spirits" (to use Keynes' famous description) of households and firms. The world economy was embarking on a massive economic policy experiment. Lord Keynes would have nodded with approval.

In mid-July we noted that a pessimist is an optimist with experience. 'The debt crisis, the banking crisis, the property crisis, the oil crisis, the shift to Asia, the bear market in stocks are huge global adjustments that have all come together at the same time'. This was the summary of current economic conditions from William Rees-Mogg, a man who was born just before the Great Depression of the 1930s.[22]

Sports lovers everywhere, including many Australians, took a well-earned break on 8 August 2008. On what was for them the most auspicious day of the millennium, China's Olympics started in Beijing under clear skies (factories had been shut down for weeks) with a spectacular opening ceremony. With the Olympics behind us, there was much hand-wringing as people realised that commodity prices were collapsing.

Darwin's principle of the survival of the fittest, translated to the economic sphere meant prosperity of the fittest, and poverty or disappearance of the less fit. 'The ugly ends to booms are the economic equivalent of meteor strikes or ice ages, testing and cleansing the economy and its players'.[23] This was not, of course, a judgment widely endorsed.

On September 3, the Reserve Bank began to cut interest rates, albeit by a modest 25 basis points. Ironically, this was at a time when various local indicators were looking a bit cheerier. But it was also the month in which the Global Financial Crisis was about to reach its crescendo. No doubt the Reserve was in the loop on this, but in retrospect it is odd that a far larger initial rate cut was not made. Monday 15 September came after a frenzied weekend in New York, as Lehman Brothers and several other financial institutions teetered on the brink. It was in September-October 2008, Skidelsky said, that 'the financial crisis turned into a classic panic'.[24]

On September 7, the US government took mortgage underwriters Fannie Mae and Freddie Mac into 'conservatorship', or public ownership, after their share prices collapsed, guaranteeing $12,000 billion of debt.

Then came the shock of 15 September that changed the whole game. Against all informed judgment (except that of Martin Woolf and, presumably, of US President George Bush) the US government allowed Lehman Brothers to go bankrupt owing $600 billion. All hell broke loose, to lapse into the vernacular. After this shock, one infers that the rest of the story was minor league stuff for President Bush and his econocrats in Washington.

Merrill Lynch was sold to Bank of America to avoid the same fate as Lehman Brothers. The next day, the US government took a 79.9% stake in insurer AIG in return for an $85 billion loan facility.

On 21 September Goldman Sachs and Morgan Stanley converted their status from investment banks to holding banks. This allowed them to borrow from the Federal Reserve on more favourable terms in return for greater official supervision.

Washington Mutual failed on 25 September when depositors withdrew $16.7 billion.

Even at the time, but even clearer in the crystal light of hindsight, the decision to let Lehman Brothers fail is simply inexplicable. It was no exaggeration to say that the world's financial system wobbled on its axis. We commend Andrew Ross Sorkin's *Too Big to Fail. Inside the Battle to save Wall Street*, but it is fair to say even he is not totally clear why Lehman Brothers was let go while all other significant players were bailed out.[25] Could the judgment of history be that ultimately the failure of Lehman Brothers brings benefits that exceed its substantial costs? This too is a question which bears close attention.

At the time, many witnesses claimed that the world's financial system was in severe danger of collapsing. Skidelsky says 'panic undoubtedly gripped the Treasury and the Fed at the time of Lehman's collapse'. He quotes Ben Bernanke who told Congress on 18 September that, without a comprehensive bailout plan, 'we may not have an economy on Monday'. Mervyn King, governor of the Bank of England, said that 'Not since the beginning of the First World War has our banking system been so close to collapse'.[26]

As the banking crisis unfolded, central banks pumped billions of dollars into markets but interbank lending almost totally dried up. Bankers lost faith in each other. Rather than lending as usual to clear money transfers quickly, many bankers were asking, 'Who's next?' in the liquidation or forced merger game.

Global share prices were to keep falling until March 2009, when the main Wall Street index was 56 per cent below its recent, all-time peak. This compares with the Crash of 1929 to 1932, As Galbraith reports: 'On November 13 1929 ... the *Times* industrials closed at 224.

On July 8, 1932, they were 58'. That is a fall to just over one quarter of its peak value.[27]

It will be many years before the Global Financial Crisis of 2007-08 can be evaluated fully and assigned its place in the history of the great crises of capitalism. It may be seen as the depression avoided by swift and decisive action by wise and skilled governments and central banks. On the other hand ... Is it feasible that a crisis caused by over-borrowing and over-lending can be cured by massive further lending and borrowing?

Will a Mount Everest of debt solve the problems created by merely large mountains of debt?

Anatoly Kaletsky wrote in February 2010: 'The most important statements are often those that are left unsaid. Among the millions of words spoken at last week's World Economic Forum in Davos, the comment that nobody quite dared to utter was clear. After the crisis of 2007-09, the global capitalist system is in a period of transition comparable with the great transitions of the 1930s and 1970s.

'The question that nobody wants to raise is whether the new model of capitalism that emerges to dominate the world will be a radically reformed version of the Western democratic system or some variant of the authoritarian state-led capitalism favoured in China, Russia and some other emerging economies'.[28]

My good friend and former colleague, Ross Garnaut (writing with David Llewellyn-Smith), summarises his account of what he calls *The Great Crash of 2008* with concern for a 'lightly regulated market economy'. This version of capitalism 'has always been tolerated rather than embraced in the late twentieth and early twenty-first centuries. Following the Crash, it is now under fundamental challenge everywhere'.[29]

What a pity it will be if 'lightly regulated' capitalism, of the sort that harnesses the power and magic of Adam Smith's invisible hand, is replaced by a new capitalism which features central planning, government by official and political diktat and officious regulation. This would strangle the golden goose that is capitalism, and make the capitalist world less prosperous and less free. The challenge, of course, is to devise better regulation, not more regulation and attempted micro-management from the centre.

2

Capitalism is Crisis; and Crisis is Opportunity

Crisis equals opportunity combined with danger says a popular (but incorrect) belief about an aspect of Chinese language and culture. This idea touches a powerful nerve in many people and seems to encapsulate important elements of the great episodes of crisis in capitalist history.

The great crises of capitalism are more exciting than detective novels and action movies. There are colourful men, dastardly deeds and dramatic events. We learn of great crimes and harsh punishments, of fortunes made and lost and mistakes of governments and bankers facing fast moving events spinning out of control. We discover risks to avoid and opportunities to profit by watching events with a cool and analytical eye and acting decisively when the time is ripe.

Capitalism is the modern, now almost universal, system of social, economic and productive organisation. Its features include a dominant role for markets in allocating resources, private production of most goods and services, rational, evidence-based decision making by individuals, businesses and governments (or the appearance of this) and freedom of people to act within a framework provided by a stable, well understood 'rule of law' in what they perceive to be their own interests. It seems also that recurrent episodes of crisis cannot be avoided, but whether this is a helpful or harmful feature of capitalism is rarely discussed.

Capitalism is now largely associated with democratic political systems. But capitalism has a wider span of application than just in democratic nations. There are two main variants of capitalism – democratic capitalism and authoritarian capitalism. Variants of democratic capitalism range from laissez-faire capitalism – stronger in the USA – to socialised capitalism which is dominant in Europe. Critics of modern Europe point to its sclerotic economy and critics of American capitalism cite its vast inequalities of wealth and income.

Capitalism is mankind's greatest economic system, which in the past four centuries has created unprecedented wealth and technological innovation. The means of production – land, labour, capital and technology – are (mostly) privately owned. Supply, demand, price, distribution, and investments are determined mainly by private decisions in the free market, rather than through state planning. Profit is distributed to owners who invest in businesses, and wages are paid to workers employed by businesses. Capital is accumulated as profits are reinvested.

Human beings have traded for as long as records exist – indeed, mankind's earliest written records include business accounts. Forms of money have also existed since the dawn of history and, as the historian Niall Ferguson puts it: '... financial innovation has been an indispensible factor in man's advance from subsistence to the giddy heights of material prosperity that so many people know today'.[1] The pre-history of capitalism is the prevalence of trade, the use of money and the seemingly inherent desire to accumulate wealth. Capitalism from the sixteenth and well into the eighteenth century was largely dominated by beliefs summarized as 'mercantilism'. The mercantilist theory assumes that wealth and monetary assets are identical and that the ruling government should advance a nation's goals by playing a protectionist role in the economy, encouraging exports and discouraging imports through the use of subsidies and tariffs.

Vestiges of the theory remain in the minds of some modern-day politicians, but most politicians and almost all economists have accepted the benefits of free trade, flexible currencies and international specialisation of production and trade rather than a limited self-sufficiency behind tariff walls and other forms of protectionism.

Protection of rice farmers in Japan and farmers generally in the EU and USA are influential remnant mercantilist policies.

The chroniclers and reformers of capitalism emerged in Britain and France in the late 18th century. The classical political economists Adam Smith, David Ricardo, Jean-Baptiste Say, and John Stuart Mill published analyses of the production, distribution and exchange of goods in a market that have since formed a body of knowledge and doctrine accepted by most contemporary economists.

Adam Smith's attack on mercantilism and his reasoning for what he called 'the system of natural liberty' in *The Wealth of Nations* (1776) marks the beginning of classical political economy. Smith devised a set of concepts that remain strongly associated with capitalism today, particularly his theory of the 'invisible hand' of the market, through which the pursuit of individual self-interest produces good overall results for society. Smith was brilliant, forceful and persuasive in his argument in favour of free markets. He criticized monopolies, tariffs, duties, and other state enforced restrictions of his era and argued that the market is the fairest and most efficient allocator of resources. By 1846, Britain had adopted Smith's views most concretely in its commitment to free trade and laissez-faire in most commercial matters.

In *The Principles of Political Economy and Taxation* (1817), David Ricardo developed the law of comparative advantage, which explains why it is profitable for two parties to trade, even if one of the trading partners is more efficient in every type of economic production. This principle provides the core economic case for free trade. Ricardo was a supporter of the doctrine known as Say's Law that stated that 'supply creates its own demand' and that full employment is the normal situation for a competitive economy. He also argued that inflation is closely related to changes in quantity of money and credit and was a proponent of the law of diminishing returns, which states that each additional unit of input yields less and less additional output.

The values of classical political economy are strongly associated with the classical liberal doctrine of minimal government intervention in the economy. While economic liberalism favours markets unfettered by government, it maintains that the state has a legitimate role in providing so-called 'public goods'. For instance, Adam Smith argued that the state has a role in providing roads, canals, schools and bridges that cannot be efficiently implemented by private entities. However, he preferred that these goods should be funded proportionally to their use by tolls to recover the cost, a device increasingly used by cash-strapped modern governments. In addition, he advocated retaliatory tariffs to bring about free trade, and copyrights and patents to encourage innovation.

All leading capitalist nations sought to create empires, with vast new territories repaying the effort many times. The United States fought for its freedom from Britain, and expanded its territory by infiltration, warfare and purchase. After a period of mutual hostility, the United States eventually supported the British cause in two world wars. More generally, colonies delivered substantial benefits to all the European powers, who eventually learned that trade with former colonies was more effective than trying to manage a far-flung empire.

The relationship between democracy and capitalism is contentious in theory and popular discourse. Capitalism began to flourish under the monarchs of Europe in the sixteenth century. The industrial revolution, whose development I call the Age of Innovation, flowered in Britain and spread widely and rapidly in the nineteenth century. The development of near universal adult male suffrage under a monarch, led many theorists to posit a causal relationship between capitalism and (male suffrage) democracy. However, in the 20th century, capitalism has accompanied a variety of political systems quite distinct from liberal democracies, including fascist and communist regimes, monarchies, and single-party states. Conversely, some democratic societies such as the Bolivarian Republic of Venezuela and Anarchist Catalonia have been expressly anti-capitalist.

Some people argue that, though economic growth under capitalism has led to democratization in the past, it may not do so in the future, as authoritarian regimes have been able to manage strong economic growth without making concessions to greater political freedom. States with highly capitalistic economic systems have thrived under authoritarian or even oppressive political systems. Singapore, which maintains a highly open market economy and attracts lots of foreign investment, does not protect civil liberties such as freedom of speech and expression with the same zeal as the United States or Australia. The private (capitalist) sector in the People's Republic of China has grown exponentially and thrived since its inception, despite working under an authoritarian government. Private investment flourished in Fascist states, such as Nazi Germany and Augusto Pinochet's rule in Chile led to economic growth by using authoritarian means to create an environment conducive to investment and capitalism.

In response to criticism, some proponents of capitalism have argued that its advantages are supported by solid research. For example, advocates of different measures of economic freedom point to a statistical correlation between nations with more economic freedom and higher scores on variables such as income per capita and life expectancy, including the poor, in these nations. Far more concrete is the absolute failure of Stalin's Russia and Mao's China and other leaders and nations who have tried to suppress capitalism. Among many sources, Paul Johnson's Modern Times provides the strongest possible collection of evidence on this crucial point.

The Crises of Capitalism

'Crisis' in modern English usage encompasses surprise, uncertainty as to outcomes and the possibility of great damage to important goals. The crises examined in this book were all surprising, in the sense that few people predicted their occurrence apart from those creating the boom before the inevitable bust. Even fewer anticipated crisis in trying either to issue warnings or trying to head it off. Each crisis also generated great uncertainty as events career out of control while creating both great opportunity and (especially in the case of wars and deep depressions) considerable damage.

Karl Marx is famous for predicting the end of capitalism through a process of recurrent and worsening crisis which he ascribed to competition reducing profit margins, owners of capital being forced into predatory aggregation and ultimate expropriation by a united and aggressive proletariat. While the growth of monopolies is part of the capitalist experience, the crises of capitalism are far more due to wars and episodes of boom and bust than to the internal dynamic of productive units. In addition, innovation, including development of new territories and new industries has powered growth of living standards, and growth of pension schemes is making modern countries into nations of shareholders. This has had a great effect in reducing the class conflict that was essential to Marx's vision.

Each crisis we examine can be described as the result of a series of broadly similar and interconnected events, probably because the surprise was so great, the uncertainty so marked and the danger so obvious. But, as we shall see, the crises of capitalism also benefitted some people and each crisis gave the existing structure a shake that delivered great benefits of a more general kind. The Austrian economist Joseph Schumpeter in his book *Capitalism, Socialism and Democracy* said that the 'process of Creative Destruction is the essential fact about capitalism'.[2]

The graphs provide some general indications of the numerical effect of the asset booms and busts that are characteristic crises of capitalism. These indicators are asset values – specifically share prices. Share prices are the result of millions, nowadays billions, of decisions that require an attitude to the future, and which can reasonably be considered as reflecting varying degrees of optimism or pessimism among the investing public. Share prices therefore can claim to be a highly relevant indicator of a nation's state of confidence, or at least that of its moneyed class. In the case of the Tulip 'mania', which some writers say was not really a crisis anyway, only qualitative estimates of movements in the prices of tulip bulbs can be provided.

This graph on the following page shows the US Standard and Poors (S&P) index with a log scale to best summarise the relative sizes of swings in confidence and the booms and busts of US share prices from 1914 to 2010. Visual inspection suggests that the boom of the Roaring Twenties and the subsequent bust was the biggest and the best. America made great progress during the 1920s and suffered greatly in the 1930s. Economists argue that with better economic policies it would have been possible to capture more of the gains and experience less of the pain, but this is by no means proven.

USA - S & P 500 - 1914 to 2010
(Log Scale)

Types of investors

We need now to make a slight detour. There are broadly two types of equity investors, 'macro' investors and 'micro' investors. Macro investors focus on trying to predict and take advantage of movements in share price indexes, bond yields, currency fluctuations and complex variations on the theme with 'leverage' (using borrowed money) and buying or selling options over any of the investment types to increase both the risk and the potential reward. George Soros, the man who broke the British pound, is a prime example of such an investor.

'Micro' investors are more interested in the opportunities offered by individual stocks or commodities. Peter Lynch's investing book, *One Up On Wall Street*, published in 1989, made the case individual investors could outperform highly educated (and remunerated) Wall Street stock pickers by taking advantage of special knowledge gained in the normal course of life. Lynch pointed out that, as consumers, workers, mothers and fathers, individual investors are much closer to real world developments than the people in Wall Street's ivory towers. When new products are introduced or new businesses opened up, consumers get first-hand information that Wall Street firms wait months for analysts to come up with.[3]

Peter Lynch specialises in 'multibagger' opportunities, shares that produce returns that are some multiple of the initial investment. We have applied this terminology to the moves from low to high in the share price indexes used to illustrate the degree of optimism in each of the episodes we examine in this book. A measure of the swing to pessimism is provided by the proportion of the peak value at the post boom low. The following graphs show each of these measures for the main episodes discussed in this book.

It is worth noting that while a tenbagger or twentybagger is relatively common for the prices of individual stocks, when dealing with whole markets, such numbers are rare indeed as market indices summarise the average performance of whole groups of stocks including ten and twentybaggers, total duds and average performers. In the cases of the Mississippi and South Sea bubbles we are dealing with the prices of individual stocks, and the Mississippi Company was a one thousand bagger, a result even Peter Lynch would have been happy with, provided only he had sold at the top. After the bubble burst its value returned to its initial, near zero value, so its post-bubble value was just a tiny proportion of its peak value. The South Sea company in Britain was an eightbagger, and its post crash price gave up all of the gains, implying a value of 0.125 times its peak value, or 12.5%.

For the nineteenth century's set of more or less regular 'business cycles', some of which ended in serious asset booms and busts, American and British share price indexes are available as a proxy for the ups and downs of confidence. The case of the British Railway Mania, we also use data compiled by John Simon in a conference paper on 'Three Asset-price Bubbles'.[4] As evidence of the relative tranquility of the nineteenth century we note that the indexes used in each nineteenth century episode are all twobaggers , give or take a few decimal points.

In the later chapters discussing mainly the financial booms and busts we present graphs of share prices that show a characteristic pattern – a sharp rise over months (in the twin bubbles of 1720) or years (in the subsequent booms and busts). In most cases a dramatic uplift of share prices is followed by a severe crash that takes share prices back some way toward or (in the crash of the 1930s) far below the starting point. In the inflationary period after World War II, each crash returned to a point above its starting point, with the exception of the crash of 2007-08, which in going below the starting point of the preceding boom looks more like the crash in the early thirties. Recoveries in all cases in the twentieth century have been lengthy and usually involve at least one false start as optimism runs ahead of the reality of economic and financial recovery. There are examples of downward corrections during share price booms also, which is why profiting from large market moves is so difficult.

As we shall see, the Roaring Twenties provide a classic case. The share index used here started at approximately 150 in 1925, reached a peak of 380 in August 1929 and fell to 45 before the low point of the Great Depression in 1932. There was one major recovery followed by a steep 'correction' before the index again reached 150 in 1939, on the eve of WWII.

But the most striking feature of 20th century booms is their relative size, from the start of the 1980s increasing in size or numbers or both.

The following graphs illustrate the size of each of the main episodes discussed in this book, apart from the Tulipomania hwere reliable data is not readily available. The bars show the peak of the boom as a multiple of the starting point. The details of sources and construction are set out in the Appendix.

Great Crises of Capitalism – Asset value indicators

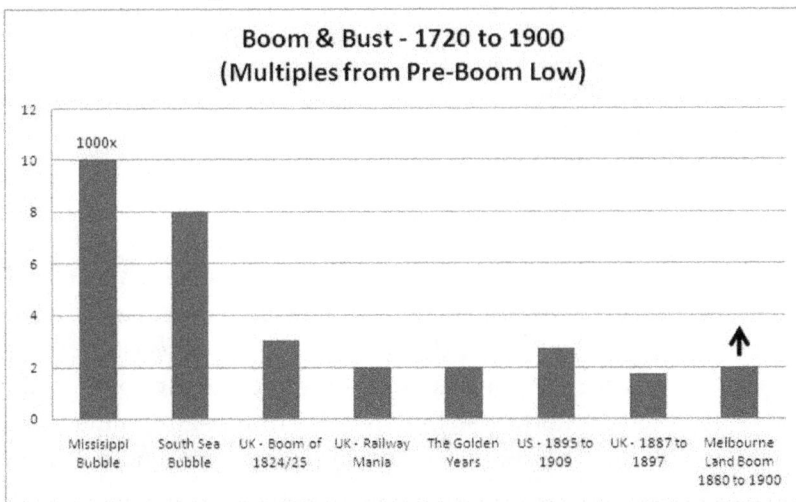

Boom & Bust - 1720 to 1900 (Multiples from Pre-Boom Low)

Boom & Bust - 1925 to 2010
(Multiples from Pre-Boom Low)

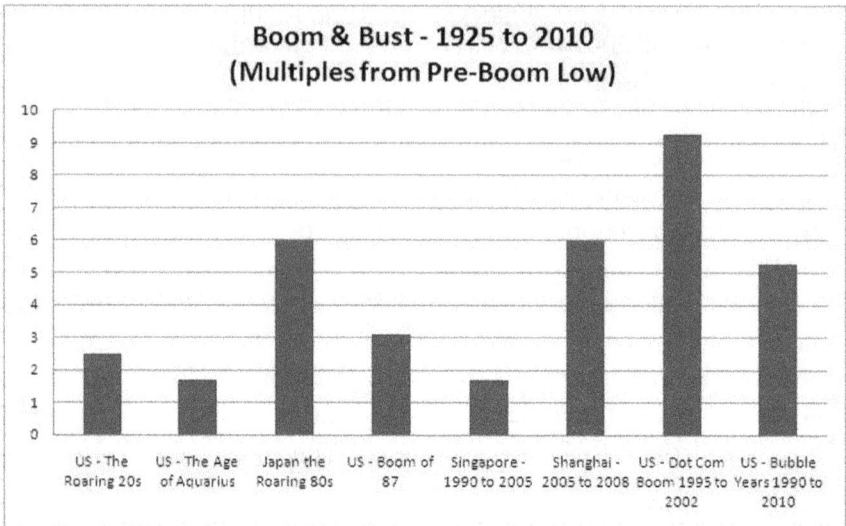

Crises and their causes

Spain's conquest of the Inca and Aztec Empires of South America in the sixteenth century was in some views the spark that set the warring states of Europe on the path to the virtually endless (despite occasional large setbacks) improvements in productivity and standard of living that still characterise the capitalist nations. The strong inflows of Spanish gold and silver gave a pronounced stimulus to economies that had stagnated for centuries.

Spain itself began its long decline following the acquisition of such unexpected new wealth. France and England, whose privateers relieved Spain of some of its new wealth, were clearer winners from the influx of

Massive injections of wealth do not always have a positive effect on the recipient, a judgment that may as often be applied to individuals as to nations.

Spanish treasure. But it was in Holland that the first widely reported crisis of capitalism exploded, and in a way it would have been difficult to predict. Tulip bulbs became the subject of a dramatic asset boom. The fashion was for rare bulbs, themselves the product of a virus, though this was not known at the time. From most accounts there was real mania in the land of clogs, dykes and windmills though we shall hear of skeptical modern economists who try, without full success, to banish any implication of what was later labelled 'irrational exuberance'.

Speculation exploded in Amsterdam in 1636, and 'Tulipomania' became a widely discussed phenomenon. There were minor effects elsewhere, but no great international impact. The Dutch authorities declined to implement new laws, or to retrospectively punish the winners from the boom. It thus recognised the great principle of *caveat emptor* more thoroughly than subsequent governments in the wake of booms and busts.

The Tulipomania was largely funded by payments in kind, as flexible bank credit was not yet available. Tulip prices rocketed up and Kindelberger and Aliber in their book on *Manias, Panics and Crashes,* report that other Dutch asset prices were powerfully influenced; shares of the Amsterdam Chamber of the Dutch East India company rose strongly, house prices 'shot up' and other 'surging investments' were made in drainage schemes, in the West Indies company and in canals. The economy slowed when the tulip bubble popped and recovered to put on a 'tremendous spurt' from 1650 to 1672. Prices of luxury housing, civic buildings and paintings rose sharply and there was a 'mania' for clocks and clock towers.[5]

The next major asset boom arose in France in 1719. Here it was the value of shares in the Mississippi Company that rose to astronomical heights, from 100 to almost 10,000 in less than a year. Massive gains were followed by massive losses when the bubble burst. Among the punishments, a nobleman who murdered someone to get his hands on Mississippi stock was broken on the wheel, an ancient and barbaric way of executing a criminal. Economists take an especial interest in this episode as it stars one of their own – a Scot named John Law, who created the bubble by his use of bank credit money and the power of what now is called leverage. Law, like many others who have followed him, seemingly overlooked the fact that leverage works in reverse when the price of a leveraged assets falls. He was not the first economist to forget that what goes up must come down.

Across the English Channel, London had its own asset bubble – the South Sea Bubble – about nine months after Paris. The symptoms were the same – people fighting for the right to invest, politicians corrupted, wealthy people buying South Sea stock with borrowed money, and a keen desire after the bubble burst to find and punish the perpetrators, or at least those who could be blamed without great damage to the rulers who had participated so enthusiastically in creating the bubble.

Retribution was harsh – public disgrace and fines that removed some or in some cases almost all of a winner's wealth. The grandfather of the great historian Gibbon was one person who lost almost all of his wealth but to his credit rebuilt a considerable fortune in the next 20 years. His grandson much later pointed out that there was no law that justified the harsh punishments metered out to winners from the bubble after the bubble had burst.

The next major crisis of capitalism was the series of wars known collectively as the Napoleonic wars, part of the ongoing, centuries-long struggle for Europe. The Napoleonic Wars ran from 1799 (when Bonaparte seized power in France) to 1815. These wars are seen by historians as sparked by the French Revolution of 1789, itself part-sparked by the Mississippi Bubble of 1720, showing the usual complex interaction among the strands of history.

French power rose quickly, with France conquering most of Europe, but collapsed rapidly after France's disastrous invasion of Russia in 1812, a mistake repeated by Hitler in 1941. Napoleon's empire ultimately collapsed after military defeat by Wellington's army in the 'nearest run thing you ever saw in your life'[6], resulting in the restoration of the Bourbon monarchy in France and the ascension of Great Britain as the world's superpower.

The Rothschild family established its wealth during the Napoleonic wars, with Nathan Rothschild collecting and transporting gold bullion and coins for the British government. Legend has it that Nathan Rothschild made a killing by superior communication skills and chicanery, but in Ferguson's account the rapid end of the war in 1815 created a major risk to the value of the Rothschild family's substantial holdings of gold. So the family used their hoard of gold to make large purchases of British bonds. Ferguson described this as 'a massive and hugely risky bet on the bond market' but I am not so sure. The alternative was to hold large stocks of gold and gold coin that was sure to fall greatly in value. When gold indeed plunged in value, bonds soared, establishing a fortune that has lasted into modern times.[7]

Economists and historians have studied the ebbs and flows of economic activity under the heading of the trade cycle in England and the business cycle in the United States. In these fluctuations the most certain regularity is that, like an apple on Mr Newton's tree, what goes up eventually comes down. It is an inescapable truth of economic history that booms are followed by busts, economics' version of gravity, though there is no simple law relating the size of the rise in asset prices to the subsequent fall. There has also been attempts to define so-called 'long-waves' in economic activity that mediate fluctuations of shorter duration.

The long-waves as seen most clearly in data on commodity prices, as compiled by Robert Triffin of Yale University. From 1790 until the end of the Napoleonic wars prices rose strongly in all major industrialising countries. Then from 1814 to 1849, prices fell. Gold discoveries in California and Australia led to strong commodity and share price inflation in the next quarter century, which Geoffrey Blainey describes as 'the high noon of faith in wide-ranging progress'. This optimistic time was followed by a less optimistic time, another period of commodity price deflation and lesser share price increases. Mild commodity inflation and further share price surges resumed from the late 1880s, following more gold discoveries, in South Africa, Western Australia, the USA and Canada.[8]

The century from the end of the Napoleonic wars in 1815 to the outbreak of the first world war in 1914 saw massive development and (relative to later experience) only moderate fluctuations in asset values. Trade was largely free, and flourished. Borders were relatively free, facilitating movement of people and capital. New nations arose, including the United States of America which survived a great civil war to become a world superpower in the first quarter of the twentieth century. There were dramatic technical developments, including the development of massive railway networks and great improvements in industrial production and the wealth of nations.[9]

There were at various times many of the classic signs of economic overheating – property and share booms, railway booms, imprudent lending, failure of major financial institutions, followed by sluggish economies, high unemployment and falling asset prices.

The nineteenth century exhibits, of course, a highly complex set of interrelated developments. I discuss three main episodes of boom and bust in particular asset classes, including land and shares, at times especially shares in railway companies. To provide some interesting detail I dig into the Melbourne land boom of the 1880s and the severe depression which followed in the 1890s. In this case, the rise in Melbourne land prices seems to have produced even in overall terms more than a twobagger, as discussed in Chapter 7. All the episodes examined show strong international linkages, appropriately enough as the nineteenth century was both an age of innovation and a time of accelerating globalisation.

The brilliant young Russian economist and bureaucrat, Nikolai Kondratieff used data from the late eighteenth century to the outbreak of the Great War of 1914-18 to illustrate his long wave theory of capitalist development. Geoffrey Blainey, in his book, *The Great Seesaw*, provides a succinct summary of Kondratieff's theory, which he praises for its boldness and specific allowance for cultural factors. 'In essence he argued that economic activity, war and peace, and inventions belonged to a tightly enclosed system inherent in capitalism and that every forty or sixty years this system completed a full cycle and that certain trends could be predicted by those who understood the cycle'.[10]

As Blainey says, there are mistakes and gaps in Kondratieff's writings, but his attempts to find a connection between fluctuations in gold production and inflation or deflation, the economic mood and international wars produced a 'tantalising riddle'. Blainey's version of Kondratieff's grand synthesis is summarised in the following table.

Long-term fluctuations of commodity prices, 1790 - 1920

	Price upswing	Price downswing
World's gold output	Quickly rising	Slowly rising
International wars	Many	Few
Economic mood	Confident	Less confident
Mental and cultural mood	Confident	Less confident

The first great age of innovation and globalisation ended in a period of great optimism. As Keynes put it in his passionate book *The Economic Consequences of the Peace*: 'What an extraordinary episode in the economic progress of man that age was which came to an end in August 1914. The greater part of the population, it is true, worked hard and lived at a low standard of comfort, yet were to all appearances reasonably contented with this lot. But escape was possible, for any man of capacity or character at all exceeding the average, into the middle and upper classes, for whom life offered at a low cost and with the least trouble, conveniences, comforts, and amenities beyond the compass of the richest and most powerful monarchs of other ages'.[11]

This happy state of affairs was not to last. 'Moved by insane delusion and reckless self-regard, the German people overturned the foundations on which we all lived and built'.[12] Germany's 'roll of the iron dice' (as its Chancellor called it) in 1914 is generally regarded as motivated by an almost religious desire to establish an empire that would rival England's and contain within its boundaries (including colonies) all the resources Germany would need to sustain itself and to develop its empire into the dominant global superpower.

The first great war of the twentieth century has been seen as a backlash against the first great age of globalisation, which opinion sounds a warning for us now. Whatever its value as a reminder of modern risks, this war imposed great financial and other losses through death, injury, damage and spending on armaments and soldiers. When the heir to the Austrian throne was assassinated in the Bosnian capital Sarajevo on 28 June 1914, there was no immediate reaction in financial markets, despite plenty of earlier discussion of the mighty costs that would be imposed if the major powers went to war. It was almost a month before the financial press expressed serious anxiety that the Balkans crisis might become something far more serious. When investors realised the full-scale war was coming, 'liquidity was sucked out of the world economy as if the bottom had dropped out of a bath'.[13]

Exchange rates fluctuated wildly and bond and equity prices began to slip until by July 30 1914 a full scale financial panic had developed.

Assets purchased on credit were sold at knock-down prices and the financial dominos began to fall. The major banks cancelled loans and there was a hard credit crunch that included queues of people seeking to exchange banknotes for gold coins at the Bank of England. Europe's stock exchanges closed, and the London stock exchange did not reopen until 4 January 1915. Currency and commodity markets closed. Not for the last time, the gold standard came under massive pressure and national authorities resorted to printing money.

The outbreak of war created one of capitalism's great financial crises, which would in fact have been far worse if markets had remained open to facilitate a fire sale of assets. As it was, bond and equity holders made large losses and in some cases certain asset classes were wiped out. The Bolshevik government defaulted on Russian bonds in 1918, and the Chinese declared bankruptcy and defaulted on almost all of China's external debts, a common development then and later, though the leading capitalist nations have never defaulted except indirectly although inflation. Hyperinflation in the axis nations wiped out the savings of the middle classes in the 1920s. There were bargains galore after the war for those few smart operators who had turned paper assets into gold before the wartime inflation eroded the values of paper assets.

Despite its defeat in the war of 1914 to 1918, Germany was to try again in 1939, but not before one of history's great share price booms and busts helped to create the world's greatest depression. After climbing between two and three times its starting point US share prices fell by approximately 80% and the rate of unemployment reached 20% or more in most capitalist nations, perhaps twice that number if allowance is made for severe underemployment. The Great Depression plus the great wars before and after it ranks as capitalism's greatest crisis. This is especially so as there is as yet no definitive and widely accepted economic analysis of just why the Great Depression was so serious. I say more about this in chapter 8.

The Great Depression led to the first serious analysis of the case for deliberate intervention to try to turn the course of global economic crisis, in the form of JM Keynes' *General Theory of Employment, Interest and Money*, published in 1936. As we have seen, the Global Financial

Crisis of 2007-08 provided the first real test of the *General Theory*, and it is perhaps appropriate to say 'so far, so good'.

The war of 1939 to 1945 was the first modern war to be ended by the dramatic destruction of two cities, Nagasaki and Hiroshima, each obliterated by a single (nuclear) bomb. No surprise, perhaps, that despite massive tension between Soviet Russia and the leading capitalist nations there was no global nuclear war, nor in later years (so far at least) resort to use of 'tactical' nuclear weapons by any state or terrorist group.

No surprise, also, that the defeated nations resolved to behave better than in the aftermath of the first great twentieth century war. More surprising, perhaps, that the

The recent performance of 'Keynesian' policies has been strongly praised by many. The fact not widely known is that in the capitalist heartland in the early months after the Global Financial Crisis production, jobs and asset prices fell at least as sharply as in the early months of the Great Depression. Then powerful fiscal stimulus, interest rates set to zero and bailouts of major financial institutions stemmed the falls. But the impacts of the Global Financial Crisis of 2007-08 are far from over and final judgment will be a decade or more in the making. My final two chapters canvass some issues bearing on this matter.

victorious powers, led by the USA, the UK and the Soviet Union agreed to softer peace terms than their predecessors in 1919. Germany was partitioned and the US, UK and French sectors quickly became a modern, democratic capitalist nation. The Russians created the People's Republic of Germany (GDR), with The Wall between it and the democratic, modernising part of Germany.

Very few people tried to escape from democratic, capitalist Germany into the GDR, whereas the flow in the other direction was substantial despite the communist rulers' attempts to ban it, often with extreme prejudice to the potential escapees. When The Wall finally crumbled in late 1989 the most graphic comment came from a man from the East: 'They have lied to us for 70 years'. A similar story is told by Li Cunxin in *Mao's Last Dancer* when he finds the skyscrapers and shopping malls of Houston are real.[14]

Another contrast between the post-war situations was the economic performance of the former belligerents and the health of their peoples. Following the first great twentieth century war there was an influenza plague that killed at least 50 million people, more than twice the number who died in the war. Economic recovery was halting at best – made far worse than it needed to be by misguided attempts to restore the gold standard at pre-war rates in the UK and some other nations. Germany's massive obligation to pay reparations, the UK's debts and other burdens inhibited recovery. There was also resort to protectionism, rolling back the reforms of the nineteenth century that had helped to create a golden age of trade with free movement of people and capital.

Instead of recession morphing into depression, following the war of 1939 to 1945 the world economy boomed. The Korean War (1950 – 1953) helped to create a wool boom that gave Australia one of its biggest economic boosts since the gold discoveries of the 1850s. Europe formed a 'common market' which encouraged trade and whose initial success created a mood for further experiments in economic liberalisation.

The 1950s and 1960s are remembered in many nations as a second golden age. Trade, employment and incomes expanded rapidly and economic deregulation added impetus to the boom. Despite the surge in commodity prices in the Korean War boom, inflationary expectations remained low and stable, and occasional resort to the fiscal and monetary policy brakes served to maintain that situation. The (conservative) Australian government brought down a 'horror budget' in 1951-52 that quickly restored stable expectations and sustainable behaviours of both unions and corporations. The same government, with a different Treasurer (Finance Minister), in 1960-61 imposed a credit squeeze that again restored stability.

Gradually, however, governments tried to do too much. The US government declared war on poverty with President Johnson's 'Great Society' program. At the same time, America was involved in an unwinnable war in Vietnam. Inflation and antiwar protest began to build and the rise of US inflation initially gave other nations an advantage in trading with the USA, an advantage that was eroded as inflation began to increase elsewhere. The fundamental causes of what became a global trend to inflation were masked for almost all analysts.

Australia's example was typical of the experience of small open economies with fixed exchange rates, each of which experienced a similar crisis due, fundamentally, to lack of a clear understanding of what was happening in the world economy. Australia's Treasury (Finance Department) declared inflation was caused by excessive wage demands and the fiscal brakes were applied. Monetary policy was also tightened but with a fixed exchange rate this increased capital inflows which expanded the money supply despite futile efforts to rein it in.

President Nixon in 1971 cut the US dollar's convertibility to gold, signalling the end of the gold standard. With the 'anchor' of the gold standard finally severed, the global economy sailed effortlessly into an inflationary future. It was a time of drugs, sex and rock'n'roll and someone christened it the Age of Aquarius, a time of love, light, and humanity.

This writer demonstrated with the aid of a modified version of the large 'Keynesian' econometric model at the Reserve Bank of Australia that Australia's inflation was far more due to global inflation than it was to domestic factors, including above normal wage hikes. This was controversial at the time but withstood searching scrutiny by other economists. Two years later, whilst living in London, I had the satisfaction of being told by a senior Treasury official, the late Dr Chris Higgins, that Treasury accepted that I had been right. Together we took in *The Rocky Horror Show.*

I had by then moved to work at the London School of Economics where there were similar-minded economists, including one of my thesis supervisors, Professor Harry Johnson. I was in London when the first of the oil price shocks hit the world economy, as OPEC formed an effective cartel to exploit the strong global demand for oil. In late December 1973, OPEC decided to raise the posted price of marker crude oil from US$5.12 to US$11.65 per barrel effective January 1, 1974. OPEC's oil price inflation reinforced other global inflationary forces to bring stagnation to the industrial economies.

The ugly word 'stagflation' was coined to describe the previously rare combination of price inflation combined with industrial stagnation. Gradual economic recovery was reversed following the Iranian revolution and Iraq's invasion of Iran when oil reached a new peak of US$ 36 per barrel and this time there was greater resolve to find ways to economise in the use of oil. The price of US$145 per barrel in July 2008, while adding to the sense of panic, was nowhere seen as such a problem as the equivalent peak in 1973. Share markets mostly moved in relatively narrow bands in the Age of Aquarius, though from the start of the period to the end there was a modest annual increase in average share prices, mirroring the goods and services inflation that so bedevilled the times.

Once out of the lamp in the 1970s, the genie of inflation was to take a decade or two to conquer. The USA acted soonest and with most force. The US Fed under Chairman Paul Volcker instituted so-called 'new operating procedures' in 1981, creating a short sharp shock that quickly returned sanity in the setting of wages and prices in the US economy. It was to take another decade and the adoption of a flexible exchange rate for Australia to undergo a similar anti-inflationary shock, and other countries followed the US example with varying time delays and in their own fashion.

Paul Volker in my view is the world's greatest central banker, with a towering reputation matching his great height. Though in his eighties now, he continues to be influential, though sadly his call for the return of the Glass-Steagall Act to provide a saner and safer financial system in the United States has (so far) been rejected.

The Japanese economy was the next to experience a crisis. This ranks as one of the great crises of capitalism because it heralded the change in status of Japan from miracle economy to a stagnant one. It is far from certain that this experience is yet fully understood. If only because the Japanese crisis of 1989 in some ways resembles the American crisis of 2007-08, it deserves careful study.

During the 1980s, Japan boomed, with share prices and land prices reaching previously undreamed of levels. The Australian embassy in Tokyo, to take one example, provided the Australian government with a massive capital gain when its garden – about half of its land – was sold during the bubble of the late 1980s for a reported US$ 600 million. The Nikki index of share prices peaked at a value of almost 39,000 on December 28 1989 – more than six times above its level a decade earlier. The subsequent fall was also dramatic and the Japanese economy has experienced mildly depressed conditions since.

Japanese banks had loaned against the value of land and owned shares in Japan's great manufacturing and trading companies. The banks were kept alive as 'zombie banks' with zombie customers. Failure quickly and ruthlessly to write down asset values helped to create the longest post World War II recession in what had been one of the world's most dynamic capitalist economies. An economist for Nomura Securities, Richard Koo, has developed an interesting theory of 'Balance Sheet Recession' to explain Japan's lost decades.

The analogy with the American situation now has many elements: major banks and other financial institutions have been bailed out; asset values are depressed; economic activity is low; confidence is weak; and there is fear of deeply rooted deflation despite massive fiscal and monetary stimulus. It is noteworthy that even by the end of 1999 – that is a decade after the Nikki share index reached its all-time peak – this index was less than half of its peak value.

Even putting the Japanese boom and bust aside, the 1980s and 1990s were eventful decades. Indeed, Kindleberger and Aliber, authors of *Manias, Panics and Crashes*, say there were more asset price bubbles between 1980 and 2000 than in any earlier period.[16] There was a dramatic US share price boom in the 1980s, when the index more than doubled and then dropped suddenly and dramatically. The so-called Asian crisis saw serious trouble in the fast-growing economies of South East Asia in 1998 and then a boom and bust in Russian asset prices. Then there was a classic share price bubble in America centred on 'new economy' stocks that produced a nine-bagger win for the IT crowd and eventually behaved like old economy stocks and crashed after a heady boom. It was this boom that elicited US Fed Chief Alan Greenspan's determination not to try to fight the bubble. Paradoxically, Greenspan reacted to the *crash* in share prices by slashing interest rates, with the US Fed's cash rate reaching a then record low of 1%.

Niall Ferguson notes that the stock market boom of the 1990s reminded some investors of the Roaring Twenties, and indeed their respective share price graphs look remarkably similar. He argues that however the nineties reminds him far more of the 1720s. The Enron Company, Ferguson says, used its 'impeccable' political connections, clever reinvention of the rules of finance (and, one is forced to add, ethics) and fraudulent manipulation of global energy markets (and relevant investment analysts) to create vast paper wealth, as did John Law with similar innovative tactics in the great Mississippi bubble. It should come as no surprise that the aforementioned Alan Greenspan received the Enron Prize for Distinguished Public Service from the modern John Law, Kenneth Lay, shortly before the Enron story began to fall apart.[17]

The Greenspan doctrine treats asset booms and busts asymmetrically, so there should be no confusion about why the 1990s and 2000s have seen massive volatility of asset prices, with an upward bias.

It was appropriate really that Greenspan's career was celebrated by Enron's Chief, Kenneth Lay, as it was Greenspan's loose monetary policy that set up the great share price boom of the first decade of the twenty-first century. Together with excessive risk-taking by lending institutions and excessively clever financial engineering by investment banks and even previously boring home loan institutions, fund managers and financial officers of industrial companies like Enron, loose monetary policy led directly to the Global Financial Crisis of 2007-08.

Modern communications, the globalisation of trade, capital flows and news broadcasts all suggest that crises might come and go more quickly than in the past. Certainly it is a theme of Kindleberger and Aliber, that the twentieth century experienced more and larger crises than earlier centuries. These writers head their final chapter 'The Lessons of History and the Most Tumultuous Decades Ever.'

The approach and main conclusions of this book

This book covers the most exciting of these crises in detail and most of the rest to a greater or lesser extent. My approach is to rely on the best of the detailed accounts by others of the historical episodes. For the post World War II crises, beginning with the rise of inflation in the 1970s, I write from personal experience, having lived through the period first as an economist employed in Australia's central bank and then as an investment professional and businessman who maintained a special interest in economics.

Taking the facts as read, recognising inevitable limitations of understanding, my contribution is to suggest what the evolving history of capitalist crises tells us about how capitalism works and the lessons for governments, central bankers and people trying to maximise wealth and protect it. War is horrible, and should be regarded as an absolutely last resort by any sane national leader. It is often assumed, implicitly or explicitly, that financial boom and bust is also a negative development to be avoided if possible. This is incorrect. Great things are achieved in the buoyant times, and the hard times that inevitably follow purge the economy of most of the excesses and the frauds of the boom. It is when asset booms get totally out-of-control that great damage occurs, and this is why national and world leaders need to find ways to create a more stable financial system.

For those who see the speed of events increasing, I note that the Tulip boom, the Mississippi Bubble and the South Sea Bubble all ended in less than a year. In strong contrast, the financial fluctuations of the nineteenth century and the Roaring Nineteen-twenties in America, the great inflation of the Seventies, the Roaring Eighties in Japan, the New Economy Nineties in America and the Rampaging 2000s just about everywhere all lasted for a decade, give or take a year or two.

My conjecture is that this is because the increasingly global financial system has created a degree of complexity and resonating responsiveness between multiple markets and policy responses that prolongs both the expansion and contraction phases of economic life. Indeed, the experience from the start of the nineteen-eighties might eventually come to be seen as a continuous process of interacting expansionary and contractionary forces. If leading nations and international agencies do not implement different, less discretionary, financial policies, my concern is that there will be increasing economic instability leading to a crash that provides a crisis of capitalism at least as serious as that of the 1930s.

I shall with appropriate modesty consider some defences against excessive buoyancy that should prevent the worst features of uncontrolled financial excess. My conclusion is that semi-automatic reactions, such as requiring banks to increase their reserve ratios as booms develop, would be a sensible way to test the degree to which buoyancy is based on solid foundations. I have in mind financial system equivalents of the so-called 'automatic stabilisers' of good fiscal policy. I strongly believe that central bankers should be required to 'lean into the wind' by targeting a broad measure of asset inflation as well as some suitable measure of goods and services inflation.

Since share price inflation everywhere tends to be far more strongly influenced by Wall Street than by local economic factors, taking account of global share prices may be largely a task for the US Fed, or perhaps as China rises in influence a task for the US Fed and the People's Bank of China acting in concert. In the final chapters I shall also consider a more radical approach, inspired by Paul Volcker's bold change of operating procedures in 1981, as well as my youthful research with some of the world's leading monetarist economists.

Marx said that capitalism is crisis. I respond that crisis is opportunity.

Wars and financial crises provide great opportunity as well as great dangers. My chief conclusion for individuals is that people need to take personal charge of their investment strategies if they wish to maximise their wealth and their family's wealth. Given the tendency for the biggest financial crises to be separated by decades, a family interested in becoming (or staying) wealthy needs to take a multi-generation view of matters financial, and to find ways to benefit from asset booms while avoiding the worst of the downturns. This is my most important message for individuals and families in the great and complex world of modern capitalism.

The numerology of financial crisis

I now report some technical matters that may, perhaps with profit, be skipped by readers uninterested in the more technical reaches of the great modern economic ocean.

Numbers of crises listed by Kindelberger and Aliber are as follows: Seventeenth Century, 3; Eighteenth Century, 9; Nineteenth Century, 22; and Twentieth Century, 12.[18] There is no doubt that financial innovation and technical progress generally changed the ways in which crises manifested themselves, but whether the Twentieth Century included 'the most tumultuous decades ever ' is probably unproven. What can be stated with greater certainty is that the twentieth century included two of the worst wars and the greatest depression so far experienced. The second half of the nineteenth century perhaps deserves further consideration as 'most tumultuous ever'. Starting with the gold discoveries of California and Australia, the rapid development of new territories, new modes of transport and new products and services leading to the massive property booms and busts toward the end of the century, this time certainly rivals the second half of the twentieth century as an exciting boom time, with inevitable busts since we all have to pay the piper when the parties are over.

A recent major study to address the overall question of stability is Reinhart and Rogoff's *This Time is Different. Eight Centuries of Financial Folly.* Chapter 16 discusses 'Composite Measures of Financial Turmoil'. Composite indices of crises in the twentieth century are presented on their pages 253 and 254. Both graphs feature the Panic of 1907, World War 1 – hyperinflation, the Great Depression, banking, currency, default and inflation crises during the 1930s, World War II, the Oil Shock – Inflation crisis of the 1970s, the emerging market crises and the Nordic and Japanese banking crises in many post WW II years, the dot-com bubble and bust and the Global Financial Crisis of 2007-08, called by these authors 'The Second Great Contraction'. Both graphs show far more volatility in the first half of the twentieth century than at any other time.

Later, on page 258, is a graph from 1800 to 2008 of 'Average number of Crises per Country per Year'. Peaks are in the 1820s, the 1850s, the 1880s and at the time of WW1. Until WW1, each peak was larger with the later peaks in the 1930s and early 1940s and again in the 1990s being slightly lower.

Reinhart and Rogoff also present a table of 'Selected episodes of global, multicountry, and regional economic crises'. This features the crisis of 1825-1826, the Panic of 1907, The Great Depression, the Debt Crisis of the 1980s, the Asian Crisis of 1997-98 and the Global Financial Crisis of 2007-08.

3

War and Peace and Capitalism;
a many stranded rope

*Are war and economic progress allies or enemies? Does
economic prosperity make nations more inclined to make
war than to find ways of prolonging peace? What is the
connection between economic fluctuations and war and
peace? These are important questions rarely answered
with conviction. What is far more certain is that war
represents a major, recurrent challenge to the capitalist
system.*

In the early days of capitalism wars did not always impinge greatly
on civilians and involved fewer fighting men (and casualties) in relation
to a nation's population. Potentially, then, victory in war could produce
rewards that exceeded the costs. War has always been horrible, but full
on global war with all the modern weapons of war would do immense
damage to everyone involved, and is practically unimaginable.

The nuclear bombs used against Japan changed the rules of war.
Two cities and most of their inhabitants were killed or severely hurt
with just two explosions. The damage was so great that no sane leader
could unleash such weapons again, except perhaps in a last desperate
defence against a completely ruthless enemy. Proof of this lies in the
failure of the United States and the Soviet Union to turn their cold
war into a hot war.

The even more devastating weapons now available add to the need for restraint by leaders. But the spread of modern technology, including weapons technology, makes an act of state or ideological terrorism potentially far more damaging, and capitalism has a number of ideological enemies. Sadly, we cannot ignore the connections between war and the economies of modern nations. We start at the dawn of the modern capitalist era.

The sixteenth century saw Spain at the peak of its power. In 1519 Cortes sailed to South America, burnt his ships and conquered the Inca Empire. Vast riches were returned to Europe, and Spanish gold was the spark that set Europe on the path to global dominance as the first great capitalist civilisation.

The vast riches that resulted from Spain's conquest of the Aztec and Inca empires of South America did not just go to Spain, as French, Dutch and English navies and privateers took sizable shares by intercepting and capturing Spanish gold fleets. Queen Elizabeth was a considerable shareholder in the syndicate that financed the enterprise that captured the prodigious spoils brought home by Drake in his *Golden Hind*. One sees capitalism red in tooth and claw in this example, with no complaints about the political arm participating as an insider in the accumulation of great wealth.

The faint echo of this attitude is the view of some but not all commentators that managers should also be shareholders of the companies they run. Queen Elizabeth would presumably fail to understand the largely standard strictures against modern companies run by families, and in most cases controlled by those families.

John Maynard Keynes in his 1930 essay 'Economic possibilities for our grandchildren', calculates the value of the great treasure captured by Drake. With her share of Drake's treasure, Queen Elizabeth paid off all of England's foreign debt, balanced her budget and invested her remaining 40,000 pounds in the Levant Company, which prospered. The profits of the Levant Company were used to found the East India Company, and Keynes says that the profits of this great enterprise were the foundations of England's subsequent foreign investment'.[1]

He asserts that England's foreign investments have yielded an income of about 6.5%, of which half has been brought home to enjoy, and the other half has been left to accumulate abroad. 40,000 pounds accumulating at 3.25% from 1580 to 1930 is 4 billion pounds, the approximate value of Britain's overseas assets in 1930. Such is the magic of time and compound interest.

Mining booms bring great wealth to a nation, but economists have concluded that there are many negatives to offset the obvious positive of a major new source of wealth. The influx of gold and silver into Spain was a major source of inflation, and we have learned in the twentieth century that inflation weakens nations in many insidious ways. For Spain the new riches no doubt provided a sense of effortless dominance leading to hubris and then inevitable nemesis. But the influx of treasure gave already highly competitive powers a stimulus that helped transform the nations of Europe.

Perhaps the lesson is that people who best handle sudden new wealth are the likely winners in the race for economic and political dominance.

The calculus of conflict

Preparation for war or recovery from war creates jobs and restores economic prosperity. Even if it is a fact, the judgment ignores the possibility that spending on armies and armaments could have been directed to far better causes, such as improving health or education, encouraging scientific or cultural activity or other causes more worthy than waging war.

Of course, even in the twenty-first century, 'more worthy causes' are only a viable objective if a nation maintains a strong defence capability. There are currently enough real or perceived geopolitical threats that virtually no nation is willing to lay down its arms and trust to providence or the innate decency of other nations.

Another simplistic view is that repairing the ravages of war provides meaningful work for the post-war generation. This may be true but, in thinking about a balance sheet of war, one immediately recognises that restoration by definition means repairing existing damage. The existing damage caused by modern war almost certainly exceeds any benefit from the work of restoration and in any case this calculus ignores the vast differences of intergenerational outcomes - loss of life or limb among those involved to the war verses the gains of those constructively employed in war's aftermath. The severe economic consequences for Germany of the peace settlement of the World War I, and its contribution to the second world war, shows how the calculus can easily be negative, if impossible to analyse with precision.

A more sophisticated view is that, while wartime destruction sweeps away irreplaceable people and great buildings and costly infrastructure, it sometimes also destroys the oligarchs who went to war. Sometimes this leads to democratisation and a more sustainable future for the survivors of war and in ways impossible to calculate this may suggest ultimate net benefits. Possibly the invasion of Iraq was an example of such an outcome, though clearly the costs to both sides were enormous. The democratisation of Japan and Germany after the second world war are clearer examples.

A view of some writers, usually implicit rather than explicit, is that war is a useful evolutionary tool. Demented people may imagine that war winnows the weak, but in fact it typically destroys the flower of a warring nation's youth. It is surely stretching matters to see the loss of so many strong and idealistic young men in the two great wars of the twentieth century as good for the human gene bank.

Wars in the capitalist era

Paul Kennedy's fine book *The Rise and Fall of the Great Powers* says that in 1500 the 'power centres' included Ming China, the Ottoman Empire, Muscovy, Tokugawa Japan and the cluster of states in west-central Europe. However impressive the 'oriental' powers were, they 'all suffered from the consequences of having a centralised authority which insisted upon uniformity of belief and practice in many things including religion, weapons development and even commercial development'.

'Warlike rivalries' within Europe, says Kennedy, stimulated a constant search for military improvement, which interacted fruitfully with technological and commercial developments thrown up by Europe's 'competitive, entrepreneurial environment'. With few obstacles to change, stimulated by Spanish treasure, European societies 'entered into a constantly upward spiral of economic growth and enhanced military effectiveness'.[2]

By 1600, when our story begins, the warring states of Europe were the dominant powers, but also the only nations which comprised the emerging capitalist world. At various times the 'oriental powers' provided military challenges, but mostly it was the capitalist nations that were bent on imposing their will on other powers and subjugating less developed peoples. Whatever the ideological motivation, expanding the rule of the market provided a classic capitalistic imperative.

Now Japan is part of global capitalism, and its dramatic asset market crash in 1989 heralded the onset of one of the great crises of capitalism. Russia is the dominant part of what was the Soviet Union, for decades confronting the USA until America's much greater wealth gave it victory. Russia is, however, again today becoming an economic and military force.

The Ottoman Empire disintegrated in 1919, but its radical Islamic offspring pose ongoing real and present threats to capitalism. Turkey, whose capital Constantinople (now Istanbul) once ruled the Ottoman Empire, is trying to join the European Union (EU). Other parts of the Muslim world are having trouble co-existing peacefully with the Judeo-capitalist Israel in the Middle East and modern capitalism elsewhere. Muslim immigrants to mainstream capitalist nations like Australia often seem disinclined to accept the local culture.

Communist China is best classified as an authoritarian capitalist nation, like nominally democratic Singapore, South Korea and Taiwan. China is growing rapidly and has massive (but still poorly equipped) armed forces. If there is a serious military challenge to democratic capitalism in the next 100 years, China is currently the most likely candidate. Its people integrate well into democratic capitalist nations, however and, with India, China is a strong candidate to become a reliable member of a generally democratic capitalist world.

The struggle for dominance of Europe

'The struggle for Europe', which for Europeans must have seemed like the struggle for the world, is the simplest explanation of the many internecine wars within Europe, often spreading to the wider world of European colonies or spheres of influence.

There were many contending states jostling for power in Europe from the sixteenth century. Spain was the first to stake its claim. Spain's defeat of the Incas and Aztecs in the sixteenth century resulted in large shipments of gold and silver but some of this early flow was captured by French, Dutch and English pirates or privateers. From the middle of the sixteenth century mining replaced plunder as the primary source of precious metals. Vast gold fleets were protected by armed warships, and Spain had started a major fort building program. During the 17th century, Spain was beset by many enemies and the only thing that kept it as a world power, assert some writers, was the flow of precious metals from the Americas.

Philip III initially kept Spain out of the Thirty Years' War that broke out in 1618. Philip III died in 1621, and his son, Philip IV became king. He was younger, and probably sillier, so he joined the war. Warships that were being built for the Spanish Treasure Fleet were reassigned to the war in Europe. In the 1630's, the tides of war turned against Spain, and she found herself in more trouble than she could afford. While the French were making gains in Europe, the English and Dutch were plundering and settling the Spanish Main. In 1624 The English built a settlement in St. Kitts, and, in 1627, Barbados. In 1627 and 1635, the French were in Guadeloupe and Martinique.

In 1621 the Dutch formed the Dutch West India Company and in 1628 sent a fleet of over 30 ships into the Caribbean under Admiral Piet Heyn – his mission, to capture the Spanish Treasure Fleet. The Dutch fleet was spotted by the Spanish and the Treasure Fleet stayed in port in Cartagena and Vera Cruz. When some of Heyn's ships returned to Europe, the Spanish thought the danger had passed and their fleet sailed for Spain, only to be captured off the coast of Havana. The Dutch booty was 90 tons of gold and silver worth about 3,000,000 pesos. King Philip IV suffered a nervous collapse when he heard of the loss of the Treasure fleet, and did not appear in public for over 5 days. Nowadays such behaviour would be proof of a leader's unduly sensitive soul.

Catalonia and Portugal revolted in 1640. It took Spain 20 years to recover Catalonia and in 1668 it was forced to grant Portugal's independence. Between 1650 and 1670's, the English, under Cromwell, rebuilt their fleet, and turned it into a professional navy. In 1652, Cromwell sent a fleet under the command of William Penn, father of the founder of Pennsylvania, to capture Santo Domingo. He failed in this effort, but the fleet was able to keep the Treasure ships in port, and the gold and silver did not go to Spain that year. The English did not return empty handed, because they captured Jamaica.

For the next couple of years, no Treasure fleets sailed to Spain, for fear of capture by the English. In 1656, the English navy, under the command of Robert Blake, captured the fleet off the coast of Spain. Blake captured the Treasure fleet the next year too, this time off the Canary Islands. Other English expeditions followed.

Spain's power continued to decline, and the French started to move into the Caribbean in the 1660's with the capture of the western side of Española, colonised after visits by Christopher Columbus on his voyages in 1492 and 1493. In 1683, French buccaneers attacked Veracruz and liberated over 800,000 pesos in silver and other merchandise. In 1697, French regulars and buccaneers attacked Cartagena, and the people of Cartagena paid a ransom of 8,000,000 pesos to save their city.

By the end of the seventeenth century, Spain was politically, financially and strategically weak. The War of Spanish Succession from 1701 to 1714 finally brought about the collapse of the Spanish Empire. This war was fought among several European powers, principally the Holy Roman Empire, Great Britain, the Dutch Republic, Portugal and the Duchy of Savoy, against the Kingdoms of France and Spain and the Electorate of Bavaria. The overt reason was a feared unification of the Kingdoms of Spain and France under one Bourbon monarch. Success of such unification would have drastically changed the

European balance of power and the other powers refused to accept such an outcome.

The war was concluded by the treaties of Utrecht (1713) and Rastatt (1714). As a result Philip V remained King of Spain but was removed from the French line of succession, averting the threatened union of the two kingdoms. The Austrians gained most of the Spanish territories in Italy and the Netherlands. As Spain and then Holland fell into the second group of European powers, from 1660 to 1815 five other nations – France, Britain, Russia, Austria and Prussia – gradually achieved greater dominance.

This was the time that France, under Louis XIV and then Napoleon, came closer than at any other time to dominating Europe. Always, however, in the final analysis, some combination of other powers would block such an outcome. The costs of standing armies and national fleets, and conflict itself, had become 'horrendously expensive'[3] by this time, and so relative economic strength had its usual effect.

The Napoleonic Wars were a series of conflicts between Napoleon's French Empire and changing groups of European allies that ran from 1799 (some say 1803) to 1815. As a continuation of the wars sparked by the French Revolution of 1789, they revolutionized European armies and played out on an unprecedented scale, mainly due to the application of mass conscription. French power rose quickly, conquering most of Europe, but collapsed rapidly after France's disastrous invasion of Russia in 1812.

Napoleon's empire ultimately suffered complete military defeat resulting in the restoration of the Bourbon monarchy in France. Meanwhile the Spanish Empire continued to unravel as French occupation of Spain weakened Spain's hold over its colonies, providing the preconditions for nationalist revolutions in Latin America. As a direct result of the Napoleonic wars the British Empire became the foremost world power, a position it maintained until the massive costs of the two world wars of the twentieth century.

No consensus exists as to when the French Revolutionary Wars ended and the Napoleonic Wars began. Possible dates stretch from 9 November 1799, when Bonaparte seized power in France with the coup of 18 Brumaire to 2 December 1804, when Bonaparte crowned himself Emperor. The Napoleonic Wars ended with Napoleon's final defeat at Waterloo on 18 June 1815.

Kennedy speculates that Britain and Russia, located in the wings of Europe, had disproportionate influence as they had more opportunity to opt out of middle European wars until the best possible time. He also argues that Britain's relatively honest and efficient financial system gave it a strategic advantage in its struggle with France in the eighteenth century. Growing military expenditures had to be financed by borrowing and wartime spending stimulated industry. An overcommitted French army was finally if narrowly defeated by Wellington at Waterloo.

Perhaps exhausted, certainly financially weakened, the leading nations of Europe were more peaceful for a century after the final defeat of Napoleon. Geoffrey Blainey in *The Causes of War* discusses the weariness theory of war and peace, and especially Toynbee's. 'According to his "tentative psychological explanation", a general conflict such as the Napoleonic wars made such a deep impression on the mind and spirit that men were reluctant to inflict this experience on their children. And so, for a generation, strong restraints impeded the coming of war'.[4]

The next generation, so the argument runs, 'bred in peace', then leaped lightheartedly into a series of wars, including the cluster of wars from the Crimean to the France-Prussian, but were still restrained by the lingering aversion to war which their parents had handed down. These wars therefore did not last long, and were followed by spells of peace. 'Slowly, however, the memory of the devastation of war was completely effaced, leaving a peace-bred generation who ultimately began a world war which was fierce and unrestrained'.[5]

However well this theory fitted the past, the 'premature' outbreak of the World War II provides a difficulty. So do various other details, such as the ease with which Napoleon recruited soldiers when he returned unexpectedly from Elba on his way to Waterloo. Blainey concludes that enthusiasm for war, or weariness of war, did not have any simple and predictable effects.

The period of massive capitalist development in the second half of the nineteenth century saw a 'frantic jostling' by the European powers for colonial territories in Africa, Asia and the Pacific. The so-called 'Unequal Treaties' imposed on Japan had the effect of introducing Japan to the European world. After some domestic struggle, Japanese leaders opted to modernise education, the capacity to wage war and some aspects of politics on European lines. Russia's war with Japan is attributed in part to its attempt to secure a warm water port, and Russia's defeat in that war was an early sign of the rise of the 'oriental' powers. Germany in 1914 sought the wheat fields of Eastern Europe, which Germany believed, probably correctly, it could manage more efficiently.

Kennedy argues that by 1914 from Europe only Germany and Britain were still capable of being regarded as great powers, France, Austro-Hungary and Italy having all declined in economic and military capacity. Russia, despite its inefficient autocratic governance, and the vigorously democratic United States, were the rising powers.

Keynes wrote the *Economic Consequences of the Peace* in a burst of passionate energy after the then young Treasury officer's attendance at the conference of victors in Versailles in 1919. The book famously predicted economic and geopolitical disaster as a result of the draconian terms imposed on Germany by the Treaty of Versailles. An important part of Keynes' message was that the global economy was already fragile by 1914, and that a sane treaty was essential because the economic omens were already so perilous.[6]

Before 1870, different parts of the small continent of Europe, Keynes observed, specialised in their own products but, taken as a whole, Europe was largely self-sufficient. 'After 1870 there was developed on a large scale an unprecedented situation, and the economic condition of Europe became during the next fifty years unstable and peculiar. The pressure of population on food, which had already been balanced by the accessibility of supplies from America, became for the first time in recorded history definitely reversed. ... Larger proportional returns from an increasing scale of production became true of agriculture as well as industry.'[7]

Germany was a 'vast and complicated industrial machine' which needed to be run continuously at full blast to maintain employment and subsistence for her strongly growing population. 'The interferences of frontiers and of tariffs was reduced to a minimum, and not far short of three hundred millions of people lived within the three Empires of Russia, Germany and Austria-Hungary'. The various currencies, all related in a stable way to the value of gold, facilitated the free flow of capital and trade. 'Over this great area there was an almost absolute security of property and of person'.[8]

Europe was organised 'socially and economically' to secure the maximum accumulation of capital. There was some regular increase in the daily conditions of life for the masses, but most of the returns went to the rich. 'In fact, it was precisely the inequality of the distribution of wealth which made possible those vast accumulations of fixed wealth and of capital improvements which distinguished that age from all others'. World War I destroyed this unusual and fragile situation. The war disclosed 'the possibility of consumption to all and the vanity of abstinence to many'.[9]

Keynes produces one of those rare sentences that seem to summarise the history of one of mankind's most tragic centuries. 'Moved by insane delusion and reckless self-regard, the German people overturned the foundations on which we all lived and built'.[10]

Of all the wars in the struggle for Europe, the two major wars of the twentieth century were by any measure the most devastating, and thus presented the greatest challenge to the capitalist system. In the German historical museum in Berlin is featured a saying of the German Chancellor Theobold von Bethmann Hollweg, that 'war is a leap in the dark, and a roll of the iron dice'. How right he was. At the end of this war, Germany was devastated, Russia had experienced the Bolshevik revolution and the other European belligerent nations were exhausted. The terms of the Treaty of Versailles sought to ensure that Germany would never again threaten other countries in Europe.

Coming on top of the unsustainable fragilities of capitalism in the early years of the twentieth century, retribution was swift. Deep depression globally was deepest in Germany, and gave Hitler's Nazis the chance to seize power. Hitler's aggression was explicitly about conquest, securing resources for his Reich, to which was added extermination of Jews and other 'undesirables'. The very different treatment of Germany (and Japan) after World War II was explicitly about bringing a tamed Germany and a compliant Japan into the global capitalist community. With the rise of the European Economic Community (EEC), and the success of democratic Japan, this must be seen as an objective brilliantly achieved

One might conclude that the second of two wars to end war succeeded. The post World War II generation of Europeans were, it now seems, determined to change their warring traditions. Now, renewal of war among the nations of the European Union (EU) is almost unimaginable. Now the most likely war within the EU is a civil war against bureaucracy, which resides in Brussels. Whether such a large and diverse grouping of nations could ever decide to wage war on another nation or group of nations must be doubted. But will the EU survive? That is a vital question.

Wars of conquest

There is clearly something deep in the human character that is driven toward expansionism. The lure of the untamed American frontier is the stuff of popular legend as well as history's driving force, and forms the basis of many of Hollywood's finest movies. America fought for Independance and to avoid dissolution, and it launched several wars of conquest. These wars included the Mexican-American War (1846-1848), the Spanish-American War (1898) and the Philippine-American War (1898-1913). All were won by the United States and all expanded its territory and influence.

Much earlier, in 1803, President Jefferson completed the Louisiana Purchase, possibly the world's largest real estate deal so far. The United States paid approximately 15 million dollars to France for over 800,000 square miles of land. Ironically in view of America's current situation as a mendicant nation, Jefferson's United States did not have the money to pay the $15 million outright so it instead borrowed the money from Great Britain at 6% interest. The Louisiana Purchase was an action not specifically authorised in the American constitution, so was according to some lights unconstitutional, as was the later (1867) purchase of Alaska from Russia for a mere $7.2 million. The struggle for Europe produced mirrored struggles for colonies, which were perhaps primarily struggles for distant lands. The wars of Europe were fought also in distant places. Ownership of or even heavy influence over territories of the 'New World' gave scope for additional trade, and we shall see in Chapter 5 that even the perception of vast riches available in the new world fuelled boom and bust in the old world.

The efforts of the European nations to engage with Qing China form a less than honourable chapter in the history of capitalism. The Opium Wars from 1839 to 1842 and from 1856 to 1860 were the climax of trade disputes and diplomatic difficulties between China under the Qing Dynasty and the British Empire. Opium was smuggled by merchants from British India into China in defiance of Chinese prohibition. The First Opium War, between Britain and China broke out in 1839 and Hong Kong was ceded to Britain in 1842 under the Treaty of Nanking.

Britain was granted a perpetual lease on the Kowloon Peninsula under the 1860 Convention of Beijing, which formally ended hostilities in the Second Opium War (1856-58). The United Kingdom, concerned that Hong Kong could not be defended unless surrounding areas also were under British control, executed a 99-year lease of the New Territories in 1898, significantly expanding the size of the Hong Kong colony.

In the late 19th century and early 20th centuries, Hong Kong developed as a warehousing and distribution centre for U.K. trade with southern China. After the end of World War II and the communist takeover of Mainland China in 1949, hundreds of thousands of people fled from China to Hong Kong. Hong Kong became an economic success and a manufacturing, commercial, finance, and tourism centre. High life expectancy and per capita income, widespread literacy and other socioeconomic measures attest to Hong Kong's achievements under British rule.

Britain's interference in Chinese history illustrates the utter ruthlessness of a dominant superpower in pursuit of its aims. It also illustrates neatly that trade and war are closely interrelated – 'evil twins' as someone said. Many Chinese people naturally found the treaties imposed on China humiliating and these sentiments contributed to the Taiping Rebellion (1850-1864), the Boxer Rebellion (1899-1901), and the downfall of the Qing Dynasty in 1912, putting an end to dynastic China.

The creation of Hong Kong and other dynamic capitalist outposts in Asia has given China direct access to the machinery of modern wealth creation, and can only be viewed as doing this oriental power a good turn no matter how humiliating the process was at the time. And with the fall of the Emperors, the officials in the British foreign office must have quietly (if prematurely) celebrated the success of their predecessors' efforts to engage China in the modern world of commerce.

Wars of conquest may be more rational than wars for ideology, especially if the aggressor is confident of winning against a clearly weaker opponent. The trouble with the struggle for Europe is that the dynamics of that struggle produced vast swings in the balance of power, with nations or alliances defeated in one war preparing sooner or later for the next war.

Successful wars of conquest expand opportunities. The opposite question is whether new opportunities discourage war? This is certainly a view that has been popular among historians and armchair theorists of the causes of war. 'Perhaps a long era of peace reflected the existence of strong outlets for militant energies and ambitions' observes Geoffrey Blainey.[11] Certainly the relatively peaceful years from 1815 to 1914 were years of great development and great opportunities.

Gold discoveries, development of railways, the motor car, inventions and discoveries galore and new continents to develop provided enormous challenges for the ambitious. 'That the vast Anglo-Saxon spaces of the United States provided not only an outlet for millions of Europeans but also the burial grounds for perhaps 600,000 soldiers between 1861 and 1865 is a slight blow to this argument'.[12] The view that leaders will make war when commercial or technological challenges and opportunities are lacking is another theory that fails to survive Geoffrey Blainey's rigorous assembling of evidence.

Wars of 'ideology' – really economics in disguise?

The many wars that are, superficially at least, about ideology may be largely the capitalist struggle in another guise. The American civil war is generally seen as primarily about ideology. Holding the Union together seems deeply ideological, as at first blush is limiting the extension of slavery into new territories and ultimately freeing all slaves.

If the American civil war was primarily ideological, its horrendous human and economic costs seem curious, though this judgment may reflect this writer's intellectual bias. One has to value highly the preservation of the Union and the freeing of all slaves sooner than might otherwise have been achieved to see net benefits in this war. The ultimate costs were surely not predicted, or Americans might have devised a different solution to their differences in 1861.

But economists can imagine another explanation for the American Civil War, demonstrating the inherent imperial ambitions of the subject. Due to the 'free' labour represented by slavery, actually cheap labour, the Southern States had the possibility of developing a distinct economic advantage over the North. Despite its smaller population, the Antebellum South already had disproportionate political and economic influence over the Federal Government. Cheap labour meant that crops produced in the South had an inherent advantage over goods created in the North, and the flow of free workers from the South to the North was keeping wages low in the North, and presumably spreading 'Southern values' in the process.

Limiting slavery in the new territories, and ultimately freeing all slaves, was on this logic a rational economic objective for the larger population of the North. A large cost might be justified for ultimate political and economic control of the United States of America. Ideology cannot be totally banished with this approach, since if the economic argument holds water the North might simply have accepted slavery. The generally unrecognised economic roots of wars of ideology, however, make up a strong strand in the rope that connects war and economic progress.

The Chinese civil war was another case in which 'ideology' was, in superficial terms, the primary motivating cause for a long and costly military struggle. In reality, this struggle was a direct threat to capitalism, a struggle that ultimately took one quarter of the world's population out of the capitalist system and into the very different economic system that was communism of the Maoist variety.

The feudal system ended in China in 1908, when the commanding figure of the empress dowager died. The 'boy prince' who succeeded her was unable to maintain the Manchu dynasty, and abdicated in 1912, to be succeeded by Dr Sun Yatsen, a Christian Cantonese educated in American Hawaii and British Hong Kong. China's first quasi-democratic election was held in 1913, but the reformers failed and China was ruled for a time by a succession of warlords.

The great Chinese civil war of the modern era began in 1927. It was fought between the Western-supported Kuomintang (KMT or Chinese Nationalist Party) and the Communist Party of China (CPC). In the People's Republic of China the war is more commonly known as the 'War of Liberation'. The civil war carried on intermittently until it was interrupted by the Second Sino-Japanese war, resulting in the Chinese combatants forming a united front. Japan's campaign was defeated in two nuclear firestorms in 1945, marking the end of World War II, and China's full-scale civil war resumed in 1946. After a further four years, 1949 saw a cessation of major hostilities – with the newly founded People's Republic of China controlling mainland China and the Republic of China's overtly capitalistic jurisdiction being restricted to Taiwan and several other islands. To this day, since no armistice or peace treaty has ever been signed, there is controversy as to whether the Chinese Civil War has legally ended. Today, the two sides of the Taiwan straits have close economic ties, but many people believe that Taiwan provides a potential flash point between the USA and China, a potential future crisis of capitalism.

Many other recent wars seem more obviously about ideology. The invasion and occupation of Iraq (2003-2010), the so-called War on Terror which began on 11 September 2001, the Vietnam War (1945-1975), the Korean War (1950-1953) and the Spanish Civil War (1936-1939) all fit this description. These overtly ideological wars all involved severe economic and social costs, including loss of lives, prestige and treasure for the losers, with little apparent gain even for the winners. This lose-lose perspective is especially acute to outside observers for whom the combatants often seem virtually indistinguishable. While one cannot forbid consenting adults from fighting, an advocate of democracy cannot help thinking that there should be better ways – like voting under the watchful eye of a genuinely international police force – to resolve essentially ideological differences.

The United States and its allies (including Australia) said that they were 'fighting for freedom' in Korea and Vietnam. These wars were the real world hot war equivalent of the Cold War between Russian communism and American capitalism. In the end, the superior industrial muscle of the capitalist allies, and the decay of the communist ruling party, produced a decisive victory over the 'evil empire' that was the Soviet Union; although Korea saw an eventual division into North and South; and Vietnam produced a win for the communists. Now Vietnam and China are the remaining communist nations with economies closest to the capitalist ideal. Whether an authoritarian political system can co-exist with an essentially capitalist economic system is one of the great unanswered questions of the modern world.

One reason for this question is simple. Capitalism involves increasing areas of life to be the subject of market transaction. Such transactions do not depend much on power relationships that dominate 'political' transactions. People in well-functioning markets become used to buying goods and services. As Adam Smith famously wrote: 'It is not from the benevolence of the butcher, the brewer, or the baker, that we expect our dinner, but from their regard to their own self-interest'.[13] People who have experienced the freedom of markets, and the technologies (including the internet) provided by markets, are unlikely in the final analysis to accept the arbitrary rule of unelected despots.

Of course, some people ruled by despots have never, or not often, experienced the freedom of the marketplace, and are habituated to taking orders from higher authority or obeying the mad ideas of religious leaders. The 'war on terror' was started when democratic, capitalistic nations were attacked in New York, London, Madrid and

Bali by people who just do not accept democracy, the rule of secular law or the capitalist system that the democratic nations have taken as central to their way of life.

However, maximising wealth and the power of individual self-determination are hardly the stuff of which crusades are made. We know from interactions between individuals that in many dialogues often the more fanatical, driven person prevails. A key question is whether capitalism can survive the twin challenges of radical Islam and Chinese Communism.

The fact that the Muslim world supplies much of the western world's oil, and the failure of Israel to form a lasting peace with its neighbours, are reasons for pessimism. China as America's banker may be a neutral factor, an economic version of the doctrine of mutually assured destruction that prevented nuclear holocaust in the second half of the twentieth century. The flood of refugees from dysfunctional authoritarian nations to western democracies is a reason for optimism, as we see very little movement in the opposite direction.

War and capitalism – a many stranded rope

A standard and sensible observation is that the nation or alliance with the stronger economy will defeat an economically weaker nation or alliance. Superior leadership in a poorer region may cause an upset, as Robert E. Lee nearly did in the American civil war, but that is a rare example where in any case the basic theorem remained unchallenged. An exception is when guerrilla forces are defending their own land, and there is a credible view that if Robert E Lee had used such tactics there might now be four nations in North America rather than three.

In dealing with geopolitical considerations, national leaders must achieve a balance between economic development, defence capability and services such as health, education, welfare and other support for economic development – the classic problem of guns, books and butter. America under President Reagan famously engaged the Soviet Union in an arms race it could not afford. Small capitalist nations such as Australia have to shelter under America's defence umbrella, and renewed American isolationism would provide such nations with severe concerns.

Blainey's powerful final chapter is called 'War, Peace and Neutrality'. He points out that war and peace are 'more than opposites'. There can be no war unless at least two nations prefer war to peace; even fighting in self-defence involves a decision not to simply surrender. The same framework should be used in explaining the outbreak of war, the widening of war by the entry of new nations, the outbreak of peace, surmounting crisis during a period of peace and 'of course', the ending of peace. 'When leaders of rival nations have to decide whether to begin, continue or end a war, they are, consciously or unconsciously, asking variations of the same question: they are assessing their ability or inability to impose their will on the rival nation'.[14]

In deciding for war or peace, national leaders appear to be 'strongly influenced' by at least seven factors: military strength; predictions of how outside nations will behave; perceptions of internal unity or discord in their nation and the land of the enemy; knowledge or forgetfulness of the realities and sufferings of war, nationalism and ideology; the state of the economy and its ability to sustain the kind of war envisaged; and the personality and experience of those who share in the decision.

In considering the economic factor, it is plausible to suggest that many of these factors will lean toward war at a time of economic prosperity. People's assessment of their position and that of their nation are more likely to be overly optimistic in times of strong economic prosperity. Government revenues will be stronger, industry will be booming and people, including political leaders, will be more confident. Clearly the perceived ability to sustain war will be regarded as stronger when the economy is strong than when it is weak. Especially in a closely integrated global economy, all nations or groups of nations are likely to be experiencing prosperity or hardship at the same time.

So here is a strong strand in the rope connecting war and the economy. War is more likely than diplomacy as a solution to conflict when both nations or groups of nations in conflict are experiencing strong economies. With the weaker strands operating in the other direction, including war spending creating jobs, there are two-way, self reinforcing links between the likelihood of going to war and the state of economies.

We know from the history of economic boom and bust that ordinary citizens may get caught up in irrational schemes and that powerful but misguided 'animal spirits' can lead businessmen and individual investors to make foolish mistakes. Going to war may be a national leader's equivalent folly. This point cannot be pushed too far, of course, because if it were always true there would be declarations of war whenever an economic boom reached its strongest point.

But if this hypothesis has some validity the economic effect will also be detected in the aftermath of war, but working in the opposite direction. In the aftermath of war, a nation's economy is likely to be weak. There is the sheer devastation of war, there is malnutrition and epidemic and recent memories of horrendous suffering to keep leaders more focussed on reconstruction and diplomacy than on war. This was the experience, to varying degrees, following most wars of history, providing another strong strand in the rope linking economic circumstances with decisions about war and peace.

Yet this too is not the whole picture. World War II occurred very soon after World War I, indeed well before the end of the Great Depression, whose severity was itself due to the devastation of the first world war and the fragility of capitalism at the end of the first Age of Innovation. And there was an economic boom after World War II, not the usual four horsemen of the apocalypse.

This unexpected boom was partly, perhaps largely, due to the very different views of the victorious nations about the nature of the post-war peace. Led by the USA, the victorious allies set about restoring the western part of Germany as a peaceful vassal state. Japan, too, was assisted to become a modern capitalist democracy. Then freeing of trade and other forms of economic deregulation gradually removed many of the restrictions on capitalism imposed during the Great Depression of the 1930s.

Niall Ferguson's book *The War of the World*, is about twentieth century wars but considers 'violence' generally rather than just wars between nations. In relating violence to economic events, Ferguson considers economic volatility rather than the level of economic activity. In explaining the 'extreme violence' of the twentieth century, Ferguson cites 'ethnic conflict, economic volatility and empires in decline'. 'By economic volatility I mean the frequency and amplitude of changes in the rate of economic growth, prices, interest rates and employment, with all the associated social stresses and strains'.[15]

Economic volatility can be volatility in both directions. Economic booms create volatility in an upward direction – faster economic growth, inflation of asset prices and inflation of goods and services prices, rising interest rates and rapidly increasing growth of jobs. Boom-time conditions may well encourage national leaders to choose war-war rather than the tedious jaw-jaw of diplomacy.

The reconciliation of Blainey and Ferguson may be that economic booms make war between nations more likely but both and boom and bust, by creating economic volatility, encourage the general 'violence' that has so bedevilled the world in the past century.

But in considering 'violence' generally and its relation to economic conditions generally, we must not forget that economic booms inevitably lead to busts. As any sufficiently hard-headed person realises, asset booms or 'bubbles' always lead to asset busts. Severe asset busts may or may not trigger economic depression but by any definition increase the volatility of economic conditions.

4

The Dutch Tulip Boom of 1636; with brief comments on the modern market for art

This episode of national mania has been the subject of many claims to be the first great crisis of modern capitalism. It affected mainly a small though ambitious European nation, but gave the Dutch a fright that caused them to become one of the world's most cautious people. At least, that is the folklore.

Colin Clark was a wonderful British-Australian economist who worked to great good effect from the late 1920s until his death in 1989. Clark was a Catholic man of the old school, who rejected both birth control and Malthusian constraints on economic growth. Holland was his prime example. This writer remembers an argument with Professor Clark on the subject. My example was taken from research on a small Pacific Island nation, the Gilbert and Ellice Islands. Its problem, as I saw it, was that its population was growing at a logarithmic rate whereas production of coconuts and capture of fish (its only industries) were growing at an arithmetic rate. This was, I asserted, a simple Malthusian disaster in the making – unless the people embraced birth control.

'Nonsense', Professor Clark responded. 'Holland in the sixteenth century faced similar constraints. Its choice was to conquer large parts of the world and become the great trading nation that it still is today'. 'What is the global equivalent of that argument?' I asked, not willing to give up my point too easily. 'Mankind must colonise the galaxy!' the professor responded, unwittingly endorsing my leisure time reading of science fiction if not my essentially protestant views of the Catholic Church's ban on modern forms of contraception. With the world's population now six billion, and headed for a projected peak of nine billion, this is a subject which is even more relevant today.

Holland in the seventeenth century was in its golden age. Great churches and universities, imposing administrative buildings, fine avenues and canals provided the features of wealthy cities and towns. Great painters such as Rembrandt, Frans Hals, Peter Brueghel the Younger and Vermeer were plying their trade. Dutch armies were the crack fighting force of Europe. The Dutch navy was preparing to smash Spain and rival England. It was nation of tradesmen, sailors and soldiers, with many trophies brought home from the Orient.

Holland at the start of the seventeenth century had already established a number of small East India companies to exploit the new sea route for the spice trade. Each company had a charter to operate for a limited term that was normally for one voyage after which the capital was returned to investors. The Dutch parliament, with strategic advantage in mind rather than profit, established in 1602 a unified East India company, with a monopoly on all Dutch trade east of the Cape of Good Hope and west of the Straits of Magellan.

Niall Ferguson, in his fine book *The Ascent of Money*, says the greatest Dutch invention was the joint stock company. The Dutch had also created lottery loans to help finance their public debt and a central bank the Amsterdam Exchange Bank which provided a 'reliable form of money'. By 1690, Amsterdam was, Ferguson says, 'the world capital of financial innovation'. It was a fine place for the Scottish gambler, convicted murderer and economist John Law to lie low.[1]

The Dutch East India Company had shareholders and a limited, although longer, charter than its predecessor companies. With cash in short supply – another precedent for new companies through the ages – one dividend was paid in spices. In 1612 someone decided the enterprise would not be wound up, and thus shareholders who wished to exit had to find a buyer for their stock. Thus a stock market was born. Gradually various reforms to what is now called corporate governance were made – auditors appointed, dividends paid and protection of the rights of shareholders implemented. A tough young man, Jan Pieterszoon Coen, became the first Governor-General of the Dutch East Indies, dealing ruthlessly with the locals and officials of the British East India Company as he established a strong Dutch presence. He is reported to have said: 'We cannot make war without trade, nor trade without war'.[2]

Given later events in France and London, and the example of Tulipomania in Holland, what is amazing is that there was no bubble in Dutch East India stock. The company's stock rose gradually with the Dutch empire and declined gently with the Dutch empire. Perhaps the Tulip boom served as a warning, or perhaps Holland never had a Jan Pieterszoon Coen of Commerce, or a John Law or even a John Blunt. What is clear, Ferguson says, was that Dutch finance 'came as a revelation' to Law.[3] This shows *The United States from the late 1990s and again in 2007-08 provides a prominent example, with financial innovation using complex derivative products that no-one properly understood causing great damage to the financial world.* how a leading edge in innovation can so easily become a bleeding edge. This is a result that has often been repeated.

Sheramy Bundrick is an 'Art Historian, Professor, Writer & Traveler'. She came across *A Satire of Tulip Mania* by Jan Brueghel the Younger, ca. 1640, in the Frans Hals Museum in Haarlem. This painting is a 'singerie', a painting in which 'monkeys are used as an allegory to expose the foibles of humankind'. Here is the museum's own description, from its website (quoted by Bundrick):

> One monkey points to flowering tulips while another brandishes
> a tulip and a moneybag. This is how artist Jan Brueghel indicates

that this painting is about the tulip trade. A sale is concluded by hand-clapping. Bulbs are weighed, money is counted, a lavish business dinner is savoured. The monkey on the left has a list of names of expensive tulips. The sword at his side is a status symbol. Farther back, a monkey sits like a nobleman astride a horse. Another in the mid-foreground is drawing up a bill of sale. The owl on his shoulder symbolises folly. Brueghel is ridiculing tulip mania by depicting the speculators as brainless monkeys. The painting also shows what happened when the tulip trade crashed: a monkey on the right urinates on the - now worthless - tulips. Behind him a speculator who has run up debts is being brought before the magistrate. A monkey sits weeping in the dock and in the centre at the back a disappointed buyer is wielding his fists. At the back to the right a speculator is even being carried to his grave.

Bundrick continues:

Vincent van Gogh knew about tulip mania; in a letter to his mother, he provides a comparison to the art market of his day that proves an odd premonition: "Those high prices one hears about, paid for work of painters who are dead and who were never paid so much while they were alive, it is a kind of tulip trade, under which the living painters suffer rather than gain any benefit. And it will also disappear like the tulip trade. But one may reason that, though the tulip trade has long been gone and is forgotten, the flower growers have remained and will remain. And thus I consider painting too, thinking that what abides is like a kind of flower growing. And as far as it concerns me, I reckon myself happy to be in it".[4]

Delusion and madness

Charles MacKay's *Memoirs of Extraordinary Popular Delusions and the Madness of Crowds* names his chapter on this outbreak of collective madness simply as 'The Tulipomania'. This much quoted, much reprinted, account has been challenged by modern scholars, as we shall discuss. Even if its 'data' were based on unreliable sources, and its 'irrational bubble' interpretation is flawed, the work itself has so strongly influenced the history of boom and bust that it must be taken seriously for its cultural significance.

The questions raised by MacKay's work are many: was the undoubted boom and bust in the prices of tulips really a 'mania', or rather rational behaviour in a market for rare bulbs; did the bust bring on a more general economic crisis, or was it no great crisis after all; was there international contagion? The fact that the Tulip Mania is the subject of a satiric painting by one master painter, and referenced by another, proves it was a dramatic event, almost certainly influencing the culture of its time. The frequent reference to MacKay's account during modern episodes of boom and bust shows its enduring cultural influence.

Van Gogh is Henry's favourite artist. That he had so little commercial success or artistic acclamation during his lifetime is testament to the fickleness of judgments about such matters, and also the inability of conventional opinion to separate merit from implied judgments about the personality of an artist, especially a truly innovative artist.

It is believed that the tulip was first imported to Holland from Constantinople in the middle of the sixteenth century. A collector of rare exotic plants was seen in 1559 to have one or more tulips in his garden at Augsburg. In the decade following this period, tulips were much sought after by wealthy people, especially in Holland and Germany. The esteem in which the tulip was held increased steadily to embrace the middle classes and even the poorest people.

Keen collecting and cultivation was overtaken by an extraordinary episode of what can only be seen as collective mania, hard to credit by those familiar with the modern Dutchman. The extent of the mania can be glimpsed in this table of prices extracted from MacKay's text.

1635   100,000 florins for 40 roots – paid by 'many persons'; 4400 Florins – one Admiral Liefkin, weighing 400 perits (a perit is a small weight, less than a grain); 1260 Florins – one Admiral Van der Eyk, of 446 perits; 1615 Florins – one Childer, of 106 perits; 3000 Florins – one Viceroy of 400 perits; 5500 Florins – one Semper Augustus of 200 perits ('thought to be very cheap')

1636 Semper Augustus, Harlem – 12 acres of building-ground given in exchange; Semper Augustus, Amsterdam – 4600 Florins, a new carriage, two grey horses and a complete set of harness. (Neither of these bulbs were regarded as being of the highest quality.); Viceroy – Two lasts of wheat, four lasts of rye, four fat oxen, Eight fat swine, Twelve fat fat sheep, two hogsheads of wine, four tuns of beer, two tuns of butter, one thousand lbs of cheese, a complete bed, a suit of clothes and a silver drinking cup, collectively worth 2500 Florins.; Semper Augustus – 3000 Florins, (allegedly eaten for an onion by a sailor); Admiral Van der Dyke – 4000 Florins, (supposedly peeled and cut up by amateur English botanist).

This price data is now regarded as unreliable. MacKay also provides more qualitative information which is today regarded as not totally objective but whose very exaggeration can be regarded as indicating the impact of what is an early great disturbance to the capitalist system. The demand for tulips of a rare species increased so much in the year 1636, that regular marts for their sale were established on the Stock Exchange of Amsterdam, in Rotterdam, Harlaam, Leyden, Alkmar, Hoon and other towns. Tulip-jobbers speculated in the rise and fall of tulip stocks, and made large profits by buying when prices fell, and selling out when they rose. 'Every one imagined' that the passion for tulips would last forever, and that money would flow from 'every part of the world' in pursuit of rare tulips. 'Nobles, citizens, farmers, mechanics, sea-men, footmen, maid-servants, even chimney-sweeps and old clothes-women', dabbled in tulips.[5]

Tulip inflation put pressure on the prices of other assets and even ordinary goods. 'The prices of the necessaries of life rose again by degrees: houses and lands, horses and carriages, and luxuries of every sort rose in value with them, and for some months Holland seemed the very antechamber of Plutus'.[6]

All good things, and especially all extraordinary ways of getting rich, come to an end. MacKay comments dryly: 'At last, however, the more prudent began to see that this folly could not last forever. Tulip bulbs were not brought to plant, but for resale at a profit. 'It was seen that somebody must lose fearfully in the end'. ... 'As this conviction spread, prices fell, and never rose again. Confidence was destroyed and a universal panic seized upon the dealers'.[7]

Deals were reneged upon and there were many defaulters. Men accused each other of dud dealing and 'the cry of distress resounded everywhere'. When the bubble burst, some people lost the fortunes built by trading tulips in the boom, and those left holding roots recently acquired were mostly ruined. A few people had sensibly hidden their new-found wealth and invested it in other assets, including the English and other funds.

Sadly, it seems losers outweighed the winners, or else the losers were noisy and the winners discreet. 'Many who, for a brief season, had emerged from the humbler walks of life, were cast back into their original obscurity. Substantial merchants were reduced almost to beggary, and many a representative of a noble line saw the fortunes of his house ruined beyond redemption'.[8]

These facts may be exaggerated, or even correct, but presumably this was a zero sum game, as in every transaction there was a voluntary exchange. Those who bought early, sold before the crash and invested their money in other assets were presumably winners. Those who bought late in the boom and were left holding greatly depreciated bulbs after the crash were losers. Winners were presumably inclined to remain quiet, feeling good about their sagacity. Losers were inclined to feel bilked and to demand restitution.

There are many lessons from this episode, even if it is exaggerated or somewhat fanciful. Perhaps most important, speculating in assets of no intrinsic value is doubly dangerous and success depends on taking a profit before average opinion realises that the intrinsic value of such an asset is less than commonly realised.

The real story

Scientifically inclined economists have in recent years questioned both the facts and their interpretation. The first to do so in a convincing way was Peter Garber in a 1989 article on 'Tulipmania' in the *Journal of Political Economy*. I base my comments on this article and his later book called *Famous First Bubbles. The Fundamentals of Early Manias.* This book focuses on the Tulip 'mania' but also discusses the twin bubbles of 1720 which is the subject of the following chapter in this book.

Garber is anxious to establish the truth of the matter because that is what a good scientist must do. His research is designed to cast doubt of the irrationality of the 'mania' because he believes all economic transactions are grounded in rationality and because he believes accusations of irrational behaviour will encourage killjoy regulators of the type we Australians call wowsers.[9]

Garber's bias is from what I call the 'continuous equilibrium' school of economics dominated by economists from the University of Chicago. I note with only slight exaggeration that the mindset of this school is that people and therefore economies are always in equilibrium. Someone who jumps from the Eiffel Tower, having weighed all the costs and benefits of continuing to live, is in an equilibrium of a sort (provided he does not find a flaw in his calculations on the way down) until he hits the ground, at which time he instantaneously changes state to a different sort of even more final equilibrium.

Despite this comment, I have always admired efforts to show that there may be 'continuous equilibrium' in economies and 'rational fundamentals' behind events that others see as involving 'disequilibrium' or 'irrationality' of some sort. Garber tries very hard to achieve such an outcome in the case of MacKay's *Tulipomania*. Fortunately for the romantics amongst us, he does so without quite getting there. But I leap ahead of the story.

Garber starts with definitions of the word 'bubble'. 'Bubble is one of the most beautiful concepts in economics and finance in that it is a fuzzy word filled with import but lacking a solid operational definition'.[10] Put differently, a bubble is that part of asset price movement that in not explainable by changes in 'fundamentals' – those things that we believe ought in a fully rational world influence prices. If we cannot explain price movements, we call them a bubble and 'appeal to unverifiable psychological stories'. Clearly this is unsatisfactory. The trouble, of course, is that with sufficient ingenuity one can construct 'fundamental' explanations for just about anything.

The long-serving Chairman of the US Fed, Alan Greenspan,

famously labelled a strong boom as due to 'irrational exuberance'. Whether asset price movements have any 'irrational' component is something you can only know after the fact, so Greenspan's phrase is another example that sounds good but, Garber asserts, is empty of all meaningful content. Palgrave's *Dictionary of Political Economy* published in 1926 defines a bubble as 'Any unsound undertaking accompanied by a high degree of speculation'.[11] This too is devoid of meaning because no-one can tell if a speculative venture is unsound until it is tried. This is a more powerful criticism. Highly speculative ventures may be highly successful, or they may fail. A serious investor in highly speculative ventures expects some to fail, some to just about 'wash their faces' and a few to win big. In my experience trying to help governments stimulate useful innovation I have often had to remind the ministers and officials involved that one can never guarantee success in a risky venture, and this sometimes seems to come as a fresh insight.

Speculation is one of the essential features of capitalism, and labelling it, even by implication, as 'unsound' is to weaken capitalism. On this point I am in full agreement with Peter Garber.

Kindleberger's much read book on *Manias, Panics and Crashes,* asserts Garber, defines a bubble as follows: 'A bubble is an upward price movement over an extended range that then implodes'. Garber describes this definition as a 'sort of chartist view of bubbles'.[12] So long as one does not go on to assert that 'bubbles' are necessarily irrational, the result of mob psychology or the madness of crowds, I see no danger in this definition. The vital point, it seems to me, is whether one is automatically predisposed to see asset price booms, or 'bubbles' as crazy and therefore worthy of regulation that seeks to stop the upward movement of asset prices or to punish those who promote 'speculative ventures'. The urge to punish is usually far stronger in the case of failed speculations. There is perhaps a case to punish people for proven fraud, but even in that event it may be better to allow the people who believed the fraudster to suffer the consequences of their folly – a point that MacKay makes in his discussion of the South Sea 'bubble', as we shall see.

There is one variety of bubble that Garber admits into his dictionary of bubbles – the 'rational bubble'. This is a severe price movement that people rationally expect to end, but buy the asset concerned with the aim of getting out before the inevitable crash. The rational buyers in such a bubble may be relying on less well informed people or even less rational people to do the final buying before the bubble bursts. The historian Geoffrey Blainey observed when we were discussing this matter that many things in life start being entirely rational and become irrational only toward the end. Of the various definitions of 'bubble', this is my sort of bubble, and I do not much care if it is called a bubble or a merely powerful boom.

The appearance of the word 'bubble' may itself be a warning sign, equivalent to a taxi driver giving stock tips.

I will also quote the summary on this matter of definition of John Simon, who has written of bubble episodes for a conference at the Reserve Bank of Australia: '... a bubble is an asset market event where prices rise, potentially with justification, rise further on the back of speculation, and then fall dramatically for no clear reason when the speculation collapses. Furthermore, they typically occur in an environment of general optimism, for example, at the end of a long expansion. Commonly associated with these price changes, but not necessarily, are an easy availability of credit, new technology, and an increase in company formation'.[13]

Garber is also somewhat skeptical about the data and anecdotes used by MacKay. He says MacKay 'plagiarised most of his description from Beckmann with a little literary embellishment'.[14] Ouch! This is an uncharitable thing to say about a man who wrote one of the classics of finance and economics. Perhaps we should regard it as a masterpiece of creative writing. Perhaps MacKay was a master bubble-maker himself, with the rare ability to turn the dismal science into the intellectual equivalent of a good bodice-ripper. We might forgive him at least his 'literary embellishment' and observe that, if he were a plagiarist, so too were many people who followed in his footsteps.

Garber has made a very fine contribution in collecting and assembling data, and relating it to the facts of tulip reproduction and market dynamics in a convincing manner. In his 'Tulipmania' article and later book he compares the market dynamics in rare bulbs with market dynamics of rare bulbs in later eras, including tulips and hyacinths – the latter replacing tulips as the fashionable flower at the beginning of the eighteenth century. The prices of rare bulbs surge because wealthy collectors are keen to be the first to own the latest horticultural marvel. But rare bulbs either become common or disappear, which explains why prices decline rapidly after a surge. As Garber says at the end of his important 1989 article: 'the results of the study indicate that the bulb speculation was not obvious madness, at least for most of the 1634-37 "mania". Only the last month of the speculation for common bulbs remains as a potential bubble', although in this case he says there are too many uncertainties to be sure.[15]

Garber's final comment on the 'wonderful tales from the tulipmania' in his 2000 book describes them as 'catnip irresistible to those with a taste for crying bubble, even when they are so obviously untrue. So perfect are they for didactic use that financial moralisers will always find a ready market for them in a world filled with investors ever fearful of financial Armageddon'.[16]

The consequences of the Tulipomania

According to MacKay, meetings were held around the country and 'deputies' were elected to travel to Amsterdam in an attempt to consult with government to find 'some remedy for the evil'. The government suggested the deputies devise a solution. Several 'stormy' meetings were held for this purpose; but no measure could be found 'likely to give satisfaction to the deluded people, or repair even a slight portion of the mischief that had been done'.[17] No way to restore the status quo was possible, and any attempt to do so would create irresolvable conflict between winners and losers. This, surely, is equally a feature of the more complex booms and busts of modern life.

The Dutch government of 1637 was asked to sort out the mess but wisely took time to reach conclusions and eventually endorsed the same unworkable plan devised by the deputies. The courts refused to consider cases involving tulips based, as they saw them, on simple gambling.

Trading in company shares in sixteenth century Holland had involved spot transactions, stock options and futures trades. Organised bear raids involving short sales of stocks and the spreading of negative rumours about the affairs of the company happened, Garber asserts, 'a tactic employed to this day'. An edict published in 1610 prohibited such 'manipulative activities'. Futures trading as regarded by the authorities as 'immoral gambling', but no one was prosecuted for using such tactics.[18]

Ignoring foolish laws is not a modern practice, as it often leads to prosecution. The modern approach to a crisis in which there are winners and losers is to strengthen the rules against speculative ventures, which in the long run weakens capitalism.

Curiously, the Dutch still hold the tulip in particular esteem. And even in England, Charles MacKay said, in his day, strange as it may seem, a tulip was worth more money than an oak. More money than an oak infected with the fungus that produces truffles? Sadly, there is in history no mention of 'Trufflemania', and neither MacKay nor Garber has studied the matter.

Garber observes that there is very little mention of economic distress in Holland at the time of the Tulip boom, although there were many deaths from the bubonic plague. Perhaps, as well as being a doubtful 'bubble', the Tulipomania was not even a crisis. This question is addressed directly in a wonderful recent book by Anne Goldgar, published in 2007 by the University of Chicago Press. Goldgar concludes: 'Tulipmania did not destroy the economy, or even the livelihoods of most participants'.[19]

Tulipmania however had deep consequences, consequences which explain why the episode has had such a strong grip on succeeding generations. Tulipmania was again in the news during the time of the Mississippi Bubble and the South Sea Bubble. It has been repeatedly invoked at other times of boom and bust, including during the Global Financial Crisis of 2007-08. The persistence of the story of the first 'crisis of capitalism' is tribute to its deep impact as well as the skill of MacKay's colourful even if flawed account.

The damage was, for the most part, not financial Goldgar says: 'It was the confusion of values, the breakdown of honor, and the destruction of trust bound up in the events of the 1630s that caused this damage to Dutch society. These led, at the very least, to bitter disputes and anger, and even, it seems, to a questioning of truth and reality itself'.[20]

It is fair to say that similar damage was done to standards of honor and trust in the Global Financial Crisis of 2007-08. Indeed, the essence of the financial gridlock that so worried many people when the US government declined to bail out Lehman Brothers was widespread lack of trust among and between bankers. And it may be doubted that the word honor is much used in modern finance, and that talking even of 'honor among thieves' is likely to produce quizzical raised eyebrows in the highest towers of finance.

The modern market for rare objects

The closest modern example of Tulipomania is probably seen in the market for fine art. Winners from great stock market booms, if they are smart, take profits before the equity bubble bursts and diversify into assets such as property or fine art. In the final stages of the great share boom of 2003-2007, the London art market was also booming. Adrian Ash reported in a magazine called *MoneyWeek* in February 2007 that Sotheby's midweek sale of contemporary art in London netted £45.7 million – some US$90 million. Indeed, it was 'the most successful contemporary sale ever staged in Europe,' for a total of $173 million; Christie's achieved $177 million with its own Impressionist and Modern auction; the next two days brought Sotheby's Contemporary sale, followed by Christie's auction of Post-War and Contemporary art which netted $138 million, including a new Francis Bacon record, nearly double the previous high of $30 million.

In summary: 'Four days...one city...$578 million. That's more than gross inflows for the entire UK mutual fund industry over the same period. But don't forget Sotheby's commission on top!'[21]

Fortunately for the modern regulator, the dominance of the art auctions by people who are seriously rich means that 'Caveat emptor applies ... even if the art is to your taste. Doig's *White Canoe* isn't all that bad, but you wouldn't know it from the Saatchi Gallery's description' (quoted by Ash):

Is the market for fine art based on 'fundamentals', 'speculation' or 'irrational exuberance'?   Dare   I say all three in varying proportions?

> [Doig] paints white like it's got every colour in it; he paints dark like it's got every colour on it. A mirrored image of a lake at night, White Canoe is a wishful infeasibility where the reflection is more detailed than the landscape itself. The boat is aberrantly glowing. The landscape has the all-consuming blackness of an oil slick, deafening and motionless; all other colours seem to slide across it in a rustic laser show. The blue stains of tranquil moonlight have the eerie effect of erasing; Peter Doig's perfect night seems to be melting like celluloid stuck in the projector....

Japanese billionaires set the pace in buying art during their great asset bubble of the 1980s. They were buying trophy properties all over the world, including Hollywood studios in California and the Exxon building in New York. Japanese buyers purchased a Renaissance chapel in France, complete with stained glass windows, intending to dismantle it stone by stone and ship it to Japan. This provoked the French to pass a law prohibiting the export of national treasures.

Japanese buyers were prominent at major art auctions in London, Paris and New York, where they bought famous works of art for phenomenal prices. Just as American tycoons would do ten years later, the Japanese began buying art as if they really liked it. An alleged crime boss, Susumu Ishii, discovered common stocks in 1985 and influential friends helped him to make vast gains. He invested a small part of his fortune to buying works of art by Chagall, Renoir, Monet and others. The Yusuda Fire and Marine Insurance Company paid nearly $40 million for Van Gogh's *Sunflowers*. Ryoei Saito spent $82.5 million on another of Van Gogh's paintings, *Portrait of Dr Gachet*, and a further $78 million for Renoir's *Au Moulin de la Gallette*.

The Australian billionaire beer baron and yachting superstar, Alan Bond, also made headlines in 1987 when he purchased Van Gogh's *Irises* for a then world record $53.9 million. Controversy was redoubled when it emerged that Sotheby's had lent him half of the purchase price and held the painting under lock and key in a secret location. 'What troubles critics of the transaction' said Rita Reif of *The New York Times*, 'is that the extraordinary price paid for *Irises*, less than one month after the Wall Street crash on Oct. 19, 1987, fuelled an atmosphere of euphoria in the art market. The price became the bench mark most often cited as proof that art was a commodity that had weathered the economic crisis'.[22]

To those of us who are merely well-off, such prices may seem extraordinary, perhaps even irrational. But the price of works of art by the world's celebrity artists is a very concrete thing, and its purchase by very rich people surely does no great harm to society. Indeed, many such works of art end up donated to great galleries where they become available for viewing by all people either freely or for a modest sum.

Controversy increased when Bond's business empire collapsed, and again when Bond went to gaol. While he was in goal bond became a competent painter of pictures himself; a self-portrait is held by Australia's National Portrait gallery in Canberra. All that is needed to close the circle is for some future rich person to buy one of Bond's paintings for an outrageous sum of money.

Henry had the great good fortune to be entertained at the New York Yacht shortly after Alan Bond wrested the America's cup away from this venerable institution for the first time. The atmosphere was frosty, to put it mildly, and the occasion was great fun.

Ash concludes: 'The Japanese were awash with money by 1989. Their cheap money pump – flooding the bond, commodity and derivative markets with carry-trade Yen – finally was washing across Old Masters and New Pretenders alike yet'. Yet the hubris, or perhaps just sensible asset diversification, that made Japanese billionaires acquire so many fine art works and expensive buildings soon faced nemesis in the form of the market crash that started at the very end of 1989.

Here is another fact that overturns conventional wisdom. Such wisdom has it that a portfolio of very different assets provides protection against a meltdown in any one asset class. Often this is 'proved' by studies purporting to show that the 'correlations' between prices of different asset classes are low or negative. This may be so for particular periods of time, perhaps carefully selected to make it so, but in the case of the major crises of capitalism such correlations usually become irrelevant as all asset classes boom together and crash together, or within short time periods from the date of the first asset class to crash.

Following the crash in the prices of equities which began in late 2007, the bubble in old and new art took its time to mature, but in November 2008, Miriam Kreinin Souccar observed in *Crain's New York Business*: 'The bubble has finally burst in the art market. The frenzy that made art students stars overnight, spawned scores of fairs around the world and turned young investment bankers into major collectors has come to an end'.[23]

The market was down by a third, and canny buyers with deep pockets were quietly strengthening their collections. An optimistic art sales executive observed philosophically that what was happening seemed like 'a return to normalcy after the hyperreality of the past three or four years'. He added, no doubt after a reflective pause: 'It will give the artists a chance to focus on their work instead of trying to sell out their studio during the first year of their M.F.A. program'.[24]

It is not unknown for people rich and poor to bet on horse races, or in casinos, or to buy lottery tickets. People with deep pockets have been known to invest in trying to make new drugs, or to drill for oil or even to make movies in the hope of extraordinary gains or in some cases the expectation of tax losses. Howard Hughes was obsessed with building and flying better aeroplanes, a highly speculative venture.

Tulipomania was succeeded by the Mississippi bubble, the South Sea bubble, new territory bubbles, railway manias, land development delirium, Miningmania, Iris- and Monet-mania, the 'new economy' (Internet) boom and the excitement of many other fashions in capitalist development. It seems clear that some people at least are inveterate gamblers. It is fashionable to be critical of gambling, but is the gambling spirit an essential part of being human? Is a propensity to take bets one of the chief drivers of human progress? Are the gamblers among us some of our most valuable citizens?

It can be asserted that Tulipomania was no 'crisis of capitalism'. But it was at least a proto-crisis in a proto-capitalist economy. As such it contains features that we see repeated throughout history, especially and typically very substantial asset price inflation in a relatively short period of time. Unlike modern crises of a similar type, it did not spread internationally, nor was the asset price bust serious enough to produce

Maybe the chief lesson is that the Dutch officials who failed to act against the winners from Tulipomania were far wiser than they seemed to be at the time.

massive economic dislocation. Tulipomania adversely impacted on 'honor and trust', and in this sense it was a clear precursor of the type of crisis that has subsequently become both more widespread and more serious.

5

The twin bubbles of 1720; France and England gulled by professionals

Almost 100 years after the time of Tulipomania came the twin bubbles of 1720. The Mississippi Bubble was centred on Paris and the South Sea Bubble occurred largely in London. Despite their exotic names, these were crises of capitalism's heartland. Tulipomania spread to some extent from Amsterdam to nearby cities. The contagion in 1720 spread far more decisively from Paris to London, and to other European cities, making these twin events a clear precursor to the age of globalisation.

In both England and France in the early eighteenth century there was a key challenge for governments. Modernisation was in the air, but governments were grappling with debts that could not be managed well due to antiquated tax systems and a raft of curious and ad hoc debt instruments. Both nations focussed on converting the national debt into equity, with some success it must be said. Governments were helped by financial entrepreneurs, one of whom, John Law, has been described as an eminent economist. The events described here show that such eminence is not necessarily a qualification for high office in government.

The boom conditions of 1720 fostered hundreds of projects that students of those times have recorded – proposals for a wheel for perpetual motion, for carrying on a trade in the river Oronooko, for furnishing funerals, for insuring and increasing children's fortunes, the Puckle gun which fired round or square bullets, and the list goes on.[1]

The boom in France spread to England, and both bubbles spread to other parts of Europe, particularly to Holland and Germany. Larry Neal has provided the most thorough analysis both of the domestic booms and their international ramifications, using data on capital flows to unravel the fullest account of this first great international crisis of capitalism. Neal's chief diagnostic tool is a combination of two effects. The first is what he calls the 'Ashton effect' – a short-lived currency appreciation indicating a scramble for liquidity. The second is called a 'Kindelberger effect' – a subsequent currency depreciation which, if it fails, will deepen the crisis. Neal brings economic science into the picture to buttress the anecdotes, which he fully appreciates and includes in his work.[2]

The events of 1720 showed the rulers of both France and England to be corrupt, at least by standards of probity that we would applaud today. They exposed monarchs who were poisonous or ineffective, or both, unethical ruling classes and corrupt elected politicians. The lessons learned led ultimately to reform in all three houses. It may be that 1720 provided a blow which meant France failed to maintain her status as an economic superpower and which led inexorably to revolution and misery.

In England the players were John Blunt, a 'shallow schemer, who conned a nation'; and Robert Walpole, a 'scheming Whig politician from Norfolk with an ambition as large as his girth'.[3] The key to the French mania was the Scottish economist and entrepreneur, John Law, aided and supported by the Regent to the French throne. Law has been described by master economist Joseph Schumpeter as 'in the first rank of monetary theorists of all time'.[4] Like the Nobel Prize winning economists whose wildly profitable hedge fund lost far more money than their brilliant minds could comprehend in 1998, academic brilliance is no guarantee of success with innovative ideas or in solving the problems of highly indebted nations.

This writer in the early 1970s was with a bunch of economists at a conference held in Australia's first legal casino. Much alcohol had been drunk when the group devised a scheme that one member of the group asserted 'could not possibly fail'. Members of the group enthusiastically contributed ten dollars each (I seem to recall) and the intellectual leaders were sent off to break the bank. They returned shortly after, having lost all of our modest stake on the first roll of the dice. If only Robert Merton and Myron Scholes, the Nobel Prize winners and hedge-fund owners, had been with us in Hobart that night, their 'Long Term Capital Management' business might not have needed to be bailed out by a consortium of Wall Street's leading banks twenty-five years later.

Blunt and Law devised schemes to dissolve burdensome national debts, restore national prosperity and create vast wealth for themselves and their friends. Their schemes ultimately failed and both men were disgraced - but it was a heck of a ride for so long as it lasted. Walpole through great ability and cunning gained and held unparalleled political power for many years.

John Law was the son of a Scottish goldsmith. He went into exile after killing a man in a duel and made a fortune from gambling. In Amsterdam, as we saw, he observed the success of the Bank of Amsterdam in making sense of the many gold and silver coins of Europe and in funding trade, especially through the Dutch East India Company that it half owned. He read widely and began to work out his own theories. He wrote *Money and Trade*, a persuasive economic treatise of insight and clarity. This he sent to Scotland, with a plan for paper money, backed by land, to replace debased gold and silver coins whose supply was erratic and dependent on mines owned by Spain. The Scottish parliament eventually rejected the plan and proceeded to strengthen its formal ties with England, meaning that Law's exile was extended to Scotland.

Law travelled Europe, seeking a ruler who would back his plan. After years of false starts, he arrived in France in 1713 with a substantial fortune. France had such an unmanageable national debt that default had been discussed. The shortage of credit was universal, trade was depressed and most peasants were poorly dressed and malnourished. Louis XIV died soon after Law arrived and his place was taken by the Duke of Orleans as regent for the heir to the throne, a lad of only seven summers.

The Mississippi Bubble

In the early eighteenth century, the finances of France were in the 'utmost disorder'. A profuse and corrupt monarch, whose profuseness and corruption were imitated by almost every functionary, from the highest to the lowest grade, had brought France to the verge of ruin. The national debt amounted to 3000 million livres, the revenue to 145 millions per annum, and the expenses of government 142 millions per annum; leaving only three millions to pay the interest upon 3000 millions'.[5] One advisor suggested declaring a state of bankruptcy; others opposed such a drastic remedy and were backed by the Regent. The gold and silver coins were called in and reminted with only four-fifth of the original weight – a classic debasement of the currency.

Tax collectors were investigated, with incentives for those who testified against them. 'The Bastille was soon unable to contain the prisoners sent to it, and the gaols all over the country teemed with guilty or suspected persons'. Only one was condemned to death; others were pilloried, sent to the galleys or fined and sent to prison. A mere one hundred and eighty livres were collected from this campaign. About eighty paid for the scheme and the rest found its way into the pockets of the courtiers and their wives and mistresses. The people become 'indignant that such severity should be used to so little purpose. They did not see the justice of robbing one set of rogues to fatten another'.

Law arrived in the midst of this confusion. The Regent saw that something should be done but lacked the energy or virtue to do anything effective about it. Law said that a metallic currency, unaided by paper, could not meet the needs of a modern nation, and that credit was required to again make France a great and prosperous nation. He had his book on *Money and Trade* translated into French and no doubt spent a lot of time lobbying the great and the good.

Eventually Law won the support of the Regent (a previous gambling companion) and in 1716 established a bank and a new paper currency, strictly backed by coin. The Regent backed Law in insisting that taxes be paid in the new currency and in other ways, and the new currency gained acceptance. Charles MacKay says: 'He made all his notes payable at sight, and in the coin current at the time they were issued. This last was a master-stroke of policy, and immediately rendered his notes more valuable than the precious metals'. The French government, desperate for revenue, had already debased the coinage, and was to resort again to this expedient. The Regent was innocent of matters commercial, and clearly lacked common sense, and (MacKay again) 'appears to have been utterly astonished at his success'. If paper currency could do such good, even more paper currency would do even more good. This was the fatal logical error, one that condemned Law's plan to eventual total failure, indeed catastrophe.

Law wanted to do more than this, to create a 'motor' that could create wealth by granting credit. The motor of credit is a vital part of a modern economy but history shows that when this motor runs too fast it burns out. Excessive credit growth is almost always part of an asset bubble and the end of credit growth almost always a prime reason for the *In effect, asset prices get to a level that is too good to be true and first one and then others and finally the whole herd decides if it seems too good to be true it probably is too good to be true.* type of crash that afflicted both Paris and London in 1720. But asset bubbles can burst simply because asset prices stop rising, or fall due to loss of confidence, and it seems that was a factor in both the twin bubbles of 1720.

It was the very success of the East India Company and the Bank of England in creating wealth by funding trade – creating in the process valuable shares, 'another form of currency' – that gave Law his next idea. Law merged his bank with the Mississippi Company in mid 1719 and sold shares in the venture. The competition for shares in the Mississippi Company was fierce. France laid claim to a territory, 'Louisiana', almost half the size of the United States of America as it was then. Law planned to raise money, send settlers and watch the money roll in. Share prices at first declined (to about half the issue price) until Law provided a guarantee to buy them back at their par value. This created a free option on making money, as the guarantee was backed by 40,000 livres of Law's gambling profits. The Mississippi Company was granted exclusive rights to the Alsatian salt mines and to trade with the Barberry States. The right to the entire profit of the Royal Mint was sold to the company.

Law's bank was granted many further favours – the monopoly of the sale of tobacco, the sole right of refinage of gold and silver until, finally, it was 'erected' into the Royal Bank of France. Once the bank became a public institution, the Regent immediately 'caused a fabrication of notes to the value of one thousand million livres'. This was the first departure from sound principles, and MacKay insists this was the responsibility of the Regent, not John Law. Law, however, must be blamed for allowing himself to be talked into actions which his own thinking must have doubted. Members of the French parliament were naturally jealous of Law's influence as a foreigner and many questioned the soundness of his projects. When they threatened to have Law tried and if found guilty hung, he threw himself on the protection of the Regent, who quashed the rumblings by arresting the president of parliament and two of his councillors, who were sent to distant prisons.

Law focussed now on the affairs of the Mississippi Company. Its shares were rising despite the parliament's questioning. Rumours of the supposed riches of Louisiana's mines helped. In early 1719 the Mississippi company was given the exclusive right to trade with the East Indies, China and the South Seas, and to all the assets of the French East India Company. Law promised large dividends and the public enthusiasm could not resist such a vision splendid.

MacKay provides several pages describing what are by now classic signs of a bubble building to its climax. 'Dukes, marquises, counts with their duchesses, marchionesses and countesses, waited in the street for hours every day before Mr. Law's door ... At last, to avoid the jostling of the plebeian crowd, which, to the number of thousands, filled the whole thoroughfare, they took apartments in the adjoining houses, that they might be continually near the temple whence the new Plutus was diffusing wealth. Every day the value of the old shares increased, and the fresh applications, induced by the golden dreams of a whole nation, became so numerous that it was deemed advisable to 'create no less than three hundred thousand new shares at five thousand livres each, in order that the Regent might take advantage of the popular enthusiasm to pay off the national debt'. This was truly a fantastic early example of privatisation, the fashionable activity of the 1980s and 1990s. 'Law was now at the zenith of his prosperity, and the people were rapidly approaching the zenith of their infatuation'.[6]

England had been watching developments in France with some anxiety – would Law restore France's fortunes and would that create a serious geopolitical adversary were the questions. 'Money flows like water in the Seine' concluded a newspaper, and there was no drought that year in Paris. People flocked to Paris from the countryside, and then from Holland and England, to buy shares in Law's company.

Law was like a modern rock star, with the qualification that it was virtually everyone who sought his attention and the right to obtain a share of the action, not just the young folk.

The share boom generated a property boom, then a building boom. The winners bought horses, furniture, books, works of art and jewellery. Law himself bought vast tracts of land. This pattern of asset diversification is typical of great asset bubbles, and often there is also substantial inflation in the prices of the necessities of life. This writer fondly recalls being invited to stay with the Deputy Chairman of the stockbroking company James Capel several years after the partners of this company had sold half of their shares to the Hong Kong and Shanghai Bank. His was a Tudor Mansion of impressive proportions with a great dining hall whose walls were filled with the portraits of the 'instant ancestors' he had acquired from the local antique store.

In 1720, the British Embassy as well as newspapers reported events for their readers in London. 'How long, feared England, would it be before Law's schemes led to a revival of France's military ambitions? How long before it asserted its economic supremacy and crushed British business overseas?'[7] 'Come back John Law, all is forgiven' was no doubt the view of some officials and politicians.

The graph shows that the peak in the price of shares in the Mississippi Company was reached in November 1719 but extended, by various more or less honest means, well into 1720, with a peak of almost 10,000, compared with a starting price of 100.[8] The extended 'plateau' is an unusual feature of this time series and is due to Law's ability to fix the stock price for a time by manipulating the news and the rate at which new stock was issued.

Neal infers from his study of exchange rate moves that capital actually started to leave France when Law's currency debasement began, and that a substantial number of speculators took their profits to England in late November of 1719 when Law stabilised the share price at his target of 10,000. In early February 1720 there was a short-lived plunge in the price of the stock and further capital flight when Law suspended all dealings in stock, foreign exchange and bank notes. Pressure from investors caused Law to reopen the stock market and to buy and sell unlimited amounts of stock at the price of 9,000. Law held the line for several months but the inevitable crash came in May 1720, which is when London's South Sea Bubble began in earnest.[9]

Shares in John Law's Mississippi Company
1719-1720

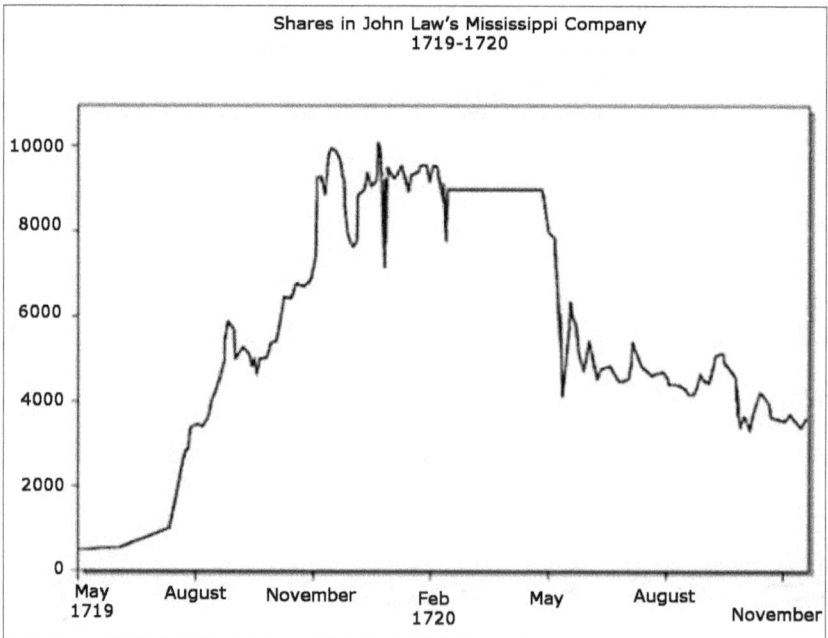

Asset booms spreading internationally has become the norm, with virtually instantaneous spread of information and hundreds of thousands of traders reacting to every scrap of news. Now asset inflations in different countries are more closely related in time, and in the case of share prices there is a distinct tendency for Wall Street to dominate price action in other equity markets. In the case of the bubbles of 1720, sharp and well informed operators could take profits in Paris and travel to London for another heady ride.

One hypothesis is that the asset booms of the twentieth century were more soundly based and therefore lasted longer. Another is that globalisation with its many centres of finance creates much greater complexity and opportunities for mutually reinforcing booms and busts.

But the booms and busts of the twentieth century each lasted far longer than either of the twin bubbles of 1720, a puzzle in search of an explanation.

The South Sea Bubble

The British government at the start of the seventeenth century was also groaning under a massive public debt. There were many complicated arrangements and no certainty as to the full extent of the debt. Malcolm Balen estimates it at 31 million pounds when it was sold to the South Sea Company for seven and a half million pounds after a blind auction whose loser was the Bank of England.[10]

John Blunt was the son of a shoemaker, personally unattractive but highly ambitious, full of ideas and energy. He proved himself to be an inspired promoter of companies and became secretary of the Sword Blade Company, whose initial purpose was to manufacture under licence and sell in England the supposedly more elegant French rapier. The company's first effort in expanding beyond armaments was to buy large tracts of cheap land in Ireland at a time of depressed prices. The purchase was bankrolled by shares in the company issued in return for 'army debentures'. The company had first quietly brought up the debentures at a discount and the share for debenture swap on favourable terms (to the company) raised their price and provided a handsome capital gain. The government got cash for its land in Ireland and was lent money by the company at a low rate of interest as a sweetener.

I cannot pretend fully to understand this example of creative financing but it seems all the principal players were happy. Presumably the original buyers of the 'Army debentures' were the ones who lost out, but for them any compensation was perhaps better than none. Here was the classic 'win, win, win' scenario so prized by writers of books on modern management. 'It was a key moment in its history, the turning point in what became a growing, and corrupt, entanglement with affairs of state'.[11]

The Bank of England was not amused, as it saw the Sword Blade Company turn into the Sword Blade Bank. When a mysterious syndicate, its backers unknown but almost certainly including partners from the Sword Blade Company, offered to lend the government 1.5 million pounds at a low rate of interest, the Bank of England was even more unamused. It was forced to outbid Sword Blade and was rewarded with

Such short-sightedness is well known even in modern politics. Contrast the massive fiscal stimulus applied during the crash of 2007-08 with the many calls for fiscal restraint in 2010. Again must be asked the question – could they not do the sums in 2007-08? Was it so hard to imagine that fiscal stimulus in 2008 would produce damaging debt burdens in 2010?

an extension of its charter to 1732. But it struggled to raise money for the profligate government.

The Chancellor of the Exchequer, Robert Harley, consulted John Blunt in 1710. Blunt persuaded Harley to resurrect the old Whig solution of the lottery. Blunt made the prizes far larger than those in past lotteries and, not surprisingly, the lottery was a great success. This success triggered a succession of similar enterprises over the next decade, but the annuities to be paid to subscribers increased the pressure on the government's finances. Could the Chancellor not do the sums, one is forced to ask, or was he expecting to be safely retired when the vultures flew into the chicken coop?

Back in 1720, John Blunt was riding high. The size of the lotteries, and the prizes, exploded; stock-jobbers created syndicates so many more people could participate; and an already strong gambling culture was greatly entrenched. The challenge of course was to reduce the national debt. The Chancellor's idea was to form a trading company, a conventional enough move. 'Trade and war were the unholy twins of commerce'.

Harley's plan, however, was politically radical. He envisaged that the new trading company would become a financial institution to rival the Bank of England and the East India Company. It would not only trade in the South Seas, but also would take over 9 million pounds of the 'floating' portion of the national debt. The company would ask the owners of this debt to exchange the debt for stock in the new trading venture. There were several challenges to overcome. Peace with France and Spain needed to be established, trade concessions negotiated and 'supposed riches' of the relevant territories yielded up. Daniel Defoe and Jonathan Swift provided propaganda for the government.

On 10 September 1711 the South Sea Company was formed, with the Chancellor as Governor, nine of thirty appointments political, five from the Sword Blade Company. Balen notes that not one of them had any experience of trading with South America. The Bank of England was even more unamused at this highly innovative example of what we might now call a private-public partnership. There was serious political opposition, and Defoe's skills as a propagandist were put to a stern test.

Balen quotes one of Defoe's paragraphs that might well be recycled in a decade or two from now, if not sooner: 'Now we see our treasure lost, our funds exhausted, all our public revenues sold, mortgaged, and anticipated, vast and endless interests entailed upon our posterity, the whole kingdom sold to usury, and an immense treasure turned into an immense debt to pay; we went out full, but we are returned empty'.

Harley's peace vote was lost by one vote. He overcame the objections of the House of Lords by creating a dozen new lords and he charged the Duke of Marlborough and Robert Walpole with corruption over the Army's accounts. Walpole went to the Tower where he nursed his resentment and planned his revenge.

The army was ordered not to fight, the French advanced at a great rate and eventually 'It was peace, but not with honour'. A formal peace took another 18 months to achieve, and Harley, by then Earl of Oxford, gave up his demand for trading settlements in South America. He did not inform his fellow directors of the South Sea Company of this backflip and began to stay away from directors' meetings. The company had hundreds of tons of merchandise rotting in stores. When the peace treaty was finally signed only one merchant ship per year was allowed to visit nominated ports. Put not your trust in princes. The Spanish levied heavy taxes, Queen Anne declared she had the right to one quarter of any profits and the company as a trading enterprise effectively 'lay at anchor'. Now it was a ship to float the national debt.

The national debt had grown by another 9 million pounds, and Harley was unable to cope. He succumbed to the demon drink and was dismissed by Queen Anne, who promptly died a week later. Walpole returned to government, again Paymaster-General of the Forces but nursing a deep grudge from his time in the Tower of London.

Meanwhile, John Law was presiding over 'resurgent, resplendent France' as first minister, the Mississippi affair reaching 'an unaccountable height'. 'The rue Quincampoix, all madness and money, proved to be the precursor of England's equally febrile fate at the hands of the South Sea Company'.[12]

John Blunt held secret discussions with the government. The bigger the debt, the bigger his potential profit was his view, although with the debt 'almost beyond imagination' the risks were immense. Blunt was offering to float the national debt by selling shares in this vast multimillion-pound liability in order to make a profit. Balen adds wryly: 'It was as implausible a way of trying to make money as had ever been invented ...'[13]

The plan of course was to sell shares to investors for more than he was required to pay the government to discharge the national debt.

Provided he could engineer a share price bubble, his profit would be enormous. John Blunt pulled it off. To do so he had to corrupt key government members (who received heavily discounted notional shares, which were sold on their behalf to give a riskless profit), outbid the Bank of England and pay seven and a half million pounds to Treasury for the right to fund England's massive debts.

Walpole endorsed the scheme while buying stock that he later sold for a handsome profit. His main effort at opposition was to try to force Blunt to agree to a fixed price for conversion of debt to stock which, if accepted, would have destroyed the scheme. Lord North and Lord Grey attacked the scheme in terms that are used today by people from Main Street about the financiers: they deplored 'the pernicious practice of stock-jobbing which produced irreparable mischief in diverting the genius of the people from trade and industry'.[14]

Neal concludes, as already noted, that capital flowed from Paris to London. Indeed, with insiders and outsiders among the directors of the South Sea company, a 'rational bubble' existed for the time of the great price surge from late February to mid-June. The Dutch were dominant among foreigner investors, shrewdly observing the South Sea directors' attempts at market rigging. The final surge in the price of the stock is a statistical artefact, as it represents what Neal calls an 'enormous forward premium that represented the pressures of a tightening credit market' on those manipulating the stock. The collapse of the bubble from late August to late September was influenced again by tight credit positions requiring speculators to unwind purchases made during the final stages of the bubble. Then price declines were driven by uncertainties about the outcome of necessary restructure of the company's activities. Evidence from the currency movements says both French and Dutch speculators went home in September and October of 1720, when the final collapse of the South Sea share price was occurring.[15]

The graph shows the movement of the South Sea Company's share prices in 1720. The peak was in late July, around three months after the bursting of the Mississippi bubble. This bubble was much smaller than the Mississippi bubble, as the rise from 128 was to almost 1,000 rather than 10,000. Modern asset busts usually follow far more closely on the heels of one another. A crash in the afternoon on Wall Street infects Asian markets as they open next day and the contagion is passed with the sunrise to the markets of Europe and so the bubble bursts in all the languages.

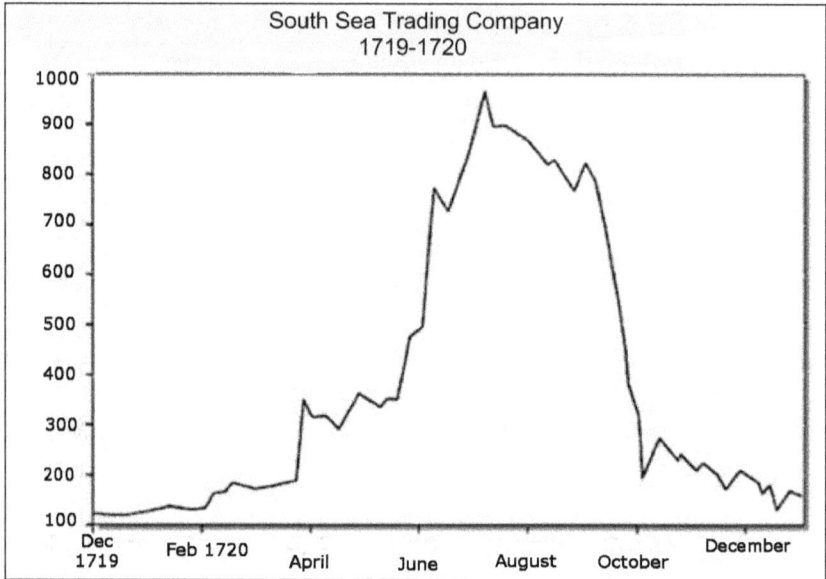

South Sea Trading Company
1719-1720

The bubbles burst

The French bubble was the first to burst in 1720. At its peak, the price of the Mississippi Company's shares were almost 1000 times the initial price. On this measure, and on more literary reports, the mania in Paris was an order of magnitude larger than that in London and the retribution both more savage and more arbitrary.

'The pernicious love of gambling diffused itself through society, and bore all public and nearly all private virtue before it'.[16] But, while it lasted there was substantial stimulus to trade. People flocked to Paris, intent on making and spending money. The mother of the Regent calculated that the population was increased by 350,000 people at the peak of the boom. There was a great shortage of accommodation, traffic was practically at a stand-still and prices of rich laces, silks, broad-cloths and velvets increased four-fold.

In early 1720, a disgruntled prince demanded of his bank so much specie that three wagons were required to move it. Law appealed to the Regent who demanded that Prince de Conti return two-thirds of the amount withdrawn. But the initial damage was done, and there were imitators. It is strange, says MacKay, that so narrow an escape should not have made both Law and the Regent more anxious to restrict their issues. But the more acute stockjobbers knew that that prices could not continue to rise for ever. Smart operators began to convert their stock to specie and send it away – one clever chap loaded an old cart with gold and silver worth nearly one million livres, covered them with hay and cow-dung, disguised himself as a peasant and drove the load to Belgium.

Anyone so clever, and with an ego so controlled, deserved to live well for the rest of what one hopes was a long and happy life.

Shortages of specie quickly led to an inquiry, and restrictions were imposed on the amount of specie a bank could provide. Also tried was a limit of the value of coin to 5 and then 10% of notes. As matters grew worse, with the price of specie rocketing up, Law tried to ban the use of specie altogether. This destroyed the value of paper totally and, according to MacKay, drove the country to the brink of revolution. Rewards were paid for information about people with more than 20 livres in their possession or found buying jewellery, plate or precious stones. Privacy was violated and a mere accusation could lead immediately to the granting of a search-warrant. The courts groaned under the weight of business. The Regent and Law were both held responsible, but there was complaint rather than revolution.

By May 1720, the price of Mississippi stock was falling, and there was little belief in the supposed wealth of the new colony. A last, desperate attempt was made to save the situation. Six thousand of the 'very refuse of the population' were impressed, fitted out with clothes and tools, paraded through the city and sent off to be shipped to America. Two-thirds of them never reached the new world but dispersed through France and sold their tools and clothes for what they could get for them.

In France, in contrast to England (as we shall see), the remedy was left in the despotic hands of those who had perpetrated the mischief. All payments were ordered to be made in paper and many more notes were fabricated. But the alarm once sounded, no argument could restore the slightest confidence in paper that was not exchangeable into specie.   A council of state was held to find a solution. It was calculated that notes on issue were valued at 2600 million of livres, and coin almost half of that. It was eventually agreed that notes should be gradually depreciated until they were half their value. Great protests were made and the Regent was forced to issue another edict restoring the nominal value of the notes. Never, said an author of the times, was seen a more capricious government – never was a more frantic tyranny exercised by hands less firm.

The mob was very restive, and it is said that Law narrowly escaped being torn limb from limb. A detachment of Swiss guard could not protect his home, and with his family he sought and found refuge with the Regent, who of course had already blamed Law for the whole disaster.

Eventually, in May 1720, the Chancellor, D'Aguesseau, who had been dismissed and treated most unfairly in 1718, was recalled to help in the restoration of credit. On 1 June a new proclamation abolished the law that made it criminal to amass coin of more than five hundred livres, and everyone was permitted to have as much specie as he wished. Old bank notes were withdrawn and burned and new notes issued on the security of the revenues of the city of Paris. The bank had sufficient coin to issue in exchange for notes but such were the crowds that on one particularly bad day 15 people were squeezed to death and soldiers fired into the crowd who were also threatened with bayonets. Law, having narrowly escaped being torn asunder, became the subject of satire in the form of cartoons and risqué songs. One of these songs suggested the application of the notes to the 'most ignoble use to which paper can be applied'.

Finally, edicts were promulgated that deprived Law's notes of any value. All the privileges of the Mississippi Company were taken from it, and this was the death-blow to the whole system. Shareholders were ordered to place their shares on deposit with the company and pay massive sums to complete the purchase of partly-paid shares.

Most of the latter group left France although there were orders to hold them to check if they had plate or jewellery with them, or had been involved in stock-jobbing. Those who escaped had sentence of death passed against them and others were treated with harsh and arbitrary fines, imprisonment and confiscation of property.

Law was helped to leave France by the Regent, a friend to the end, and ended up resuming his life as a gambler, all property in France being stripped from him and his family. He was eventually allowed to return to England, where he remained for four years. He died in Venice, in distressed circumstances.

One of many stories told by MacKay concerns the behaviour and demise of Count d'Horn, younger brother of the Prince d'Horn and related to several noble families. The Count was 'dissolute, unprincipled and extravagant'. With two similar friends, he formed a plan to rob a rich broker. They met in a low class tavern where after a few moment's conversation the Count sprang upon the broker and stabbed him three times in the breast. He began to rifle his person, to steal his Mississippi and Indian scheme bonds, whereupon one of d'Horn's accomplices stabbed him again. The victim's cries brought other customers to his aid and the Count and his friend were caught in the act. Count d'Horn's eventual punishment was to be broken on the wheel, a terrible end which was insisted upon despite many appeals to the Regent by friends and relatives, supposedly because Law persuaded him not to be merciful. d'Horn himself when offered poison chose to accept his horrible punishment instead, finally showing a princely virtue.

In England, MacKay writes, occurred the same madness that infected France. But, 'thanks to the energies and good sense of a constitutional government, [this] was attended with results far less disastrous than were seen in France'. In London, the peak price of South-Sea stock was around eight times the original price, an order of magnitude lower than the equivalent peak during the Mississippi bubble.

When the South-Sea Stock began its inexorable decline the pain began. Most stock had been effectively purchased on margin, as stock was issued in tranches. Many people had borrowed to buy stock and were liable both to pay for the various tranches and to repay their borrowings. Smart, or merely lucky, buyers bought early and sold at a profit before the inevitable slump. Those who mortgaged their property to buy stock near the top of the market were quickly bankrupted as the stock declined in value. As we shall see more explicitly in the case of the crash of 1929, buying on margin allows for the magic of leverage.

Leverage is white magic in a rising market but quickly becomes black magic in a falling market. People seem destined to forget this lesson in two or three generations no matter how painful the learning is for their forbears.

A lesson that did not need to be learned on this or similar future occasions was that those deemed responsible for the crisis had to be punished. Great criticism was made of the directors of the South-Sea Company in England, heightened when rumour had it – no doubt correctly – that they had sold some or all of their stock before the crash. The ministry was seriously alarmed at the state of affairs. Directors were insulted in public and serious riots threatened life and property. Goldsmiths and bankers who had lent vast sums on the security of stock were forced to abscond. The Bank of England declined (after a brief failed attempt) to participate in an attempt to save the South-Sea company.

'And thus', says MacKay in the words of the Parliamentary History, 'were seen, in the space of eight months, the rise, progress, and fall of that mighty fabric, which, being wound up by mysterious springs to a wonderful height, had fixed the eyes and expectations of all Europe, but whose foundation, being fraud, illusion, credulity, and infatuation, fell to the ground as soon as the artful management of its directors was discovered.' And MacKay adds in his own words: 'Nations, like individuals, cannot become desperate gamblers with impunity. Punishment is sure to overtake them sooner or later'. But this was by no means the view at the time, nor is it now when people are gulled by experts. In 1720, the King was asked to return from his sojourn in Hanover. Meetings were held throughout the country and petitions sent to the parliament demanding vengeance against the South-Sea directors.

Back in 1720, the King asked the parliament to find out and apply the 'proper remedy' for the national misfortune. In reply several parliamentary speakers indulged in the 'most violent invective' against the directors. It was said that there was no law that could be invoked against the directors, and they should be sown into sacks and thrown in the Thames, like parricides in Roman times. Walpole was more measured and reminded his colleagues that the first task was to restore the nation's credit. The parliament passed a resolution requiring the government to seek a remedy for the national distress, but also to punish its authors.

Punishment of the guilty was easier than restoration of the national credit. The necessary inquiry was quickly established and many wild statements were made, and strong resolutions passed, for example blaming 'vile stock jobbers' for the crisis. Directors and officials of the South-Sea Company were banned from leaving the country for 12 months, and a secret committee of thirteen was appointed with power to send for persons, papers and records. There was extreme public excitement and interest.

The calls for vengeance against modern villains are equally vigorous. In Australia, Alan Bond, Brian Quinn (once a director of the central bank) and Christopher Skase are all 'tall poppies' who have been excoriated with many others. Each of these men was hailed as a hero before he was revealed as a villain, as was Britain's Robert Maxwell, Enron's Kenneth Lay and indeed all the CEO's whose companies required bailout in the Global Financial Crisis of 2007-08.

While all this was happening, Knight, the treasurer of the company, entrusted with all the dangerous secrets of the dishonest directors, packed up his books and documents, and made his escape from the country. Now directors, including Sir John Blunt, were taken into custody, and messengers were sent throughout the continent requesting the arrest and return of the hapless Knight. Sir John Blunt was an uncooperative witness, and refused to answer questions as he 'thought it hard to be compelled to accuse himself'. After several ineffectual attempts to 'refresh his memory' Blunt was 'directed to withdraw' and 'violent discussion' ensued. Earl Stanhope 'warmly resented' an imputation of The Duke of Wharton and became ill and died shortly afterwards. This caused 'great grief' to the nation, and George I 'shut himself up for some hours in his closet, inconsolable for his loss'.

Knight was apprehended in Tirlemont, near Liege, and lodged in the citadel of Antwerp. The British authorities tried many times to have Knight returned, but the State of Brabant refused, appealing to their right to try any criminal apprehended in their country. While this debate raged, Knight was allowed to escape and was to remain in exile for 20 years or more. That this was due to a secret deal was suspected but unproven for the best part of three centuries when (Balen reports) a letter dated 11 September 1721 confirming the long-standing suspicions was discovered in the Vienna state archives.

When the Committee made its first report to the House, it stated that its inquiry had been 'attended with numerous difficulties'. Witnesses had been unhelpful, books presented to them had false and fictitious entries, other items had been erased or altered and pages had been torn out. The most important books had been destroyed or taken away. But it was clear that fictitious stock had been assigned to members of the government, sold at a profit and (presumably) withdrawn or recycled after the profit had been passed on. The practices discovered were deemed to be 'corrupt, infamous and dangerous', and the perpetrators were ordered to make restitution to the unhappy sufferers from their own estates.

One Charles Stanhope was the first person required to account for his role. His defence was that the Treasurer, the absent Mr. Knight, had handled all relevant matters and whatever had been done was done without his authority. Great efforts were made to protect him, but even so he was acquitted by the tiny margin of three. This acquittal was met with great unhappiness through the country and menacing mobs assembled in different parts of London.

The next two men to appear had a far harder time of it. After brief hearings, Mr Aislabie and Sir George Caswell were expelled from the House and committed to the Tower. Sir George was ordered to refund 250,000 pounds and Mr Aislabie's was required to provide details of his estate so his refund could be determined. (In those days, the modern practice of having all property in the name of one's spouse had not yet become popular.) There was much rejoicing by the mob, bonfires were lit and danced around. The next man to be examined was acquitted and the menacing mobs again formed. Then the next man to face British justice died the night before his examination, and it was generally believed he had poisoned himself. The directors were examined one by one, and over two million pounds was taken from them toward repairing the mischief they had occasioned. A reside was allowed each of them, the amount presumably depending on their degree of guilt and appearance of remorse. MacKay's account does not say whether or on what basis the money so obtained was distributed.

The twin bubbles of 1720 left a large mark on modern capitalism. The authorities sought retribution but in many cases were handicapped by their own involvement. The natural reaction was to strengthen the case for separation of powers between the monarch, the parliament and the judiciary.

Edward Gibbon, of *Decline and Fall* fame, was the grandson of one of the directors so harshly treated, and MacKay says that many years later Gibbon junior wrote of the proceedings. It was widely agreed, said Gibbon, that no law existed under which the directors could be charged. Parliament imposed severe 'pains and penalties' retrospectively and after the most dubious processes. Gibbon wrote, no doubt proudly; 'my grandfather, at a mature age, erected the edifice of a new fortune'.[17]

Restoring public credit took much more time and effort than punishing the directors. 'Enterprise, like Icarus, had soared too high, and melted the wax of her wings; like Icarus, she had fallen into a sea, and learned, while floundering in its waves, that her proper element was the solid ground. She has never since attempted so high a flight'.

Costs, benefits and conjectures

The twin bubbles of 1720 showed that the Tulipomania was not an aberration. As in the earlier case, the experience provided considerable raw material for analysis of the nature of asset booms and busts. My reading of this literature suggests there is indeed a role for both 'rational bubbles' and 'irrational exuberance', justifying my instincts as an economist who believes that disequilibrium is a feature of the economic world.[18]

Inherent in mankind's nature, perhaps a vital driver of the capitalist system, is the urge to get rich quick if opportunity presents itself or to invent a way to do so when no compelling idea comes to hand. And, of course, there were winners as well as losers. People who were smart, or lucky, bought early and sold before the bubbles burst. Some poor people were winners, and many rich people were losers. The rich and famous were perhaps more inclined to be sucked in, indeed in many cases they were actively courted by the schemes' promoters and in other cases they begged to be allowed to invest. When so many of the rich and famous were stupid, or unlucky, enough to be caught when the bubble burst one is forced to wonder if this was no bad thing.

In both cases beneficial side effects included reductions in the national debt, though this was achieved in an arbitrary manner with many adverse effects, including in France inflation and depression. In the case of France the economic costs of the whole episode were so devastating that Michael Balen concludes that 'France, the economic superpower, was rotting from the inside'.[19]

While Law's scheme, as modified by an incompetent and greedy Regent, ended in catastrophe and confusion, his basic ideas were sound, at least in the view of most modern economists. As already noted, Joseph Schumpeter says Law was in the first rank of monetary theorists of all time. This reminds one of the joke about the four bedraggled men at the tail of the Mayday Parade in Moscow at the height of the cold war. The Russian leader, in response to a question from his American visitor, explained 'They are the economists. They can do more damage than all the weapons and people you have seen before this'.

To make Law's scheme sound, there should have been disciplined growth of his paper currency, meeting but not exceeding the non-inflationary needs of trade. Sensible control over the growth of bank credit would also have been required, and this is a problem not satisfactorily solved even now.

In the world of 1720, neither monetary nor inflation targets had yet been conceived and restraint on bank lending, if imagined at all in the Palace of Versailles, would have been thought to be imposed by the good sense of bankers. We now know, or think we know, that bankers need to be helped to achieve good sense by the dictates and supervision of whole battalions of regulators, but this idea was a century or two in the distant future. Even now, it is far from clear that mankind has found the last word on the subject.

Both the bubbles of 1720 were flawed in concept and involved massive fraud and mismanagement. Nowadays we pay lip service to preventing repetition of such illegality, yet allow most failed financiers to escape any real punishment. No-one gets broken on the wheel today, like the unfortunate Count d'Horn. Rather the standard for those whose lawyers cannot gain an acquittal is a few years in a comfortable low security place of detention, or perhaps a fine and a few years in which the miscreant is banned from directing companies. More civilised, that is for sure, but almost certainly less effective.

There is a final point of substantial relevance. 'Nobody, says Charles MacKay, 'seemed to imagine that the nation itself was as culpable as the South-Sea Company. Nobody blamed the credulity and avarice of the people, – the degrading lust of gain, which had swallowed up every nobler quality of the national character, or the infatuation which had made the multitude run their heads with such frantic eagerness into the net held out for them by scheming projectors'.[20]

Later writers have been critical of the colour of MacKay's prose and his supposed statistical shortcomings. This quote, however, deserves to be displayed in the lobby of every financial-system regulator. Regulators should meditate upon it and devise more sensible regulatory solutions.

6

The Age of Innovation spreads the Industrial Revolution

Growth is based most securely on successful innovation, and this was the case in the golden age of the nineteenth century. With innovation producing new industries, pioneering new lands, the industrial revolution spreading from England and global monetary policy led by the Bank of England, the centre was solid. There was massive growth and occasional setbacks in both the old world and the new.

Britain in the late eighteenth century was a nation of innovators. New roads were made and old roads improved. Canals joined rivers and effectively connected the North and Irish Seas. The first railways were built. Britain's population grew rapidly, with enterprising Scots travelling south and unskilled but vigorous Irishmen travelling east. There was rapid overall growth of population due very largely to reductions in mortality. The industrial revolution was underway.

The historian T.S. Ashton attributes declining mortality to better nutrition, higher standards of personal cleanliness, more hospitals and dispensaries, better medical and surgical practices, paved and drained streets and running water in the larger towns, better garbage disposal and greater attention to the proper burial of the dead.[1] I recently discovered a heavily marked up copy of this book, which I had used in a school history class almost 50 years ago. It was like meeting an old friend after a long time apart.

There was an increase in land under cultivation in England. And a rapid increase in capital. More and more people had the power to save, and stable political conditions encouraged men to think about the power of time and compound interest. Unequal distribution of wealth and income encouraged capital accumulation.

JM Keynes, like Professor Ashton before him, emphasises 'the great age of science and technical inventions', which reached full flood in the nineteenth century – 'coal, steam, electricity, petrol, steel, rubber, cotton, the chemical industries, automatic machinery and the methods of mass production, wireless, printing, ... and thousands of other things and men too famous and familiar to catalogue'.[2] The revolutionary ideas of Newton, Smith, and Darwin were much discussed and, from 1905 those of Einstein, whose theory of relativity was destined to change the mindset of a century.[3]

Interest rates also fell as competent governments gradually got Britain's finances under control. Combined with the furious energy of Britain's entrepreneurs, growing supplies of land, labour and capital made possible the expansion of industry. Low rates of interest, rising prices and high expectations of profit provided incentive. But there were less material factors also at play. Trade had widened men's view of the world and science their conception of the universe, as Ashton puts it. The influence of philosophers was important, as well as that of inventors, contrivers, industrialists and entrepreneurs. There was greater control over nature and the beginning of a new attitude to the problems of human society. Among the role of the philosophers in the forces that produced the industrial revolution, that of Adam Smith was pivotal. His *Enquiry into the Nature and Causes of the Wealth of Nations*, published in 1776, presented a vision of 'unlimited progress in a free and expanding economy'.[4]

The nineteenth century experienced a succession of fluctuations in bank rate suggestive of more or less regular 'cycles'. These fluctuations were repeated in the measures of overall economic activity that led economists to propound theories of the so-called 'trade cycle'. My hypothesis is that in Britain at least the nineteenth century shows such regular sequences of boom and bust as the wars were not too dominating, the age of innovation provided a driving force for growth and Britain's adherence to the gold standard provided 'railway tracks' that imposed floors and ceilings on economic growth. The United States was an altogether less regulated environment, and shows more dramatic swings in economic affairs, including share prices.

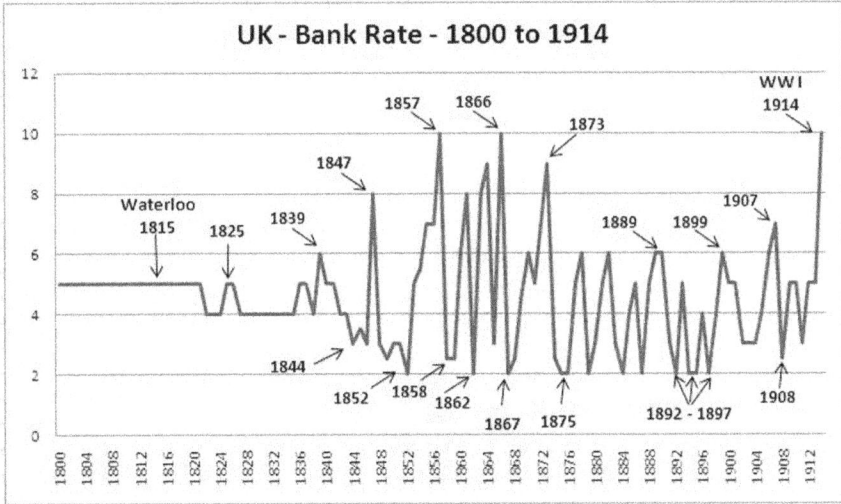

UK - Bank Rate - 1800 to 1914

The graph shows peaks and troughs in England's Bank Rate, a key contributor to economic stability under the gold standard. Bank Rate peaks and troughs generally lag behind the peaks and troughs in share prices (and in the economic cycle generally) as the Bank of England under the gold standard responded mainly to ebbs and flows of its gold stock, which itself lagged general economic fluctuations.[5]

The next two graphs show peaks and troughs in US and UK share prices respectively. As judged by share prices, clearly some ups and downs were bigger than others. There is, however, a high degree of synchronicity in the fluctuations, which suggest international linkages that we have come to label 'globalisation'. Note however, the US share index went up by almost five times from a bit over 2 to reach 10 in 1902 and again in 1909, while the UK index less than doubled from an average of around twenty (ignoring the temporary peak in 1824) to a peak of under forty in 1897.

A feature of both graphs is the clear change of trend from the middle of the century, from slightly down to strongly up, albeit with more or less regular corrections and a soft period from 1877-78 until the early 1890s. The major change of trend is primarily in my view due to the flowering of economic development and innovation, stimulated in part by the major gold discoveries in 1849 in California and 1851 in South Eastern Australia. During the soft period from 1877-78 to the early 1890s, gold was again in relatively short supply. Then there were further great mineral discoveries as the nineteenth century unfolded, including further gold discoveries in the 1890s in South Africa and Western Australia.

There is insufficient time and space to cover all the ups and downs in economic activity and in optimism in the extended nineteenth century, which ends with the outbreak of the World War I in 1914. I focus mainly on three episodes, each with a distinct peak and trough in both US and UK share prices and a clear relationship to changes in Bank Rate. These episodes are the boom of 1825, the railway mania of 1845, both far stronger in the UK than the USA, and the golden years following the discoveries of 1849 and 1851 *The table on page 125 shows the various peaks and troughs in share prices and Bank Rate. It is only in the final episode that Bank Rate peaked when share prices peaked, and thereby hangs a tale – a new man calling for more urgent action in British monetary policy.* with clear peaks in share prices in both countries in 1852 and again in 1864 and the renewed boom that peaked in 1873 in both nations. Then in Chapter 7 we focus on the astounding boom and bust in the new city of Marvellous Melbourne from 1880 to 1900.

As the graphs show, the US and UK economies marched to slightly different drums in the 1890s and early 1900s, though both had broadly familiar episodes of boom and bust within a generally buoyant economic experience. Unless I have missed some bold hypothesis, this change to a hitherto regular pattern deserves separate study.

Peaks and Troughs in economic optimism and Bank Rate

Episodes	UK Shares		US Shares		UK Bank Rate	
	Peak	Trough	Peak	Trough	Peak	Trough
Boom of 1824/25	1824	1831	1824	1829	1825	1827
Railway mania	1835	1841	1835	1842	1839	1844
	1844	1849	1845	1848	1847	1852
The golden years	1852	1856	1852	1857	1857	1858
	1864	1868	1864	1865	1866	1867
	1873	1878	1873	1877	1873	1875

USA - S & P 500 - 1800 to 1914 (Monthly)

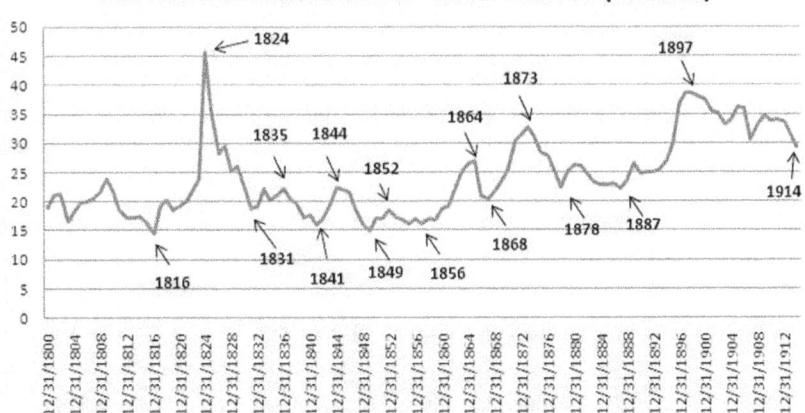

UK - FTSE All Share Index - 1800 to 1914 (Annual)

The boom of 1824-25

The end of the Napoleonic wars in 1815 produced a severe post-war downturn. But economic buoyancy gradually resumed as the wounds of war healed and normal trade resumed. John Law and John Blunt in 1720 held out the prospect of great wealth in the Americas, and a century later there was greater substance to such claims. A colourful financial entrepreneur arrived in London to raise money for 'Poyais', a small territory on the border of the present Nicaragua, and tempt immigrants. A loan of 600,000 pounds was raised, with a 6% dividend, and began to trade at a premium. In 1823, 200 colonists embarked to the capital of Poyais where, instead of a wealthy city, they found a collection of mud huts surrounded by swamps and hostile Indians. Only 50 returned.

The financial entrepreneur, like John Law before him, was a Scottish rascal, one Sir Gregor Macgregor. He fled with his family to France and, you guessed it, he took the proceeds of the capital raising with him.

British bonds were now called 'consols' after a consolidation which helped reduce the cost of borrowing by the British government and were in strong demand. The British government had sought to restrict trading in futures and options but the relevant laws were routinely overlooked. Loans were available for speculation in government bonds. British bonds were in short supply after the wars were over, and foreign loans were all the rage. Spain's South American colonies were achieving liberation with British sympathy. Getting rich by helping to build new countries in the Americas seemed like an irresistible proposition. The first part of the boom of 1824-25 was the boom in emerging market bonds, buttressed by a mining boom fed by reports of gold lying about to be picked out of the dirt.

The British government's finances were sound, confidence was high and a range of commodity prices began to rise, then as now a strong part of the 'emerging market' story. Edward Chancellor reports that Anglo-Mexican shares, on which ten pounds had been paid, rose from 33 in December 1825 to more than 150 a month later. Shares in Real del Monte, another Mexican mine, climbed from 550 pounds to 1,350, or was it 1550? (The sources vary.) With only 70 pounds paid on them, early investors were enjoying massive paper gains. Dazzled by these developments, the young Benjamin Disraeli was employed to write in support of the South American mining companies. He also invested heavily in the mining stock he was promoting so enthusiastically, and only finally discharged the debt he then incurred many years later.[6]

The second strand to the boom of 1825 was the rise of new domestic companies. Some were real enterprises. Nathan Rothschild, newly wealthy from his gamble on British bonds (discussed in Chapter 3), founded an insurance company which eventually prospered. Other ventures were more like the list from 1720. Promised was seawater piped to London for bathing, established pawnbrokers were to be undercut, cheap fish were to be sold to the poor, peaceful repose was offered for the dead, recovery of cannonballs from the seabed near Trafalgar, and the Red Sea was to be drained to capture the gold and jewels left by the Egyptians who drowned whilst chasing the Israelites. Railways began to be promoted heavily. Bankers lent recklessly to support that boom against the inflated values of shares and bonds and discounting bills for merchants speculating in commodities.

Again as in 1720, but with greater transparency, members of parliament and peers were active in promoting stocks. *The Times* complained of 'the leprous infection of avarice' but parliament recklessly passed bills to establish these companies, whether they were real, fanciful or merely fraudulent. 'Gross complacency, even contemptuous arrogance, was evident among the ruling class'. The government basked in what were claimed to be the best of times according to the King's speech at the opening of parliament in February 1825, with feelings of 'content and satisfaction ... more widely diffused through all the classes of the British people'.

There were perhaps more members of parliament concerned at the speculative excesses than during the South Sea Bubble. Chancellor quotes Lord Liverpool and Alexander Baring among others who colourfully denounced speculation and the promoters who set the bubbles in play. The government was deeply divided. There was a growing free trade movement and concern at the possibility of interfering with Adam Smith's invisible hand. There were many uses for capital in the industrial revolution that was reshaping Britain. In the event the government failed to find a balance between its economically liberal instincts and its moral repugnance to speculation, in effect anticipating ambivalence still alive in many modern legislators.[7]

The boom began to lose its strength in the summer of 1825 and investors began to ignore calls for partly paid shares. In late August the Bank of England, alarmed by the drain of its gold reserves, began to tighten credit. The so-called country banks, which had issued far too much credit during the boom, stoking asset inflation in the process, began to get into trouble, and the Bank of England

In 1826, bankruptcies increased greatly, manufacturing output plunged, there was great worker unrest as the country became mired in severe depression. The government was largely deaf to pleas to help alleviate the situation. The prevailing view was that the bust was the result of a speculative boom, and such speculation needed to be punished.

was unable (even if it had wished to do so) to be lender of last resort. Bank failures begin in October, and by December economic activity had ground to a halt. Share prices fell by up to 80%, and a director of the Bank of England remarked privately on the 'torrent of distrust' that afflicted markets. This phrase might have been used to good effect in September 2008 to focus the minds of the people trying to save the global financial system from collapse.

In emergency parliamentary session, the Bank of England was directed (or 'allowed' as Chancellor puts it) to circulate notes of small denomination, including a box of previously unused one pound notes discovered in the vaults. The Mint began coining sovereigns and Nathan Rothschild brought from France 300,000 gold sovereigns which he paid into the Bank. The liquidity crisis was averted, and the panic subsided, but the economic damage was great. To make matters worse, the mining boom came to an abrupt end and debt rescheduling and outright default hindered relations between Britain and South America for more than a half-century.

Railway mania

The Stockton and Darlington Railway opened during the boom of 1824-25, and six railway acts were passed by parliament. The bust of the following year extinguished any further tendency to euphoria until the opening of the Liverpool and Manchester Railway several years later. This venture established clearly the benefits of mobile steam engines over other methods of locomotion, including walking and travelling by horse and coach. With a dividend of 10%, the share price doubled. But in the next economic downturn following the bust of 1837 the railways began to struggle.

Gradually, however, railway networks became more extensive and their propaganda became more persuasive. The young Queen Victoria enjoyed a short train trip. Landlords discovered land served by a railroad was more valuable. Newspapers and journals began to write of the benefits, some described as almost cosmic. Despite early agricultural concerns, cows still gave milk and chickens eggs. George Hudson, the Railway King, chairman of the York and North Midlands Railway which opened in 1842, became an influential and energetic promoter of the new ways of travelling and moving freight. Penny-pinching to the point of endangering his customer's lives, Hudson paid top prices for rival companies and played fast and loose in his dealings with shareholders, even paying high dividends out of capital. 'An atmosphere of elation and ecstasy characterised the shareholders' meetings: the railway was their new religion and Hudson their Messiah'.[8]

During the first railway boom in 1836, someone floated the idea of regulating expansion of railways to create an efficient system. This was rejected, presumably due to the prevailing ideology of laissez-faire, and development proceeded piecemeal. With 66 applications for new railways before parliament in 1844, the task of framing new legislations fell to William Gladstone, then President of the Board of Trade. Regulation was opposed fiercely by George Hudson, who had his way. Watered down legislation created a Railway Act under which a Railway Department was required to study proposed new lines, but had no ability to enforce its views. After raising the deposit needed for new railway schemes from 5 to 10%, Gladstone resigned to pursue his family's railway interests, with the expectation that the new Act would receive a severe and early trial.

By late 1844, economic conditions were again benign. Interest rates were low, after a series of excellent harvests corn was cheap and plentiful, railway revenues were rising rapidly and the three largest railways were paying dividends of 10%. Many applications for new railways were in the pipeline, prospectuses provided only minimal business plans and the names of the great and the good, many of whom discreetly neglected to sign the deeds that made them liable for debts. Anthony Baring, now Lord Ashburton, complained in the House of Lords about the 'feverish state of gambling events connected with railways' though in such cases it was easier to point out the difficulties than to suggest the remedy. The government was deep in debate about the repeal of the Corn Laws with little energy to debate the regulatory issues for railroads.

Prime Minister, Sir Robert Peel, had the previous year secured the passing on a new Bank Act, designed to end the sequence of boom and bust by limiting the Bank of England's ability to expand the note issue. The gold standard would limit the Bank's reserves of gold, and there was to be a separate limit on the note issue – a belt and braces approach that seemed sure to limit speculation in the economic upswing. By August, however, Peel was concerned that a mania was developing and wrote to the Chancellor of the Exchequer about whether some sort of warning might be useful.

The mania was strongest in the North, with banks making loans against railway shares, new stock exchanges being formed, including three in the city of Leeds, and stockbrokers appearing like mushrooms in the spring. Speculation in railway shares was widespread. The poet Wordsworth wrote in his journal 'The country is an asylum of railway lunatics'. Chancellor also quotes from a letter to the *Times* which gave him the title of his book. The letter said that all the speculators knew a crash was coming, and that when the luck turned, 'and the crack play is *sauve qui peut*, or devil take the hindmost, no one fancies that the last train from Panic station will leave him behind.' This is presumably a prime example of a 'rational bubble'.

Warnings of the crash to come were regularly issued by the *Times* and *The Economist* as well as in local or specialised newspapers and magazines. The Railway King was at the height of his glory despite the general disapproval of the pace of expansion that threatened the profitability of his own lines. Facts or mere rumours about his involvement in railway business caused share prices to soar. He brought a twelve-thousand-acre estate from the Duke of Devonshire and one of the largest private houses in London for his town dwelling.

By late summer the climax of the mania was fast approaching. Capital gains and loan rates were immense, foreign railroads were planned, or dreamed about, numbers of new prospectuses rocketed and a Railway Club was established where railway enthusiasts could meet to exchange information.

As railway construction began, railway companies made calls on partly paid shares – as noted already, a form of equity effectively allowing buying on margin – and investors began to be burnt as share prices fell. The Bank of England raised interest rates by half a percent, and this signalled the end of the boom. From London, the bad news traveled rapidly by rail to the provincial exchanges, bringing paralysis to these markets. Speculation turned to litigation but there was plenty of strain on the economy as new lines were built by companies that stayed afloat, while others failed. There was a lot of merger and acquisition activity, and an anxious government passed a Dissolution Act that allowed the dissolution of railway companies on a vote of 75% of the shareholders.

Bank Rate did not rise during the build up of the mania, but only when the Bank of England's gold reserves came under strain. No inflation targeting then; not even pre-emptive action to slow the boom.

The continuing railway construction placed great strains on the economy, strains that were compounded in 1846 by a poor harvest. Some investors were wiped out, others were strapped for cash to meet calls on partly paid shares, and interest rates continued to rise. By October 1847 market interest rates had risen to around 10%, with Bank Rate at 8%, over three times the low of 2.5% in place as recently as March 1845.

In early October 1847 the Bank of England announced that it would no longer make advances on stock or Exchequer Bills. 'Until October', says Clapham, 'only commercial houses had gone down. Then came the turn of country banks, private and joint stock'. He quotes a contemporary journalist who said the Bank of England's action 'forthwith gave birth to universal panic'.[9]

The Bank Act, which three years earlier had been introduced to end speculative excess, was suspended and the Bank of England was authorised to continue its discounting operations. This brought the crisis to an end, but there was a fierce debate in which the diversion of capital from trading purposes to railways was seen as the chief problem.

The Railway King, George Hudson, was accused of much wrongdoing but never charged with any legal offence. He took refuge in the demon drink and spent much time on the continent. He repaid Company money spent on personal assets and died leaving only a tiny estate.

Great new inventions, like the railroad, usually create bucketloads of money for someone, but not always the inventor.

The laissez-faire attitude of the government meant there was much waste and unnecessary duplication of rail-lines during the boom. But with over 8,000 miles of track in operation by 1855, Britain possessed the most dense railway system in the world, providing great economic benefits.

The golden years

By the halfway mark of the nineteenth century, economic cycles – fluctuations is a better term - of approximately a decade in length were well established. The time from the French Revolution in 1790 to the end of the Napoleonic wars had been a time of inflation, typical of such times as normal economic activity is disrupted but demand for goods and services is high. When peace broke out, the inflationary wave retreated, and shortage of gold was one important reason.

The discovery of rich outcrops of gold in California in 1849 and in Eastern Australia in 1851 provided fresh impetus to the European economy. The Russian economist, Nikolai Kondratieff, later developed a theory of 'long waves' in economic life. He argued that international wars and important inventions tended to come in the upswing of the long waves. Gold discoveries tended to come when economic conditions were depressed, as pastoralists and others had more time on their hands and an incentive to keep on the lookout for signs of mineralisation.

Geoffrey Blainey argues that, in the wake of the massive gold discoveries, people expected a rise of inflation, a hint about the emphasis to come in the second half of the twentieth century on the role of inflationary expectations. The vast increase in international trade as the newly wealthy overseas territories spent freely was another sign of inflation to come. But in the period beginning in the early 1870s there was insufficient gold for the world's financial needs and the results of innovation and development of new lands was raising productivity. Prices of both commodities and shares were soft, reflecting and perhaps shaping the prevailing mood of caution. Then, late in the nineteenth century, another flood of gold, this time from the deeper mines of South Africa and Western Australia, helped start an upswing that ended in the first great global war. The vagaries of gold discoveries was a technical problem for the gold standard, but not in the nineteenth century sufficient to question the status quo.[10]

All this, of course, was taking place against a continuing background of development of new lands, new inventions, new industries and the ongoing struggle for Europe, which was becoming a struggle for global dominance.

'America's vast wilderness invited speculation', asserts Edward Chancellor in his Chapter on 'The Gilded Age'.[11] The founding fathers were land speculators, Benjamin Franklin was involved in a land speculation of sixty-three million acres in Illinois and Patrick Henry, the 'fiery revolutionary', was involved in the 'Yazoo Company' that attempted to buy ten million acres in Georgia. From its inception, the American stock and land operators worked on a far greater scale than those in Europe.

Californian gold had a massive effect in promoting both real development and inflation in America, especially in the wild west. As the population moved west, a whole raft of saloons, whorehouses and banks followed closely behind. Gold created prosperity, but led the banks to issue too many notes, and there was no central bank to moderate, or attempt to moderate, their actions. Buildings mushroomed, financed by borrowed money. In August 1857, the Ohio Insurance and Trust company failed, leaving unpaid liabilities of around five million dollars. Other insurance companies began to fall, and a 'Western blizzard' blew into New York. The bankers of New York responded by suspending specie payments, and for a time the short sellers made hay. Then share prices began to rise again and the bulls had their turn at agricultural pursuits. A 'distinctly predatory' tone developed, with survival of the fittest as the prevailing ideology.[12]

In the more stable old world, England and Russia were at war in the Crimea, from March 1854 to March 1856. Harvests in Britain were poor, and the corn trade with Odessa, an important source of supply, was interrupted. For the first time in 40 years, the British government was borrowing to wage war, long term interest rates were rising and Bank Rate was kept high, mostly 5% and above. Bank Rate would have been higher but for the steady flow of gold from the Antipodes, and the less reliable flow from the American West. 'A currency system which in difficult times', says Clapham, 'depends on the chance occurrence of nuggets in gulches and gold dust in river sands lacks stability'.[13]

Both in Britain and on the continent corporate law was being liberalised and modernised, and on the continent 'grandiose experiments were being made with joint-stock undertakings'. Following the general development model of the *Crédit Mobilier*, throughout Western Europe and well into Central Europe industrial banks promoted new developments rather than supporting existing companies. The capital goods for new industrial development mainly came from Britain, and British railway contractors were operating in half-a-dozen countries. Gold flowed both into and out of England, with an overall positive balance but occasional difficulties of timing. There was close attention to the names of the arriving ships and the gold that they carried

All the 'feverish and gold-dazzled activity' of the 1850s ended in the commercial crisis of 1857. This has been called, Clapham asserts, the first really world-wide crisis in history. Crisis broke out at 'almost the same moment' in the United States, Britain and Central Europe, and it was felt in South America, South Africa, Australia and the Far East. The spark was lit in America. In 1856 more than one-fifth of British exports went to the United States, it was believed that Britain held eighty million pounds worth of American stocks and bonds and there were many big open credits for American firms in Britain. Bad news from America was therefore bad news indeed and there were growing reports of failures of American trust companies and banks. By October, 62 out of 63 New York banks had suspended payment, and in the single month of October 1415 banks collapsed in the United States. 'Business came to a standstill along the whole of the eastern and south-eastern seaboards'.

The first European bank failures also occurred in October of 1856, in Liverpool and Hamburg, and these shocks were also passed on to London. Interest rates rose in European capitals. The Bank of England moved Bank Rate to 6% on 8 October, to 7 on 12 October and to 8 a week later, Clapham says with commendable foresight. From the main commercial centres of northern England, Scotland and Ireland came questions as to whether the Bank of England would help commercial banks and brokers in trouble. 'Scots were losing faith in their own notes, Irishmen catching panic from the air'. A powerful firm of American bankers and exchange brokers stopped payment for an amount exceeding two million pounds, and then Sanderson's the bill-brokers stopped payment for an amount in excess of five million pounds. Two days earlier, on November 9, Bank Rate had been controversially raised to a record 10%.

Bank Rate stayed at 10% until Christmas Eve, when it was reduced to 8%. This signalled the end of the monetary crisis, but the commercial crisis was to go on for some time and the industrial slump for even longer. Bank rate tumbled as activity declined and stocks of gold rose. Monetary recovery was rapid, but 1858 was 'one of the worst years of the later nineteenth century, probably worse than in

1879 or 1886'. There were no statistics of unemployment, but plenty of 'lamentable stories from well-informed clients'. The Bank voted 50 pounds for the Birmingham Unemployed Relief fund, only the second time such a charitable act had been performed.

In early 1860 came more bad news from America. Now the Union was in trouble and British capital was again at risk. Secession of Southern States began after the election of President Lincoln, and in April 1861 came the attack on Fort Sumter. Commercial interests in Britain were anxious, and Bank Rate was mostly above 5%, and for six weeks in February and March at 8%. Shortage of cotton was the major commercial concern and, while the cotton city of Lancashire had rising unemployment, most parts of the country were busier. Fresh markets were being opened for British manufactures, India was a vast new territory for railway investment and newly wealthy Australia was helping. 'The scare was in part irrational as all scares are'.

A new law of limited liability for companies was codified in England in this year. Despite the 'thundery atmosphere' spread by the Civil War there were warnings against a 'Speculative Mania' and a 'Banking Mania'. A young George Joachim Goschen joined the Court of the Bank and produced a book called *Theory of the Foreign Exchanges* – published initially as an anonymous pamphlet. Goschen advocated that, to better protect the reserves, Bank rate should be moved up not by half but rather one percent at a time. (This is perhaps the first time anyone criticised a central bank for moving 'too little, too late' to slow a boom.)   The proposal was 'most unpopular' but was later commended by the magisterial Walter Bagehot in his book *Lombard Street,* when he wrote in 1873: 'On this occasion, and, as far as I know, on this occasion alone the Bank of England made an excellent alteration of their policy, which was not exacted by contemporary opinion, and which was in advance of it'.[14]

Bank rate kept rising in one percent jumps and reached 9%. Clapham endorses Bagehot's opinion that this action avoided a calamity like that in 1857, and by the time General Lee surrendered and some European wars were resolved the 'political sky of Europe was for the moment clear'. (For the moment only, Clapham wryly observes, as Bismarck was at work.)   During these uneasy times the old firm of 'money dealers' Overend and Gurney was floated, doubtless a desperate move.

With America again focussing on business, and markets opening everywhere, 1866-67 was boomtime again, with Bank Rate again leaping up in one percent moves. In May 10 1866 the newly floated Overend, Gurney and Co. Ltd failed for five million. The families lost all their own wealth and most of the capital of the firm itself. 'New men' had joined the firm and indulged in 'reckless speculation' both in discounting bills of dubious character and in getting involved in all kinds of speculative business. May 11 was London's Black Friday. That it was only eight days after Gladstone had presented an 'exuberant' budget with no hint of a warning about the parlous state of commercial finance, which made matters far worse than they might have been. The Bank of England raised Bank rate to 9% and spent many millions of its gold reserves in discounting commercial paper. Gladstone was forced by 'deputation after deputation' to again suspend the Bank Act.

Politicians, even politicians of Gladstone's eminence, often get blindsided by economic crises. And thank goodness for George Goschen, who showed the way to better monetary policy.

The peaks in share prices were higher in 1864 than in 1852, and those of 1873 were to be higher still. Shortage of gold caused a mild deflation of commodity prices, but the United States remained united and had built the first transcontinental railroad. Germany had become united and was highly ambitious. France was beaten and penalised but far from broken. The new Suez Canal facilitated trade. Great ocean cables greatly improved global communications. Steel rails and iron ships were dominating transport; steel ships with more powerful engines were coming. There was 'furious industrial activity' in Britain during the years 1871-3, and the export of British goods and capital was at its maximum. On the continent, except in France, and in the United States, there was activity as furious but more reckless. The years from 1866 to 1873, from any perspective, says Clapham, 'look like a gigantic hinge on which the history of the later nineteenth century turns'.[15]

The Civil War in America spawned massive speculation that was to last for a decade and then collapse in spectacular style. One vital change was the government's decision to suspend payment in gold and silver and issue greenbacks. This was sure to create inflation and make gold and silver subject to speculation. But, Chancellor says, the great stock operators did not trifle with 'transient mining and petroleum bubbles'. Their focus was on railway stocks, where shareholders, especially British shareholders, 'were led like lambs to the slaughter'.[16]

The railroads had been fostered by vast Federal government land grants and loans. The Union Pacific Railroad after the war fell into the clutches of one Oakes Ames, who created a holding company, the *Credit Moblier*, through which all the construction contracts passed. The constructions costs were inflated and paid to *Crédit Mobilier* in Union Pacific stock, so that its shareholders were 'milked'. And *Crédit Mobilier* stock was given to politicians to keep them on side. When this scam unravelled, it was estimated that Ames and his cronies had plundered nearly $44 million from the Union Pacific.

Jay Gould was another railroad manipulator and robber baron, described by Joseph Pulitzer as 'one of the most sinister figures that ever flitted batlike across the vision of the American people'. 'Slight, consumptive, dark, secretive, scheming', loathed widely and passionately, 'a human carnivore, glutting on the blood of his numberless victim', the list of dark epitaphs goes on and on. At the end of 1868, Gould attempted 'the most audacious speculative feat in history', to corner the supreme prize – gold.

The opening of new lands was depressing the price of wheat, adding to the macroeconomic effects of the global shortage of gold. The US government had vast gold reserves, and Gould's plan required control of government policy. He got connected to President Grant through a lobbyist and adopted the persona of an 'inflationist' whose heart bled for the farmers. He took control of a bank to improve his access to credit. When he became (wrongly) convinced that Grant was going to pursue an inflationist plan to help the western farmers, Gould began to buy gold. President Grant began to understand the plot and declined to play. Gould realised he was in trouble and began to sell gold, Chancellor speculates, under the cover of his partner

(Fisk) who kept buying through a broker without issuing written instructions so he could not be liable for the relevant debts. The hapless broker's ruin was carefully prepared.

When the price of gold finally cracked, Gould was safely out of the market and dozens of brokers failed, at least one committing suicide and one driven mad. This Black Friday did not however end the madness. Now Jay Cooke, the banker who made his fortune selling federal bonds during the war, took his turn at a bigger game. He took over the Northern Pacific Railroad and its massive land grants, according to Cooke's publicist a 'vast wilderness waiting like a rich heiress to be appropriated and enjoyed'. The potential buyers were not convinced.

Fears of financial crisis were evident by the spring of 1873, and interest rates rose, including to half of one percent per day for margin loans. Share market turnover increased, railroad companies began to have trouble refinancing loans and there were stories of forged shares in circulation. On Thursday, 18 September, 1873, Jay Cooke was entertaining President Grant at his mansion in Pennsylvania, when they learned that Jay Cooke & Co. had failed. Initial incredulity gave way to panic and this began unravelling the speculative drama that had entranced and (it must be said) encouraged America for the past decade and a half. Jay Gould viciously shorted stocks, others hunted bargains and Cornelius Vanderbilt drove his carriage furiously down Broad Street with the intention of dispersing and calming the crowd.

When the panic continued into Saturday, the New York Stock Exchange closed for the first time in its history, and remained closed for ten days. There was no escaping the consequences of the long period of over-speculation and overinvestment. Factories closed, railroad companies shed staff, banks failed, wages were cut and money was hoarded. But there were benefits as well as costs of predatory capitalism. By the end of 1873, in the United States 30,000 miles of railway had been constructed in four years, the continent had been conquered and a dynamic new economic power was ready to take its place among the geopolitical powers.

The story in Europe was less flamboyant but in reality little different. Germany was 'lurching into every sort of enterprise, honest, on the honesty margin, or simply fraudulent'. German peasants were selling for great prices strips of land only recently enclosed. In England, Punch drew pictures of 'colliers and coal-heavers drinking champagne'. Prosperity in continental Europe produced a land and building boom in the great capitals.[17]

Agriculture was becoming modernized in the US faster than in Europe, and expanding into the endless prairie. With cheap transport both by rail and ship, much cheap grain was shipped to Europe. The Austrian banks had large investments in the European agricultural sector. With vigorous new competition from America, the banks' customers could not repay loans and many became bankrupt. In May 1873 the first banks began to fail and in the same month the Vienna Stock Exchange crashed.

Clapham says the continental *Krach* spread quickly into Germany, Switzerland and Italy. This signaled the end of the property bubble in Berlin and Paris. The policies of the governments on both sides of the Atlantic ocean (Britain apart) was to protect their own markets, yet to find new markets for their products and countries by continued colonization of large areas in Asia and Africa.

One can readily imagine the attitude of the directors of the Bank of England. Lesser men, more prone to excessive speculation, including the pesky Americans, had failed to contain their animal spirits and deserved their nemesis.

Initially Bank Rate was cut, as England was not in any apparent danger, and indeed was strengthened by a series of wonderful harvests. Soon, however, with the bad news from America adding to the danger, Bank Rate was being raised in discrete jumps to near the panic level of 9%.

During the period of crisis, Bank of England's gold reserve was always adequate, and the Governor 'politely but curtly' declined an offer of a loan of gold by the governor of the Bank of Prussia. In this crisis, it was not deemed necessary to suspend the Bank Act, and indeed the Bank of England proceeded to do some domestic lending and borrowing, for reasons nowhere recorded. By early December Bank Rate was back to 5% and shortly after to 4.5%.

Gathering momentum

While there was boom and bust in the United States of America and in continental Europe, there was little disruption to the even flow of prosperity of the world's superpower for the rest of the nineteenth century and into the first decade of the next. The technical aspects of operating with a global gold standard were well understood and smoothly practiced. Britain was a 'creditor of all the earth' and her public finance was consistently methodical, correct, and almost parsimonious. Continuous improvements to transport and new global food supplies relieved traditional anxieties about food shortages.

The even flow of business was naturally interrupted by various alarms and excursions. The Baring Crisis of 1890 is far more important for the history of Argentina than as an example of the great crises of capitalism, but also worsened the downturn in distant Melbourne. The American panic of 1907, ended by the dramatic intervention of JP Morgan forcing the bankers of New York to support the financial system, came in a year of international difficulty that also falls short of being a great crisis.[18] The gold discoveries at places with exotic names such as Cripple Creek, the Klondike, Coolgardie, Kalgoorlie, Witwaterstrand and others in the 1880s and 1890s again changed the macroeconomic picture from mild deflation to mild inflation, raising interest rates and promoting an optimistic view of the world that perhaps contributed to the outbreak of total war in 1914.

In fact, the whole of the nineteenth century was a time of regularity even in the crises. So regular in fact that Clement Juglar invented a whole theory to describe and 'explain' these apparently regular 'business cycles'. Schumpeter praises Juglar, a physician by training, as among the greatest economists of all time, echoing his high regard for John Law. This high praise is for three reasons – his systematic use of statistics, his development of a 'morphology'of economic cycles and most importantly his attempts at explanation in a way that closely intertwined facts and theory. He famously said 'the only cause of depression is prosperity'. What he meant, of course, is that booms inevitably leads to busts although Juglar failed to explain prosperity.[19]

It is clear from the history of the nineteenth century that true prosperity is created by innovation, and especially a self-confident culture of continuous innovation and improvement. Prosperity is created by exploiting new lands and developing exciting new ventures as well as the absence of war. Prosperity is supported by a well functioning financial system, with prudent financiers. During the nineteenth century the most prominent example of such a financial system was the gold standard as conducted by the Bank of England at the centre of a great empire. Prosperity often leads to over-exuberance and is often accompanied by fraud and incompetence, which helps to explain why prosperity often turns to recession or depression.

7

Marvellous Melbourne's Astonishing Property Boom and Bust; and a short subsequent history of Australia

The gold rush of 1851 set Melbourne on a course that ended in serious depression. But before that there was a boom of massive proportions, and the Colony of Victoria grew and prospered to an extraordinary degree, creating a world class city known as 'Marvellous Melbourne'. As in other cases, a great boom produced a great bust.

'Marvellous Melbourne' graduated from colonial outpost to great city in the 1880s. An ancestor of this writer, Eric Jonsson, aged 19, in 1855 travelled by the good ship *Amsterdam* from Gottenberg in Sweden. He left the ship in Melbourne to find work and a new life.

Eric Jonson (as he became) was attracted by the rich gold rush that started in 1851. Coming on top of the Californian discoveries of 1849, Victorian gold helped create global prosperity as well as immense local wealth. Victoria became a separate colony on July 1, 1851. The new colonial government quickly imposed a steep mining tax in an attempt to extract further value from the new diggers from Britain, California and Sweden. Later arrivals came from China who were in effect the multi-culturals of their day: 'They were the grasping intruders and the disturbers of the peace in the eyes of the officials, squatters, merchants and older colonists who now held power in Melbourne and Sydney'.[1]

Resistance to the tax led in 1854 to Australia's only rebellion, Australia's Boston Tea Party, with its proud flag of the Southern Cross and quick defeat at the Eureka Stockade. More than 30 soldiers and diggers were killed and thirteen surviving miners were charged with treason, but all were eventually acquitted. The editor of the *Ballarat Times*, after a long and rowdy trial, was sentenced to six months goal. Powerful popular support for the rebels marked a milestone in Australia's democratic development.

With a benign climate, many young men and plentiful flat land, Melbourne became a great sporting city. 'Australian rules' football was devised in 1858, and large teams played lengthy games with no central umpires and the rival captains enforcing the few rules. Cricket was imported from England, and victories over teams from the mother country were celebrated with great happiness. By the 1880s the day of the annual Melbourne Cup became a public holiday and vast crowds travelled to the racecourse to watch and lay down their bets. (It has been said that Australians will bet on two flies crawling up a wall.) Melbourne hosted the Olympic Games in 1956 and now boasts teams playing Basketball, 'Football' (Soccer), and both varieties of Rugby in national and international competitions. There is now a vigorous national 'Australian Rules' competition as well as a long-standing State-based national cricket competition.

Victoria in the 1850s had the richest goldfields and produced over 90% of Australian gold, and attracted most immigrants, almost 500,000 by sea and many more overland. Digging for gold was hard physical work and the prizes went to men of strength and stamina. The first great natural resource of the colony, the vast natural grasslands, were claimed by squatters in huge lots to graze sheep. The second – the right to mine gold – went in tiny lots to tens of thousands of diggers. 'The democratic flavour of the 1850s came mainly from the wide dispersal of wealth and the widespread hopes of finding it'.[2]

Geoffrey Blainey describes the inflation of prices as 'insane' and for many years in the 1850s society 'seemed to sway on the brink of chaos', with citizens concerned at the arrival of convicts from Tasmania and diggers from Canton. Inflation was due to great wealth confronted by insufficient goods and services for sale. Blainey estimates that in the first three years of gold the cost of living must have increased by 200%. This he contrasts with the worst three-year periods of inflation in the First and Second World Wars, which saw inflation of 20 to 30%. The Korean War in the early 1950s had three years of inflation of around 50%, and the three years from 1974 to 1977 saw inflation of 44%. 'In essence, inflation in the worst period of the gold rushes was four or five times as rapid as in the worst period of the 1970s'.[3]

Gold gave Melbourne and Victoria great wealth. Population surged, as free immigration boomed and transportation to Tasmania was ended. A wide range of industries became established once the immediate disruptions from new gold were remedied. Vast deposits of copper and tin were discovered, and new gold fields in a vast arc from the South Island of New Zealand, through Queensland to Darwin. Gold made Australia more democratic and optimistic. 'In fact, a surfeit of optimism was to be one of the dangerous legacies of the 1850s'.[4]

Through the 1860s and 1870s, Victoria surfed on the wave created by gold, the development of vast sheep and cattle ranches, often outside tiny Victoria, money from Great Britain and what rapidly became an entrepreneurial mining culture. In 1883 a boundary rider found the rich silver-lead lode at Broken Hill. This discovery was in fact in NSW, but the shareholders were largely in Victoria, many owning or managing sheep stations in the district. This discovery created another great wave of mining wealth, adding to the sense of endless optimism in Melbourne where most of Australia's mining companies had their headquarters.

Melbourne's population went from 268,000 in 1880 to 473,000 in 1891. People came to the city from declining gold towns and from overseas. There was also a delayed effect of the gold-rushes. In the late 1850s the single men who were gold-diggers settled down and married. There was a strong increase in the birth rate then and again in the 1880s when the gold-rush children reached marriageable age. The new generation of young married people needed houses and the building industry boomed. New train lines were needed to transport them, along with a network of tramlines. Property prices doubled in the decade to 1885.

Melbourne was designated 'Marvellous Melbourne' in 1885 by a visiting celebrity journalist, George Augustus Sala.[5] Melbourne's Collins Street became a 'street of dreams and bubble companies'. Great buildings of granite and marble and elaborate shopping malls replaced hastily built colonial structures. In the suburbs, luxurious mansions were built for wealthy colonials, thousands of suburban sub-divisions were sold and resold each time at a higher price and in the inner city industrial areas rows of terrace houses and cottages were built for a newly prosperous and rapidly growing artisan class. Money poured into the colony from abroad, mostly from England. Business boomed, banking boomed and there was a 'stock exchange saturnalia'.[6]

In the first three months of 1888 the buying and selling of Broken Hill silver shares 'verged on lunacy'. In the space of 12 months 62 new silver companies and 113 new gold companies were floated. Trading in their shares became a 'form of frenzy'. By the end of the 1880s, two mines undiscovered at the start of the decade were paying larger annual dividends than the best Victorian gold-mines had paid in their entire lifetime. The names of these mines – Broken Hill Proprietary and the new Queensland gold-mine, Mount Morgan – were magic, and in popular imagination it was plausible to imagine new undiscovered mines of equal wealth.[7]

It was the age of innovation, and Marvellous Melbourne fully shared the global enthusiasm for modern technology. Cable trams and steam trains rode steel rails, gaslight lit the night, electric light was introduced into Melbourne's Opera House and main library, telephones were introduced (confusing the elderly), the new American 'elevator' made multi-story building efficient and all this helped drive land prices even higher. Roads were paved and storm water drains were built. Schools, halls, churches, grandstands, banks and shops were needed in Melbourne and throughout Victoria. Cannon reports that by 1890 the colony boasted more than 3000 large factories, 215 brickworks, 165 large sawmills, 128 tanneries, 93 flour mills, 68 breweries and 6 distilleries.

The first overseas telegraph message was received in Melbourne in 1872 and connected the colonists with world news (and the cricket scores when test matches were played in England). For some years in the 1880s, Melbourne had five daily newspapers as well as many weekly and monthly magazines described in a fit of enthusiasm as being of extraordinarily high literary quality. South Australia granted the right to vote (for its lower house) to nearly every man in 1856, and Victoria and New South Wales followed quickly. In Victoria, in March of that year, the Secret Ballot became law by a narrow majority, followed quickly in the other self-governing colonies, a reform that was followed with great interest in Europe, Great Britain and the United States.

Allowing women to vote was a different matter. Free, compulsory and secular education became the norm in the 1870s, and girls as well as boys were subject to this enlightened law. Universities in New Zealand and Australia were opened to women once a few girls' schools and parents of girls applied pressure. A woman graduated from Auckland University in 1877, two women at Christchurch in 1880 and one at Melbourne in 1883. South Australia led the campaign for votes for women, especially in 1893 after New Zealand granted women the right to vote, although not to sit in parliament. In December 1894, South Australia granted women the right to vote, which they first did in the election of 1896.

The forty years following the discovery of gold in Australia were an age of extraordinary prosperity and great progress. Abundant natural resources included plentiful grasslands to feed sheep and cattle, soil to grow wheat and forests to provide building materials and firewood. Geoffrey Blainey says: 'Rarely in history had people explored, occupied and used such a vast terrain so quickly'.[8] A second reason for prosperity was 'strenuous application of new techniques' – developing fatter cattle, heavier fleeces and breeds of wheat more suitable to the local soil and climate. There were hundreds of labour saving devices – post and rail fences replacing shepherds, wire fences replacing post and rail, introduction of corrugated iron roofing and water tanks, artesian bores, creaking windmills and new irrigation schemes. New ploughs, strippers, mechanical harvesters and travelling steam threshing-machines greatly reduced numbers of workers needed. The Jonson family tradition records that a family member invented the stump-jump plough, but if this is true he won no great wealth and others turned the idea into a profitable invention.[9]

Rich mines provided great impetus to prosperity and, during the forty years from 1851, discoveries of gold, silver, tin and lead had provided almost constant stimulation. Techniques of mining greatly improved with many inventions later utilised elsewhere.

Transport also dramatically improved. In the 1850s men walked loaded down (some pushing wheelbarrows) to the new mining areas, hitched rides on drays pulled by horses, travelled by Cobb & Co coaches or rode horses. Sailing ships still greatly outnumbered steam-driven ships. By 1890 fast steamships dominated the passenger routes to Europe, and the Suez Canal made for a faster and calmer trip. News arrived by telegraph, and the mail steamer itself took about half the time of the fast sailing ships of 1850.

Within the larger cities cheap trams, trains and cabs replaced walking or, for the rich, horses or horse-drawn carriages. Navigable rivers were plied by paddle steamers but such rivers were few and recurrent drought made transport in this way a hazardous undertaking. The railways were the modern miracle, greatly improving travel within each colony. The railway connecting Melbourne and Sydney was completed in 1883, and the New South Wales Premier recalled that 31 years earlier it had taken him six and a half days riding horses night and day to reach Melbourne from Sydney. He missed the coastal steamer home, and it took 16 days at sea in a sailing clipper to return. Now the steam train did the same journey in 24 hours, even with a break at the border because there were different railway gauges in the two colonies.

One hundred years later my father died a week after returning from Sydney to Melbourne by train. A strike meant that, with many other elderly pensioners, he had to carry his luggage in freezing weather at 3 am from the 'standard gauge' platform in New South Wales to the 'broad gauge' platform in Victoria. The colonial builders of railways failed to agree on the same rail gauge throughout the Australian continent, an astonishing oversight that is still being rectified. Colonies became states, but to this day fight hard for their rights, including the right to oppose sensible national solutions to various problems.

Despite their isolation from the inventive nations of Europe and America, Australians made many practical inventions, often adapting machines or plants to local conditions but in some cases such as the development of the combine harvester in Victoria leading the world. There was a major focus on saving labour which was in short supply and inclined to be independent, demanding what Australians called a 'fair shake of the sauce bottle'. Gold provided what Geoffrey Blainey describes as a natural stabiliser. Whenever the economy tended to slump, so that prices of other goods and labour fell, the search for gold and its mining intensified.[10]

And there was luck. The period from 1851 to 1890 was unusually peaceful, with the Australian colonies at peace throughout. The exception was the brief Eureka rebellion, already mentioned. Throughout the forty years, the world's richest money-lender, Great Britain, sent capital, enabling Victorians to enjoy a high standard of living at the very time when they were spending heavily on railways and reservoirs, on opening up the land, building towns and undertaking a variety of debt-incurring works.[11]

The seasons were unusually benign and, in a continent later known to be subject to severe drought, this was a great blessing. The blessings of providence were shortly to be demonstrated by the great 'federation drought' in South-Eastern Australia, which stretched from 1895 to 1903. Earlier, the steady prosperity and good seasons meant Australia did not suffer the disastrous banking failures that afflicted the United States in particular. The depression of the 1890s was, however, about to change that comfortable comparison.

Australia shared one characteristic with the United States, says Geoffrey Blainey, a 'zest for taking risks which leaped beyond the bounds of common sense'. Thousands of useless mining shafts were sunk, repeatedly expensive crushing mills and steam engines were installed at mines with no ore to crush, farms large enough for England but far too small to be economic in Australia were cleared and often much hard work was wasted. In good years, pastoralists were tempted into marginal land which was later abandoned, encouraged by a theory that rain followed the plough. Compounding the folly, railways were built to districts that never could support them. Substantial towns were built in gold mining areas that were later abandoned. 'Risks were inevitable in the process of opening new natural resources but many initiatives were extravagantly risky'.[12]

Animals such as the rabbit, the rat and the cat were introduced with little thought and, finding few natural predators, flourished mightily. Rats and cats came with the ships that carried the settlers from Europe and could not have been avoided. Rabbits were a different case. They were deliberately released to provide targets for hunting, initially by one Thomas Austin on his property, Barwon Park, near Winchelsea, Victoria, in October 1859. The rabbit did enormous damage to Australia's economy and ecology, with farmers forced to spend a lot of time trying to exterminate them, on large runs employing professional 'rabbiters'.

By 1950, Australia hosted an estimated 600 million rabbits competing with sheep for the grass, and the economic damage was immense. At its worst, pessimists believed that the rabbit could destroy one of Australia's most important industries. After research carried out by Frank Fenner, the Myxomatosis virus was deliberately released into the rabbit population, causing it to drop to around 100 million. Genetic resistance in the remaining rabbits allowed the population to recover to 200-300 million by 1991, and further biological controls have since been developed.

While the balance sheet for the rabbit is strongly negative, rabbits are popular children's pets and rabbit pelts still provide the raw material for Australian bush hats. Rabbits in the past provided a cheap source of protein, especially useful in Australia's great depressions and 'thank your Mother for the rabbit' is a slightly satiric form of thanks among older Australians. Australia has become home to other feral animals, including many feral camels and wild horses, known as 'brumbies' whose economic value is low.

Marvellous Melbourne in 1890 was about to find that extravagant risks do not keep paying off. There had been earlier experiences of the bust that follows a great boom. The first land sales in Melbourne took place in 1837 and ran for about three years. Three blocks of land purchased for 136 pounds resold by auction for 10,000 pounds. Hundreds of people joined the land rush, borrowing from the Port Phillip Bank, which crashed in 1843. Wool had fetched 2 or 3 shillings per pound in 1829, falling to less than one shilling in the pound in the early 1840s. Most graziers went bankrupt and the Bank of Australasia paid no dividend for five years.[13]

The sub-prime land boom of the 1880s

Melbourne's land mania of the 1880s, so far as one can judge from contemporary anecdotes often repeated, easily matched America's build-up to the sub-prime crisis of the 2000s, without of course spreading its painful consequences globally. '... every type and degree of man was involved. Clergymen, labourers, widows, schoolmasters – all grasped the chance of quick wealth and invested their savings'. Much buying was done with borrowed money and when the bust came both the borrowers and the lenders suffered greatly.

Then new discoveries filled the colony with gold. The banks were so well stocked with gold that they stopped paying interest on deposits. With money to burn, property, like everything else available for sale, was for a time massively inflated, as people celebrated the boom with wild extravagance. Mining riches are never an unmixed blessing.

The land mania was built on two pillars, in retrospect a highly unstable structure. The first was the plethora of building societies, whose optimistic officials believed that 'every family in the colony could simultaneously build their own house, keep up the payments through good times and bad, and support an army of investors who were being paid high rates of interest for the use of their money'. If this sounds familiar to American readers, it should do so. The 'sub-prime crisis' is a recurrent theme of financial history, and those who do not learn from history are condemned to repeat it. The second form of mania was the deeply-held belief that it was impossible to lose money by 'investing' in land. This, of course, is another modern fallacy, whose denial should forever be writ large in the school-books of modern capitalist societies.

The root cause of the boom and bust was, of course, capitalism's old friends of greed, fear and panic on top of the fundamentals of rapid growth and wealth creation. But a more specific issue, seen before in the twin bubbles of 1720, was the deep involvement of legislators. The parliamentarians of Victoria were heavily involved in making money, and in land schemes in particular. When the Victorian Parliament copied the English building society legislation in 1876, it added a clause that proved disastrous. Victorian building societies were permitted 'to buy and sell or mortgage freehold or leasehold estate'.

The leading building societies made great use of this law. They used the large deposits of their customers to compete frantically for the best real estate, like modern investment banks punting their capital. To make matters worse, many of the societies' directors were conducting speculative activities of their own. In some cases criminality was added to stupidity as the directors punted in their own names using depositors' money. By 1890, the Victorian building societies held five million pounds of deposits, most of which came from the wage-earning class. Six years later this value had shrunk to a mere 800,000 pounds. 'Whole village suburbs which had been run up with building society funds were untenanted, and remained so for many years afterwards'.

Cannon describes the shady methods used to move land. Often a potential subdivision was brought by a syndicate with a low deposit and an auctioneer set to work. He advertised the land with many superlatives, provided free transport and elaborate lunches for buyers. When the bidding started several blocks were sold quickly to dummy bidders, again with tiny deposits paid. Sometimes the syndicate would build one or two impressive houses and 'sell' them at high prices to establish a fake value. Another trick was to build a railway line through the estate and claim the government would operate a railway at some early date. These techniques had changed little when this writer briefly worked as an auctioneer's mate in Melbourne during the late 1960s.

There was a brief respite from ever rising prices in 1886 following some suggestions in the distant British press that the Australians were borrowing far too much ever to repay their debts. Interest rates were increased by 1 per cent and twelve-month deposits were earning 6%. For about a year speculation waned, sales falling from twelve million pounds to only two and a quarter millions. Then in 1887 there was a new wave of speculation, the land boom proper, 'so forceful that it overrode all considerations of interest rates'. Prices rose by enormous amounts, in one case from 15 shillings a foot in 1884 to fifteen pounds in 1887, in a further suburb rising from seventy pounds to three hundred pounds per acre.

In Melbourne's central business district, prices rose even more fantastically. Prominent blocks of land sold and resold several months later for double the price. The banks again became concerned and began calling in overdrafts. This so-called 'traditional' conservative banking policy 'proved utterly ruinous to the general community' as the land promoters went looking for new sources of easy finance. The years of 1888, 1889 and even 1890 saw the formation of the most disastrous land and finance companies, the so-called 'land banks'. Under the lax banking and company laws of the times they could do all the things done by established banks, but with far less expertise and few if any cautious instincts. In the year ending June 1888, 270 new companies were registered in Melbourne, with nominal capital of 50 million pounds and paid-up capital of 25 million and the land boom soared to 'dizzy new heights'. In two of the main streets, land values rose from 400 to 1,100 pounds a foot. An insurance company paid a Real Estate Bank 2,700 pounds a foot for a prominent site. A few experienced speculators began quietly to sell and by the end of 1888 a newspaper claimed 'The land boom has spent its force ...'[14]

Cannon's account is based on numerous anecdotes, reliable in their own right but lacking macro-authority. The best overview I have found is in a conference paper by John Simon, issued by the Reserve Bank of Australia, 'Three Asset-price Bubbles'. Simon presents a graph of land values based on data from the Victorian Year-books of the time. These record the total value of rateable property and the number of rated properties for Victorian cities, towns and boroughs in a given year. Dividing one by the other gives an estimate of the average value of houses. Simon says 'At its peak, in 1888, average values rose by over 18 per cent and the stock increased by 6½ per cent'.[15]

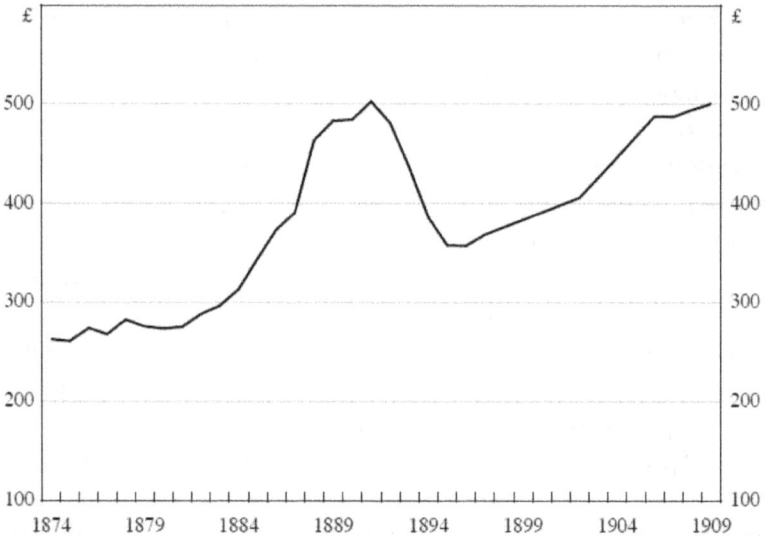

This estimate of property values, Simon says, derived as it is from traditionally conservative taxation data, probably understates the growth in house prices. I note that it probably also understates property prices in Melbourne, the focus of the boom of the 1880s. Simon therefore also quotes an alternative source, a 1975 article by Ron Silberberg on 'Rates of return on Melbourne land investment, 1880-92'. Silberberg tracked sale prices for individual parcels of land in the suburban fringe of Melbourne – those most likely to be subject to speculative attention. Silberberg estimates that the average *annual* rate of return on investment in large plots of land was around 50 per cent for much of the 1880s and peaked at 78.3 per cent in 1887. Simon comments 'These figures reflect total investment returns and, probably, the benefits of leverage'.[16]

The more conservative Victorians, including traditional bankers, knew this boom could not last. To add to the rapidly gathering clouds the conservatives discerned, industrial action was begun by unions determined to get a fair shake of the speculative sauce bottle. 'For the first time in the colony, the combined power of capital and labour were brought face to face in mutual antagonism'.[17] Employers used blackleg labour, and the Mounted Rifle Corps was mobilised to prevent disorder. In the event, the volunteer riflemen were not required but the order given - that they were if necessary to 'Fire low and lay 'em out' – entered the folklore just as if such an order had been given and obeyed. The unions lacked the power to win these disputes but their leaders became determined to enter parliament, which was achieved within a decade under the banner of Australia's earliest political party, the Australian Labor Party.

For a time, mining shares in particular continued to rise in value but, as the land banks failed one by one, it became clear that a serious economic catastrophe was underway. From July 1891 until March 1892, 20 major financial institutions, with liabilities of nearly 20 million pounds, closed down. In those 'eight desperate months' more than 120 public companies failed. English and Scottish investors, lacking accurate information, began to regard all Australian companies as 'unsafe', and refused to allow their 43 million pounds of fixed deposits to be rolled over. The major Australian banks began calling in many of their big overdrafts and building societies and land banks began 'toppling like wrecked chimneys'. There were calls on partly paid shares, and attempts to borrow to pay the calls were refused. Most speculators took the relatively easy path to the Insolvency Court or private arrangements with their creditors. And as they fell they took others with them, from timber merchants to large retailers. Directors of some failing enterprises sent out 'dummies' to prop up shares while they secretly sold their holdings, in some cases using a bank's funds for such purposes. Suicides were said to be common.

Cannon says: 'The falsifying of balance sheets, the payment of dividends from non-existent profits, and the publication of misleadingly optimistic forecasts, were among the shocking features of the crash. Men who were widely known and trusted, who had been knighted by the queen, who occupied the highest political and business positions, took leading parts in the manipulations'. Sir Matthew Davies, Speaker of the Legislative Assembly, was arrested following the failure of his Freehold Investment Co. Ltd exactly three months after it declared an 8% dividend. Many insolvent directors remained in parliament, despite specific laws forbidding this, while others made secret agreements with creditors that were not revealed for many years. It took a crusading Victorian Solicitor-General, Isaac Isaacs, to insist on prosecuting failed financiers.

During the boom, leading politicians 'gave free rein to the land boomers and borrowers. No extravagance was too absurd for it to obtain Cabinet's tacit or open approval. Huge government loans were floated in Britain; enormous railway projects were undertaken; lavish exhibitions were planned; and the boom was merrily set on its way'.[18]

It is no wonder that modern company directors are surrounded by legions of lawyers, thickets of regulation, teams of crusading regulators and vigilant politicians. But human ingenuity knows no bounds, and the case of Enron and other great recent corporate frauds, indeed the whole sub-prime crisis, shows that no amount of tough black letter law can take the place of common sense and a strong tradition of ethical behaviour.

The great depression of the 1890s

By 1880, Victoria was one of the world's richest places, and Melbourne was one of the world's richest cities. But the wealth was based too strongly on abundant natural resources, successful risk-taking and blind luck. There was no lack of hard work, and abundant British capital, to add to the mix, but Melbourne was a very confident place. The recently popular phrase 'miracle economy' may have been applied to Melbourne and Victoria for the first time. Geoffrey Blainey in *Gold and Paper*, his history of the National Bank of Australasia, says 'The swing from confidence to optimism, and from extravagant optimism to despair, symbolised this phase of Victorian banking'.[19]

In the clear light of hindsight, the boom of the 1880s was utterly unsustainable and its ending was inevitable, indeed had been foreshadowed in the English press and by the conservative bankers of Melbourne, such as the National's Francis Grey Smith. Equally painful, to add insult to injury, a young English Treasury officer, the

Hon. Arthur George Villiers Peel, later weighed in with a savage analysis published by the British government in 1894. But the real injury was far worse than any insult. However, there is a dearth of the sort of statistics modern economists and historians of the twentieth century rely upon.

Michael Cannon begins his moving account with the arresting sentence: 'The Angel of Death came early and stayed late in the Melbourne of 1892 and 1893'.[20] As in other places, there were epidemics of influenza, typhoid and measles which Melbourne's infrastructure and medical facilities were ill-equipped to prevent or alleviate. The head brewer of Foster's Brewery discovered that Melbourne's main water supply was heavily polluted with typhoid germs. He corresponded with Louis Pasteur and tried unsuccessfully to develop a vaccine in his laboratory at the brewery.

To the medical nightmare was added a savage economic downturn. The traditional, conservative bankers had adopted a cautious approach to the land boom, but fringe financiers made the running, like lenders to sub-prime borrowers in the 2000s. Blainey points out that 'Australia did not lack bold financiers who thought they could use the money, and Britain did not lack investors who thought they could safely lend the money'.[21] As the land boom peaked and began to retreat, the fringe financiers came under great pressure. The financial crisis was paramount. There was no central bank in existence and no other authority able to stem the tide when panic began. Nor could the conservative traditional banks do much to help. All too soon they were also struggling to survive.

The flow of British capital declined in 1889 and 1890. Interest rates had been exceptionally low in London but began to rise. Late in 1890 the mighty house of Baring fell, making British investors more wary about the lure of high returns in overseas nations. 'The mainspring of Australia's growth was thus shattered'.[22] Wheat was at its lowest price for more than a century, silver had slumped, there were strikes at the rich mines of Broken Hill and merino wool was exceptionally cheap, less than 8 pence a pound in 1892. Thus there was no rescue from Australia's traditional mining and rural industries.

With exports low, Australia had to curb imports or ship gold to pay for imports and interest on invested capital, much of which was in the form of fixed deposits in banks and fringe financiers. The collapse of the building societies and land-banks came early, and more traditional bankers spent much time worrying, hoarding coin and meeting to see if a plan to protect the banks could be devised. One of the group of ten leading banks, the Federal Bank, was in trouble due to its support of the building societies and suspicion fell on the state of all the banks. At the end of January 1893 the Federal Bank closed its doors, which were never to be reopened. British investors began to withdraw deposits and of course required gold sovereigns.

As pessimism was replaced by panic, it was not just British investors withdrawing deposits. The Commercial Bank, another of the ten traditional banks, closed its doors and announced it would seek a reconstruction. When it opened it provided a safe deposit facility that encouraged customers of other banks to withdraw deposits and put them into this new place of refuge.

In the six weeks after Easter in 1893, 12 banks closed their doors, through panic or fear of panic, including the highly prudent National Australasian Bank. Geoffrey Blainey says that such a drastic outcome was by no means inevitable. 'But panic did come, that unpredictable ferment of fear and stupidity and logic, and it turned depression into disaster.'[23]

At the height of the global financial panic of 2007-08 a friend told this writer that he had withdrawn $2 million from a bank deposit and placed it into a safe deposit box. Before this old practice caught on more widely, Australia's government stepped in to provide a guarantee for all deposits in Australian banks and also the overseas borrowings of the Australian banks.

As companies failed they took others with them, and their employees lost their jobs. The labour market was far harsher then than now, 'more flexible' as a modern economist might prefer to put the matter. As the savings of the unemployed ran out there was no help apart from limited private charity, which usually came too little and too late. Cannon says that unemployment was especially painful for formerly well-to-do people who had no conception of how to survive hard times. As the depression deepened for many people life became a desperate struggle for food and shelter.

The Melbourne *Age*, then a 'mighty radical force', in June 1892, published a 'grimly realistic series' of articles entitled 'Among the Workless'. The example quoted by Cannon begins as follows: 'Privation, want and semi-starvation stand gaunt and inflexible as the prospects to be gloomily faced by hundreds of sturdy fellows, who cannot, try as they may, get a day's work; while faintly, but with sharp meaning, may be heard the cry of children and the wailing of women...'

A year later, when things were much worse, *The Age* undertook another series of articles under the title 'Poorer Than The Poor', surveying each industrial suburb in turn. In South Melbourne the journalist found a house with empty kitchen shelves, a fireless grate and a solitary crust of bread placed out of reach of the children. In another house a local clergyman found a baby dead in the garret, the mother dying and the rest of the household 'drooping under their long denial'.

Another visit discovered 'sweating', a number of women working 12 hours a day in 'malodorous dens' for one third of standard factory rates. Other women took to the streets to survive or to support their families. Government work building a new railway paid 9 shillings clear a week, after the cost of food and shelter, leaving precious little to be sent home to the workers' families. People who got behind in their rent had every stick of furniture taken. 'Thus for 42/- rent, a comparatively tidy and comfortable home was wrecked, and the man and family demoralised and pauperised'.

Babies were said to be frequently found dead in gutters and rubbish bins and, in one especially sad case, a newborn was reportedly found being cooked on a backyard fire by a neighbour. Other awful stories abound. A women with six children knocked on a door to ask for help and when asked said all they had eaten for three days was the stalks of cabbages and cauliflowers mashed up, boiled and eaten with a little fat. A country magistrate reported that he sent people to gaol so they could be fed. Storekeepers in rural districts gave people food on credit but charged such high interest and fees that their customers lost their properties by the time conditions improved.

There are no reliable statistics, but Cannon says that 'Some contemporary observers claimed that every second man was out of work'. Thousands left Melbourne, many in the summer of 1892 when gold was discovered in Western Australia. Others headed for South Africa or New Zealand, where jobs were almost as hard to find. Thousands survived on scraps of food and municipal handouts. 'All we can say for certain', Cannon concludes, 'is that this was the worst depression in Australian history, before or since'.

No doubt some of the stories are exaggerated and others may have been invented. The historians I have consulted agree that the main claims in the previous paragraph are untrue. Economists point out that Australia's labour market was very flexible, and flexibility included doing casual work in return for food and moving to places where prospects for work were better. I have been chasing a Ph.D. thesis that includes an attempt to measure the seriousness of depression of the 1890s compared with the depression of the 1930s.

But this was a frontier culture of extravagant risk taking. This attitude helped to accomplish a lot during the long boom. The boom was so strong that much misery was inevitable during the bust, which undoubtedly left plenty of opportunity for the reformers who followed.

Melbourne's population had risen strongly in the 40 years since the discovery of gold. As the depression deepened, wages fell sharply, many men went 'on the wallaby' seeking work for any reward, and families left Victoria for places where prospects seemed better. In the fifteen years to the end of 1890, there was a net gain to Australia from immigration of more than half a million people. In the following fifteen years the gain was a mere eight thousand, and in some years more people left than arrived. Depression and new forms of contraception also lowered the birth rate and, with the abrupt decline in immigration, also contributed to a dramatic slowing of population growth.

Is it any wonder Australia was early in the move to provide social welfare and passed laws to modify the ideology of extreme laissez-faire that prevailed during the depression of the 1890s? At the time, this was all in the future. At the time of considerable suffering politicians first denied its existence, then claimed it was greatly exaggerated, perhaps with some justice.

And then ... a short update on Australia's twentieth century progress

After Melbourne's great boom and bust, Australia experienced relatively slow growth in the turbulent times from 1900 to 1950. There was a powerful 'Federation Drought'. The terms of Federation in 1901 produced an attitude of 'protection all round' as protectionist Victoria outpointed free trade New South Wales. Justice H.B. Higgins in 1907, sitting in the Commonwealth Court of Conciliation and Arbitration (in Melbourne), mandated a fair wage for workers covered by his award, ruling that remuneration must be enough to support the wage earner, his wife and family in reasonable and frugal comfort. The distinguished Australian economist, Edward Shann, writing in 1930, said the judgment of Justice Higgins: 'took high moral ground in claiming for the workers a wage independent of supply and demand'.[24] Over the subsequent decades, Australia's labour market was more weighted to labour than to capital, with terms and conditions for labour far superior to those in more fiercely capitalist nations such as the USA.

The Great Depression of the 1930s was seriously painful, and produced another spur to social and economic reform in Australia. My family lost the dairy farm it had carved out of the bush in eastern Victoria, and my father was sent to Melbourne to find work with his family's blessing and five pounds in his pocket. Just as he became established as a storeman and packer war broke out and he quickly enlisted. Both world wars cost many Australian lives, as young men signed on almost automatically to the cause of the British Empire. The unsuccessful Gallipoli campaign in the first war, the brutal static struggles in the European mud and the fierce battles with the Japanese invaders on the Kokoda Trail in New Guinea represented the painful and costly experiences of a small outpost of Empire coming of age. Long lists of the fallen are carved on war memorials in every small town in Australia and make extraordinarily sad reading, as do similar lists in other towns and cities of the capitalist world.

The Korean War boom saw the first of the modern commodity booms. The price of wool rocketed to a pound per pound, previously unheard of, and sheep farmers briefly became the new aristocracy. The US dollar was the international currency and still linked to gold, and extreme wool price inflation did not last very long. The 1950s and 1960s were years of gradual freeing of trade internationally and during the second decade the dawning of the Age of Aquarius with its multiple scourges of drugs, sex and rock'n'roll, and the even worse scourge of entrenched inflation.

Australia was later than most developed nations to embrace tariff reduction but made a start during the reforming government of Prime Minister Gough Whitlam, whom this writer worked to elect, much to his father's disgust. Whitlam, in the words of one old reptile, was a sound man with the fatal flaw that he 'could not tell a million from a billion'. With a strongly left-wing Treasurer (Finance Minister), Whitlam ran the economy onto various sandbanks, with poorly conceived domestic fiscal and wages policies (including uneconomic 'equal pay' for women) coinciding with the first oil price shock and the onset of global inflation. Whitlam's reign came to an abrupt end after the Senate declined to pass his government's budget in 1975 and it was dismissed by the Governor-General.

Australia in 1983 elected another reforming Labor government, led by Prime Minister R J 'Bob' Hawke, 'Hawkie' to his many admirers. This Labor government was literate in matters economic and well advised by economists such as his chief economic advisor, Ross Garnaut, Michael Porter and this writer, then working in Australia's central bank. In short order the Australian dollar was floated, financial markets were deregulated and systematic tariff reduction entrenched. More controversially the Hawke government formed an 'Accord' with the Labour movement with the aim of containing overall wages growth. Recovery was facilitated by the breaking of a severe drought and recovery from the international recession, which some people attributed to Hawkie's special powers.

When it seemed that Australia's international debt was rising too quickly, The Treasurer, Paul Keating, advised by this writer (in what was a career-limiting move), declared that Australia was in danger of becoming a 'Banana Republic'. Despite initially questioning in typically colourful language both my diagnosis and policy recommendations, Treasurer Keating followed the advice on policy almost to the letter. He moved Australia's budget from deficit to surplus, convinced organised labour to cop a 2% cut in real wages and endorsed higher interest rates following advice from the Reserve Bank. The flexible currency sank to just under 60 US cents per Australian dollar in July 1986, and this was a major factor in rapid recovery following the corrective policy actions. Fourteen years later, after peaking at 80 US cents per Australian dollar, the value was to find another low, just under 50 American cents to each Australian dollar. At the time of writing, the Australian dollar has exceeded parity with the US dollar for the first time since the currency was floated.

Clearly 'flexible' is a good description for the Australian dollar, and this flexibility has been an important automatic stabiliser for the Australian economy. A flexible exchange rate is like a share index for a whole country. It charts the weighted opinion of thousands if not millions of currency traders whose job is to monitor the economic performance of each country in order to profit from guessing more accurately than their competitors. During the twentieth century, almost every change in the Australian currency was downward, mirroring the loss of our preeminent position as one of the richest nations at the start of the twentieth century.

The Australian dollar when floated first rose. The peaks in the graph show times when international opinion was positive about Australia's economic performance and the troughs show times of pessimism. Now is a time of relatively strong economic performance and a high currency value. Indeed, if a longer run of data is graphed, it suggested that Australia's long relative decline may have stopped, and there is some evidence of a new, upward trend.

Following the government's bold policy action in 1986, the economy slowed from its excessive boom, though inflation remained stubbornly high. In 1991, after the necessary application of very high cash rates, in excess of 20%, the economy suffered 'the recession we had to have', again using the words of Treasurer Paul Keating, by then Prime Minister Keating. He won the 1993 election and introduced new reforms including the introduction of collective bargaining to labour markets. But by then Prime Minister Keating was lacking the energy shown as Treasurer and his government sank into a kind of lethargy.

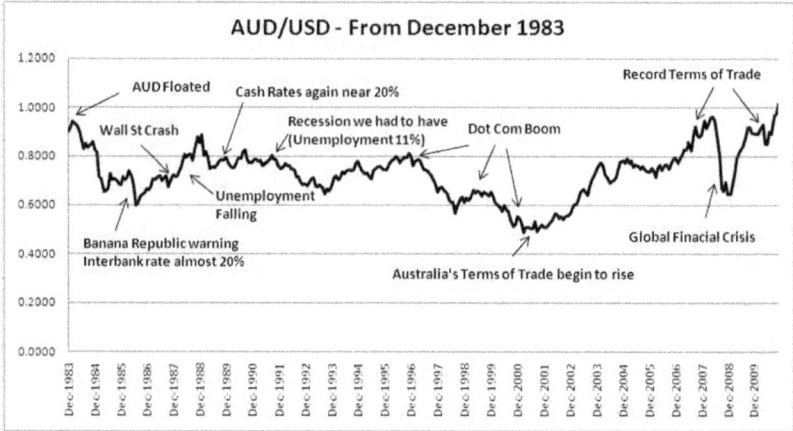

From 1996, the new 'Liberal' (conservative) government under Prime Minister John Howard continued labour market reform and signed an agreement with a new governor of the Reserve Bank offering it operational independence and requiring it to pursue inflation targeting . Howard also continued the privatisation of government businesses started by the Hawke-Keating governments. With Treasurer Peter Costello, he moved the Federal budget from deficit to surplus and introduced a goods and services tax (GST) which enabled the government both to spend strongly and introduce modest cuts to income tax, including a capital gains tax half the rate of the relevant income tax.

The executive director of the Sydney Institute said in 2003: 'In its March 2003 economic survey of Australia, the OECD has found that Australia's current and recent outcomes place it among the top performers in the OECD group of Western nations. The report's authors comment that this owes much to a good combination of prudent, medium-term orientated fiscal and monetary policies, and far-reaching reforms to labour, product and financial markets in the past two decades.'[25] The OECD has praised the 'resilience' of Australia's economy, and the fact is that it has suffered no recession since the one 'we had to have' at the start of the 1990s.

A new factor of great significance is the China boom. While this was interrupted for a short time during the Global Financial Crisis of 2007-08, China is again growing at double digit rates and Australia's terms of trade are again at record levels. In many ways, the past three decades are reminiscent of the thirty years from 1850 to 1880. With generally good policy, sizeable overseas borrowing and a lot of luck, Australia is again seen as a 'miracle economy'. To continue the analogy, this is another time in which Sydney is in relative decline while Melbourne is booming. Australia generally, led by Melbourne (and Perth), is experiencing a property boom. So far at least, this is by no means as mad at that of the 1880s, but sufficiently strong that respected international commentators claim Australia's house prices are up to 40% above fair market value.

Slightly lower estimates emerge from a thorough study by three Goldman Sachs economists published in September 2010. Depending on the valuation model they see Australia's overvaluation at either 35% or 24%, with the latter estimate their preferred measure.[26] They do conclude, however, that 'We see an acute housing shortage developing in coming years', which provides an obvious possibility of further prices rises to come.

The uncertain economic outlook for Australia

	1880s	1890s	2000s	2010s
House, land prices	Booming	Busting	Booming	???
Confidence	Sky high	Very low	Sky high	???
Credit growth	Massive	Low - Negative	Strong	???
Employment	Strong	Weak	Strong	???

The table provides a comparison of major economic trends in the 1880s and the 2000s in Australia. So far as we can tell in the absence of hard statistics from the late nineteenth century, there are a number of similar features. This immediately begs the question of whether a serious downturn is likely in the decade we are entering now.

Australia is currently seeing house and land prices rising less rapidly (Melbourne) or falling mildly (in some other major cities). Immigration remains high, and indeed strong immigration of skilled labour will be needed if wage inflation is not to explode. Strong population growth and limited supply will force house prices up..

Confidence now is lower now than it was at the height of the boom before the Global Financial Crisis but nowhere near depression levels. Credit growth is as low as I can recall as many Australian households and businesses wisely reduce their leverage. If maintained, this development will be a powerful portent of a happy second decade of the century.

Employment growth has, if anything, accelerated recently, contradicting other indications of a weak economy. For the moment, my money is on the employment data. Now the terms of trade are at record level, with a wide spread of exports, while in the 1880s exports were heavily dominated by wool. A big fall in Australia's terms of trade is a likely future shock that would provide a severe test for Australia's policy makers.

In 1929, George Meudell, a self-confessed spendthrift, concluded that 'Australia is a good country badly managed'.[27] The next decade will tell whether Australia's management has improved to any significant extent.

The outcomes for the 2010s will depend heavily on how well the government manages the resource booms - mineral and agricultural. Cutting off water to the food bowl (as recently proposed) is hardly sensible. Lack of infrastructure is limiting exports. But many other policy changes are needed to properly manage these booms.

It may be that Australia does well in the second decade of the twenty-first century. The correct comparison may be one that equates 1980 with 1850, meaning that 2010 is the modern equivalent of 1880. If this analogy holds, modern Australia is now entering the last, maddest decade of a forty-year boom. Despite the global trauma of the past two years, Marvellous Melbourne, with the mining areas of Northern and Western Australia, is growing quickly, working well (despite infrastructure bottlenecks) and playing hard.

8

The Roaring Twenties and the Great Depression

The Wall Street crash of 1929 preceded the greatest crisis of capitalism. The crash helped turn a mild recession in the United States into a great depression throughout the capitalist world. The global crisis produced a revolution in economics led by the economist John Maynard Keynes whose theories of the causes of depression are still debated fiercely.

John Kenneth Galbraith, the brilliant American economist, concluded that 'inaction [is] advocated in the present, even though it means deep trouble in the future. Here, at least equally with communism, lies the threat to capitalism. It is what causes men who know things are going quite wrong to say that things are fundamentally sound'.[1]

John Maynard Keynes, the master of depression analysis, said: 'Speculators may do no harm as bubbles on a steady stream of enterprise. But the position is serious when enterprise becomes the bubble on a whirlpool of speculation. When the capital development of a country becomes a by-product of the activities of a casino, the job is likely to be ill-done'.[2]

My focus here is on two matters. The first is the analysis of the market boom and bust. Galbraith's account of this is both sardonic and authorative. My second focus is why the market crash turned into – or was followed by – the Great Depression. The feature that attracts my attention is the entangled and interdependent falls in economic activity and stock prices. The role of confidence, and then after the market crash, lack of confidence, those states of mind described by Keynes as 'animal spirits', were of overwhelming importance. So too were policies, including tight money and fiscal retrenchment, and bank failures. Plus there was the international echo of the American slide into depression which has not, so far as I am aware, been analysed with precision or authority

Galbraith in his introduction tells of asking a lady in an airport bookshop why his book was not on sale. She asked for its name. When he said it was called *The Great Crash*, she responded firmly: 'Not a book you could sell in an airport'.

The boomtime

The nineteen-twenties was America's great decade. Confidence was high, with strong growth throughout the decade in manufacturing output, strong profit growth and a sense of what a professor called 'boundless hope and optimism'.[3] Paul Johnson says that on a 1933-38 index of 100, production was 58 in 1921 and passed 110 in 1929. Many millions of new houses were built and the number of life and industrial insurance policies passed 100 million in 1920s Real income per capita rose from $522 to $716.[4] The number of passenger cars rose from seven million to twenty-three million in the 1920s, and roads and highways were built, in a reprise of the great railway booms of the nineteenth century. With jazz and the Charlston, F. Scott Fitzgerald's *The Great Gatsby* defined the era. This writer recalls an elderly aunt described in family circles as having been a 'flapper' in her youth.

There were weaknesses; with rising inequality as the rich were getting richer much faster than the poor were improving their lot and real wages declined. Farmers were battling, black people in the South and white people in the southern Appalachians were struggling in 'hopeless poverty' and there were many dreadful slums. But America was roaring and the decade was America's Roaring Twenties.

A property boom in Florida in the mid-twenties had sounded a clear warning containing, as Galbraith says, all of the elements of the classical speculative bubble but also the essential element of substance. But, even as the Florida boom collapsed, the faith of Americans in quick, effortless enrichment in the stock market was becoming every day more evident. In 1924, share prices began to rise from low levels and, as the graph shows, the rises were to become ever faster, with only mild setbacks.

Dow Jones Industrial index 1925 to 1939

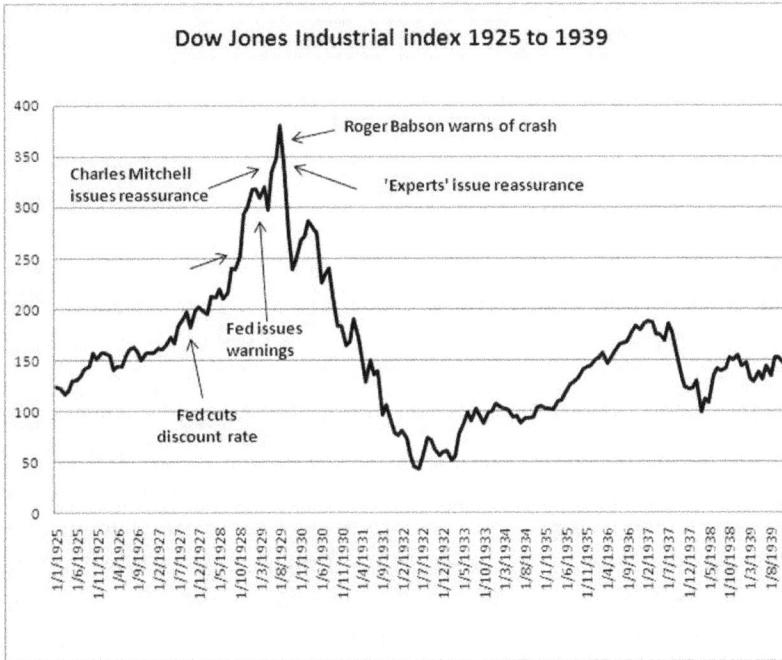

Day after day, month after month the price of stocks rose in a series of small but solid gains. Britain's return to the gold standard at the pre-war level created huge problems in that country and Europe generally and there were repeated pleas to the US to maintain cheap money. In mid-1927, three European central bankers renewed these pleas in person and the US Fed reduced its discount rate from 4 to 3.5% and undertook a bold program to buy government securities, an action a later Fed Chief, Ben Bernanke, would presumably have called 'quantitative easing'. A dissenting member of the Federal Reserve board, Adolph C. Miller, described this as one of the most costly errors committed by the Fed or any other banking system in the previous 75 years.

Galbraith does not accept cheap money as the explanation for the subsequent share price bubble, but it was presumably one important factor. 'Early in 1928', Galbraith says, 'the nature of the boom changed. The mass escape into make believe, so much a part of the true speculative orgy, began in earnest'. The market began to rise, 'not by slow steady steps, but by great vaulting leaps'.[5] Galbraith's account focuses on the people and institutions that either were, or were believed to be, influential in creating or stemming market moves.

The reassurance of great men was tested when in June 1928 arrived the first big setback in what was by then a raging bull market. Andrew Mellon said there was no cause for worry and that the high tide of prosperity would continue. 'Mr Mellon did not know, indeed could not know.' Neither did any other public figure who, before or since, has made similar statements. Mellon was participating in a ritual which in American society is thought to be of great value, but rarely is. Assert that all will be well, and this can help maintain prosperity.

Many such oracles were seeking to keep the boom rolling, but Galbraith points out several times, with apparent relish, that *the New York Times* several times wrongly called the end of the boom. Hoover won the presidential election. Hoover much later said he had all along been skeptical about the market speculation, but Galbraith describes this as an exceptionally well-kept secret. In the event, Hoover's victory boosted confidence. In November there was a further wave of buying and the *Times* observed that 'for cyclonic violence yesterday's stock market has never been exceeded in the history of Wall Street'.

December was not so exciting but, by the end of 1928, the *Times* industrial index had risen by 35%. Numbers of stocks traded set a new record, almost double that of 1927. But a far more potent sign of the times was a massive increase in buying on margin.

At some point in the development of an asset bubble nearly all aspects of property ownership become irrelevant except the prospect of an early rise in price. This had happened during the Florida boom, and in many other property booms when most transactions are effectively on 'margin'. This happened again with Wall Street stocks in the Roaring Twenties. Wall Street then had perfected the machinery of margin to an extent that was 'ingenious, precise and almost beautiful'. But no-one could confess to what was really going on or they would be forced to condemn the practice as immoral.

Galbraith's summary stands the test of time, and is certainly applicable to behaviour in the most recent boom and bust. 'Wall Street, in these matters, is like a lovely and accomplished woman who must wear black cotton stockings, heavy woollen underwear, and parade her knowledge as a cook because, unhappily, her supreme accomplishment is as a harlot'.

From 1926 to the end of 1928, broker's loans had risen from $2.5 billion to almost $6 billion – 'Never had there been anything like it before'. The costs were assumed, in the first instance, by the New York banks, but they were rapidly becoming the agents for lenders the country over, and internationally. The cost of this accommodation had risen from 5% to 12% at the end of 1928 – still, on the face of it, for a perfectly safe loan. The caveat was, so long as share prices rose. As in previous asset bubbles, this caveat was seemingly forgotten by all but the naturally prudent and the incurably cautious. In principle, the New York banks could borrow from the Fed for 5% and lend it out at 12% and, in practice, they did.

'1928, indeed, was the last year in which Americans were buoyant, uninhibited, and utterly happy. It wasn't that 1928 was too good to last; it was only that it didn't last'. Galbraith quotes Walter Bagehot, again illustrating why capitalism is subject to recurring crises: 'All people are most credulous when they are most happy'.

In retrospect, 1929 was bound to be a year to remember. Either the roaring boom would continue or it would end. A bubble can easily be punctured, but to end it with a needle so that it subsides gradually is a far more delicate task. But there was no doubt that a collapse would come. 'When prices stopped rising – when the supply of people who were buying for an increase was exhausted – then ownership on margin would become meaningless and everyone would want to sell. The market wouldn't level out; it would fall precipitately'.

Someone would be blamed when the crash came and, if it were engineered immediately, the Fed would be blamed. Responsibility rested with the President, the Secretary of the Treasury, the Federal Reserve Board in Washington and the Governor and Directors of the Federal Reserve Bank of New York. President Coolidge was leaving office and in earlier episodes of speculation he had decided it was the 'semi-autonomous' Fed's responsibility. There was, however, a serious and jarring difficulty. 'The Federal Reserve board in those times was a body of startling incompetence'.

Regulators and pundits

At a later stage in history, US Fed Chairman Alan Greenspan was to decide it was safer to clean up after the bubbles burst than try to use a needle with the relevant delicacy. In the late 1920s, those who could sense what was happening were facing the choice of an immediate deliberately engineered collapse or a more serious disaster later.

The governor of the New York Federal Reserve until 1928 was Benjamin Strong, a central banker of some reputation. He had taken the lead in giving cheaper money to Europe, and may not have paid enough attention to the local speculation. Mr Hoover later called him 'a mental annex to Europe[6]', a charge Galbraith says is unfair, since it takes more to start a speculation than a general ability to borrow money. Strong died and was replaced by a more modest man, George L. Harrison.

One of the great New York speculators, Charles E. Mitchell, Chairman of the National City Bank, became on January 1, 1929, a Class A director of the Federal Reserve Bank of New York. Now such a blatant conflict of interest would not be tolerated, although more subtle conflicts are overlooked, as when a former head of a major bank becomes Secretary of the Treasury. In 1929, the end of the boom would mean 'the end of Mitchell. He was not a man to expedite his own demise'.

Federal Reserve authorities have usually been regarded not so much unaware or unwilling as impotent. The classic instruments of central banking are open market operations and the rediscount rate. The Fed's portfolio of government securities was limited and there was a natural preference for gradual rather than abrupt action. The few sales of government bonds actually undertaken in early 1929 had no discernable effect.

The rediscount rate of the New York Federal Reserve Bank in January 1929 was 5%, while the rate on broker's loans ranged from 6 to 12%. Only a dramatic increase would have made it unprofitable for a bank to borrow from the Federal Reserve in order to lend the proceeds, directly or indirectly, in the stock market. In mid February, The New York Federal Reserve Bank proposed that the rediscount rate be raised from 5 to 6% to check speculation. The Federal Reserve Board in Washington thought this a 'meaningless gesture which would only increase rates to business borrowers'. A long controversy followed, which delayed even this feeble action. Galbraith says that 'the Federal Reserve was helpless only because it wanted to be'. Had it wanted to act, it could have asked Congress for authority to halt trading on margin by granting the board the power to set margin requirements. These were not especially low in 1929; residual caution had caused brokers to require customers to put up in cash 45 to 50% of the value of the stocks they were buying. Often, of course, this was all the cash the customers had, and an early increase in the margin to, say, 75%

The rediscount rate was eventually raised in late summer, but by then it was much too little, far too late, a problem not unknown in modern times. This is a generic problem with central banks, though they are gradually improving their performance. Even in modern Australia with an inflation target rate hikes came too slowly in the time before the Global Financial Crisis and inflation was rising sharply until the crisis struck. 'Saved by the crisis' is the summary.

would have caused many people to reconsider the risks and most would probably have sold their stocks. 'The boom would have come to a sudden and perhaps spectacular end.'

The power to set margins was eventually given to the Federal Reserve and remains in place even now. The repeated role of buying on margin in the upswing of asset bubbles suggests the use of variable margin requirements should be a regular weapon in a central bank's armoury, unless of course society does not wish to stop or even slow the bubbles.

Even such a new power might not have been needed. Galbraith

speculates that, in 1929, a robust denunciation of speculators and speculation by someone in high authority and a warning that the market was too high would almost certainly have broken the spell. Words, of course, were the most uncertain weapon in the Federal Reserve arsenal. 'Their effect might be sudden and terrible'. The consequences would be attributed with the greatest of precision to whomever uttered the words. To the cautious Federal Reserve officers in early 1929, silence seemed literally golden. The trouble was, the boom kept on roaring, indeed it was 'boiling'.

The Board decided to write a letter, which it issued on February 2, 1929. This warned banks against the practice of making loans for speculation based on borrowing from the Federal Reserve. On February 7 a similar warning was made to the general public. At almost the same time came the news that the Bank of England was raising its bank rate from 4.5% to 5.5%, in an effort to diminish the flow of British funds that was feeding the boom.

The result was dramatic. On February 7 and 8 there were two successive falls in the market, and by end February the overall market was unchanged for the month. The communications, Galbraith says, were 'incredibly feeble' but still sufficient to cause a sharp setback, despite the fact that the missives promised no effective action against speculative buying on margin.

President Hoover took office on March 4, 1929, his attitude to speculators still unstated and unknown. Toward the end of March unsettling news reached Wall Street. The Federal Reserve board was meeting daily in Washington. It issued no statements and responded to questions by journalists with 'tight-lipped silence'. The meetings were presumably about the market and extended without precedent into Saturday. With still no information, on the following Monday people began to sell. Banks began curtailing loans. 'A wave of fear swept the market'. An 'astonishing' 8.2 million shares changed hands, well above any previous record. 'Prices seemed to drop vertically.' The ticker got well behind and the only sensible inference was that things had almost certainly got worse. At the end of the day, many speculators received a 'peremptory telegram', requesting more margin promptly.

The boom could have ended then and there, but Charles E. Mitchell had different thoughts. He told the press: 'We feel we have an obligation which is paramount to any Federal Reserve warning, or anything else, to avert any dangerous crisis in the money market'. As a member of the board of the Federal Reserve Bank of New York, his word carried authority. And this was backed by his pledge to loan money to prevent liquidation. His bank would borrow in turn from the Fed, doing what the Federal Reserve board had explicitly warned against.

'Mitchell's words were like magic.' Money market rates, which had reached 20%, eased and stocks rallied. The Fed remained silent but now the silence was reassuring, as it meant it conceded Mitchell's mastery. Senator Carter Glass, who was later to sponsor the Glass-Steagall Act[7] as part of the post-crash cleanup, pointed out the conflict inherent in Mitchell's words and actions and suggested that the Federal Reserve Bank of New York should seek his immediate resignation.

The Federal Reserve board was itself criticised, in one case for 'doing its utmost to cast the proverbial monkey wrench into the machinery of prosperity'. (This was from a Mr Lawrence of Princeton.) The Fed retired hurt and, from March on, market participants had nothing further to fear from authority. Galbraith says that the Federal Reserve authorities had decided not to be responsible for the collapse.

'For now, free at last from all threat of government reaction or retribution, the market sailed off into the wild blue yonder. Especially after June 1 all hesitation disappeared. Never before or since have so many become so wondrously, so effortlessly and so quickly rich. Perhaps Messrs. Hoover and Mellon, and the Federal Reserve were right in keeping their hands off. Perhaps it was worth being poor for a long time to be so rich for just a little while.'

Leverage, and the 'wonders of the geometric series'

The story now becomes truly horrifying. The general belief was that there was a shortage of securities and the 'ingenuity and zeal'[8] with which new securities were devised was remarkable. In 1929,

Galbraith says, 'the discovery of the wonders of the geometric series struck Wall Street with a force comparable to the invention of the wheel'. A person or a group would sponsor an investment trust, consisting of common stock, preferred stock and bonds. When, as naturally assumed, stock prices rose, most of the gains accrued to owners of the common stock, which naturally included the founders. (Often common stock was issued at a premium, and founders made an immediate gain.) The trust once established in turn sponsored a larger investment trust, which sponsored a still larger investment trust. The miracle of leverage made this a relatively costless exercise for the founders, provided of course that stock prices continued to rise – that worrying but unstated, caveat.

The magic of the investment trust was based on 'knowledge, manipulative skill, financial genius and above all leverage'. The need for 'expertise' made it a golden age for professors, most of whose reputations were trashed along with the value of their investment trusts when leverage went into reverse, since it works both ways its magic to perform. (Mr Lawrence of Princeton was one prominent victim of the market crash.) Goldman Sachs made many large fortunes while the market was running for them; with their investors, they suffered great pain when the tide turned.

Except while the Fed's rather feeble warnings were operating, during 1929 stock prices rose almost every day, and they almost never fell. During June, July and August, the industrial index rose by one quarter. There was heavy trading, often between 4 and five million shares each day. Many new and exciting shares were not listed in New York. The New York Stock Exchange in those days was an institution that would accept the listing of most companies. Nevertheless, there were some who found *Sunlight is a wonderful steriliser, and much regulatory activity since the 1929 crash has been focussed on extracting information from reluctant company promoters.* it convenient not to answer the simple requests that were made by the exchange for information.

Many new shares, including shares in the exciting new investment trusts, were traded 'on the Curb', or in Boston, or on other out-of-town exchanges where regulatory scrutiny was even less. The 'normally somnambulant' markets of Boston, San Francisco and even of Cincinnati were having a boom, trading exciting speculative stocks that were not available in New York. 'By 1929, it was a poor town, sadly devoid of civic spirit, which wasn't wondering if it too shouldn't have a stock market'.

Broker's loans increased at the rate of about $400 million a month, and by the end of the summer the total exceeded seven billion. The normal rate for broker's loans was between 7 and 12% and on one occasion touched 15%. Given the apparent safety and liquidity of a broker's loan (at least while the market was rising): 'The rate of interest would not have seemed unattractive to a usurious moneylender in Bombay'. There were no warnings from the great and the good in the summer of 1929, and doomsayers were sharply criticized.

Chairman Mitchell of the National City Bank (and the board of the New York Fed) expressed anger at those who focused on brokers loans, estimates of which were available monthly and (in a less complete way) weekly. *The Wall Street Journal* reached the end of its patience, Galbraith says, and provides the following thunderbolt from its September 19, 1929 edition: 'Even in general newspapers some accurate knowledge is required for discussing most things. Why is it that any ignoramus can talk about Wall Street?' University professors provided reassurance, although in more cautious language than the strongest boosters of Wall Street.

In America in 1929, the official optimists were many and articulate. Bernard Baruch famously said that 'the economic condition of the world seems on the verge of a great forward movement'. Numerous college professors, especially those from the Ivy League universities, 'exuded scientific confidence'. Professor Lawrence of Princeton said that 'the consensus of judgment of the millions whose valuations function on that admirable market, the stock exchange, is that stocks are not at present over-valued'. He added: 'Where is that group of men with the all-embracing wisdom which will enable them to veto the judgment of this intelligent multitude'. Professor Irving Fisher of Yale made his famous estimate: 'Stock prices have reached what seems like a permanently high plateau'.

Harvard, 'by wisdom or good luck', was mildly bearish in early 1929. Its economic forecasters had said that a recession (though assuredly not a depression) was overdue. They forecast weekly, and for some time each week foretold a slight setback in business. Sadly for the reputation of economic forecasters, in the summer of 1929, when the recession had failed to appear, the dons of Harvard 'gave up and confessed error'. Modern readers have presumably heard the quip that economic forecasters exist to make weather forecasters look good.

The bankers were also a source of encouragement to those who wished to believe that the boom would go on more or less forever. 'A great many of them abandoned their historic role as the guardians of the nation's fiscal pessimism and enjoyed a brief respite of optimism'. Many of the bankers had got involved in the securities business, and individual bankers were speculating vigorously on their own account.

An honourable exception was a Paul M. Warburg of the International Acceptance Bank, whose forecasts were 'remarkably prescient'. In March of 1929, he 'called for a stronger Federal Reserve policy and argued that if the present orgy of "unrestrained speculation" were not brought promptly to a halt, there would ultimately be a disastrous collapse'... This would "bring about a general depression involving the whole country".'

Nemesis

'By the summer of 1929 the market not only dominated the news. It also dominated the culture. That recherché minority which at other times has acknowledged its interest in Saint Thomas Aquinas, Proust, psychoanalysis, and psychosomatic medicine then spoke of United Corporation, United founders, and Steel. Only the most aggressive of the eccentrics maintained their detachment from the market and their interest in autosuggestion or communism'.

Despite the extent to which the market dominated the culture, it has been estimated that in 1929 only about one and a half million people out of a population of approximately 120 million were directly involved with the market, and of these perhaps 600,000 were active speculators. 'Only in the case of the rarest individuals can speculation be a part-time activity'. Broker's offices in New York were crowded, the ticker service went national and branches of broking houses were opened on transatlantic ships. One especially entrepreneurial criminal is supposed to have carried on trading from prison, a precedent recently followed by at least one well-known Australian criminal.

On September 2, the traditional end of summer, and September 3 there was a massive heatwave. Away from Wall Street is was a very quiet day. On Wall Street, call money was 9% all day, over 4 million shares changed hands, the rediscount rate was 6.5% and broker's loans for the previous week were estimated to have reached $137 million. The New York banks were borrowing heavily from the New York Fed and the flow of gold from abroad remained strong. The effects of this were felt in far off Australia as well as in Europe and any other place that was part of the capitalist system of international lending and borrowing.

'On September 3, by common consent, the great bull market of the nineteen-twenties came to an end'. The big break in the market came on September 5, and the immediate cause was clear. One Roger Babson, speaking at his Annual Business Conference, said: 'Sooner or later a crash is coming, and it may be terrific'. He suggested that what had happened to house prices in Florida would now happen on Wall Street. In a 'burst of cheer' he concluded that 'factories will shut down ... men will be thrown out of work ... the vicious circle will get in full swing and the result will be a serious business depression'.

'As an educator, philosopher, theologian, statistician, forecaster, economist, and friend of the law of gravity, he had sometimes been thought to spread himself too thin'. Wall Street denounced him. The 'Babson break' came on a Thursday but the market rallied on Friday and was firm on Saturday. More of the usual pundits said, despite slight corrections, the 'ascending curve of American prosperity' should continue. The next week was uneven. On September 11, *The Wall Street Journal* quoted Mark Twain: 'Don't part with your illusions; when they are gone you may still exist, but you have ceased to live'.

The conventional view, Galbraith asserts, sees the stock market as 'but a mirror'. There is superficial support for this in the experience of the US economy in 1929 and afterwards. The indexes of industrial and of factory production both peaked in June. The Federal Reserve index of industrial production reached 126 in June and by October was 117. This was a convenient view for the influential members of Wall Street – 'everyone with an instinct for conservative survival [realised] that Wall Street had better be left out of it'.

But Galbraith says that any satisfactory explanation for the events of autumn 1929 and subsequently 'must accord a dignified role to the speculative boom and ensuring collapse'. Past market corrections had been reversed and there were no reasons for expecting disaster. No one [excepting Messrs Babson and Warburg it seems] could foresee that production, prices, incomes and all the other indicators would continue to shrink through three long and dismal years'.

Galbraith speculates that perhaps it was just a case of thousands of people realising that the boom could not go on. He quotes an advertisement in an investment service with the arresting headline 'Overstaying a Bull Market'. As he is with Roger Babson, Galbraith is perhaps ungenerous to those who got it right. But he is right to say that reason for the crash is unimportant. During the Indian summer of 1929, the great and the good were still spruiking the market and, indeed, the only disturbing thing was the 'fairly steady downward drift' in stock prices. What goes up, in economics as in physics, usually goes down.

Friday, October 19 saw share price falls in late trade. Saturday saw serious drops in both blue chip stocks and speculative favourites. Sunday's press was full of stories, along with the usual reassurances from experts and rumours of organised support. In following weeks the Sabbath pause had a marked tendency to breed uneasiness and doubts and pessimism and decisions to get out on Monday.

This, is seems certain, was what happened on Sunday, October 20. Monday, October 21, was a very poor day in the market. Six million shares traded, the third largest volume in history. The many people anxiously watching the ticker as it fell behind discovered they did not know what was happening – but this was a very different experience in a falling rather than a rising market.

After the Great Crash came the Great Depression which lasted, with varying severity, for ten years. In 1933, America's Gross National Product was nearly a third less than in 1929. Not until 1937 did the physical volume of production recover to the levels of 1929, and then it promptly slipped back again. In 1933, nearly thirteen millions were out of work, or about one in four in the labor force. In 1938 one person in five was still out of work.

And in distant Australia

Australia in the 1920s (as before in the 1880s) was a nation living beyond its means as governments struggled to provide social infrastructure deemed essential. It was far more vulnerable than the USA, with a far smaller economy highly dependent on exports of wool and wheat, the markets for which were highly unstable, especially so in the late 1920s. The economy was also chronically dependent on capital from abroad, highly so in the second half of the decade.

Most of the capital inflow in the twenties was in the form of borrowing by public authorities. On top of heavy debts incurred during World War 1, borrowings in New York and London added greatly to debt service. From 16% of exports in 1919-20 interest (and dividends) remittances abroad rose sharply to reach 28% in 1928-29. As Boris Schedvin says in his book *Australia and the Great Depression* 'the struggle to avoid default on public interest obligations abroad underpins the entire history of the depression'.[9] The radical Labor government of New South Wales, led by Premier J. T. Lang, declined to make some interest payments and this precipitated a vast debate which he eventually lost.

Australian unemployment reached 28% of the workforce in the horrible year of 1932, so far as imperfect statistics can tell, slightly worse than in the USA. Gross national product apparently fell far less than in America, but Schedvin's summary is that 'among the more developed countries Australia can be counted with the United States, Canada and Germany, and also much of Eastern Europe outside the Soviet Union, as the group most seriously affected by the great depression'.[10]

Causes of the crash and the consequences

Massive speculation always sows the seeds of its own destruction. In any asset boom, the point is reached that some people begin to say it is too good to be true. As more and more such people begin to sell and to tell others they have done so, the more likely is it that the selling pressure will overwhelm the buying pressure. If people have been buying on margin, or with borrowed money, the need to exit before they are wiped out is correspondingly great. So ends the boom, replaced by a bust. Irving Fisher's sunlit upland 'plateau' is rarely if ever observed.

Galbraith dismisses the 'accepted explanation' that it was easy money that fuelled the speculation in the late 1920s. He asserts that easy credit on many occasions does not lead to speculation. And, by the standards of the times, interest rates were high. This seems to contradict the point made by Galbraith several times, that banks could borrow from the Fed at, say, 6% and lend at up to 15% or even 20% to people buying stocks on margin. In this sense the 'easy money' was a reality but it was just an accommodating factor – necessary but not sufficient. One unanswered question is whether speculation of the sort that occurred in the 1920s has ever happened *without* easy money. I suggest that the answer is 'no'.

Far more important than rate of interest and the supply of credit, says Galbraith, is the mood. This echoes Keynes' emphasis on 'animal spirits' and is surely relevant. In every asset boom we have studied there is a public mood of optimism; in every market mania the mood is by definition one of madness. Geoffrey Blainey's book *The Great Seesaw* documents the vital importance of mood, of confidence or its lack, in generating the swings from boom to recession that some economists know as the trade cycle. As Blainey puts it: 'To suggest that a powerful mental seesaw is at work is to attempt to answer a vital aspect of that vast and perplexing question which Marx, Kondratieff, Toynbee and many others have raised in different forms: the relation between the economic, political, military and cultural events, and the question of whether that relationship forms a pattern in modern history'.[11]

Finally, Galbraith says, a speculative outbreak has a greater or less immunising effect. The ensuing collapse automatically destroys the very mood speculation requires. It is natural to think that the longer the time since the last experience of strong speculation the greater the chance of a fresh outbreak. A three generation break is more likely to allow for memories to fade and for the lessons to the last boom and bust to wear off. But, as we have seen, there is evidence that periods of boom and bust have occurred with far greater frequency in recent times.

It is far easier to account for episodes of boom, even speculative mania followed by an inevitable bust, than to explain the effects on the economy. Joseph in ancient Egypt achieved fame as an economic forecaster by predicting that seven fat years would be followed by seven years of famine. Using similar 'Occult or biblical' reasoning, Galbraith says, a 'great many people have always felt that a depression was inevitable in the thirties'. He dismisses this idea.[12]

Is this the influence of the generation who have avoided even family memories of war and depression, and who commonly are accused of always seeking instant gratification? Death in computer games is overcome by merely restarting the game. Does the gamer-generation implicitly believe it is necessary only to reboot to revive a failed wealth portfolio?

Nor was the American economy at the end of the twenties in need of a period of rest, as some have asserted. In 1929 the labour force was not tired. The capital plant of the country was not depleted. Raw materials were ample. Entrepreneurs were active. Presumably workers, capitalists and entrepreneurs would all have far rather soldiered on at the 1929 rate than had the 'rest' of the Great Depression. Neither did the high production of the 1920s satiate wants. On the contrary, all subsequent evidence showed (given the income to spend) a capacity for a large further increase in consumption.

So what *were* the causes of the Great Depression? As already noted, there was a minor, normal downturn in economic activity in 1929. We have already dismissed the market crash as a recognition of this minor fluctuation or as a portent of the depression to come. Often, however, those paid to 'explain' changes in equity prices, especially stock prices, hew to the theory that the market predicts economic fluctuations. However, there are many more market corrections or even crashes than there are great depressions. The crash of 1987 is one clear example, and the crash of 2007-2008 may (if we are lucky) turn out to be another.

Galbraith says that the economy was 'fundamentally unsound' in 1929. Many things were wrong but above all the distribution of income was skewed toward the rich, who were very rich. It seems certain, Galbraith says, that 5% of the population with the highest incomes received approximately one third of all personal income, a high proportion of which was in the form of interest, dividends and rent. This highly unequal income distribution meant that the economy was highly dependent on a high level of investment or a high level of luxury consumer spending or both.

Especially with this skewed income distribution, a great reduction in people's wealth, real or perceived, induced caution in decisions on whether to spend or to invest. Even with Friedman's permanent income hypothesis, a large effect on wealth as a result of the stock market crash would reduce the propensity of rich people to consume. Sagging consumption reduced business investment. With the wealthiest people tightening their metaphorical belts, many workers lost their jobs. Optimism was replaced by pessimism and hopelessness, a mood that swept America. The negative mood spread quickly to many other parts of the world as asset prices elsewhere fell more or less in line with Wall Street.

Nations other than America had their own structural weaknesses due to continuing fallout from the war and their own policy mistakes. Britain was still in 1929 adjusting to the effects of Mr Churchill's misguided imposition of too high a value on Sterling in 1925. Germany was still battling the consequences of the peace treaty imposed by the victorious but vindictive allies in the wake of the great war. In Europe generally, one consequence of this war was a great increase in borders, each with their customs houses and barriers to the previously free movement of goods and people.

As America plunged into depression, other nations' exports

began to dry up. America's Smoot-Hawley tariff hikes were designed to protect the jobs of Americans but, to the extent this worked, it was at the expense of the jobs of others. So 'echo effects' meant there was a fresh downward impetus to global economic activity, reinforced when other nations raised their tariffs and other barriers to trade.

The accepted reason for the severity of the Great Depression in America is that provided by Friedman and Schwartz in their *Monetary History of the United States, 1867-1960*. The US Fed stood by while a severe banking crisis developed. This produced a severe reduction in the stock of money and produced a retrenchment in household demand, already shaken by the market crash and loss of jobs or fears of unemployment. The Fed had the power to offset the dramatic reduction in the money supply, say Friedman and Schwartz, but chose not to act to do so, just as they had failed to act seriously against the stock price bubble.[13]

Ben Bernanke, as a young economist, focussed on the banking crisis, looking for effects beyond those of the money supply. Bankers, like many others had yielded to the optimistic mood of the times. As well, the banking structure was 'inherently weak' due, Galbraith says, to the large numbers of small banks. One failure led to other failures in a domino effect. In the first six months of 1929, while the market was still booming, we are told 346 banks failed in various parts of America, with aggregate deposits of nearly $115 million. By the end of the Great Depression, 9000 banks had failed in the United States (Ferguson says 10,000).

Bernanke constructed some clever tests of the banking crisis hypothesis. He concludes that the financial disruptions of 1930 – 33 reduced the efficiency of the credit allocation process; and that the resulting higher cost and reduced availability of credit depressed aggregate demand by more than Friedman's monetary effect.[14]

There was an international dimension to the banking failures of the 1930s also. When Britain abandoned the gold standard in September 1931, the Fed raised its discount rate in two steps to 3.5%. This, Ferguson says: 'halted the external drain but drove more US banks over the edge'. After great political pressure, in April 1932 the Fed attempted massive open market operations, but this failed to prevent another wave of bank failures. Rumours that Roosevelt would devalue led to another wave of flight from dollars into gold and the Fed again raised its discount rate, 'setting the scene for the nationwide bank holiday proclaimed by Roosevelt two days after his inauguration – a holiday from which 2,000 banks never returned'.[15]

Finally there were other policy issues, which greatly compounded the macroeconomic effects. The increases of America's tariffs are now widely accepted as unhelpful. President Hoover's Revenue Act of 1932 raised income tax on the highest incomes from 25% to 63%. The estate tax was doubled and corporate taxes were raised by almost 15%. Both political parties agreed the budget should be balanced. Attempts to achieve this meant cutting government spending or raising taxes, or both. There was an irrational fear of inflation while the country was experiencing the most violent deflation in the nation's history.

Our generation saw the beginnings of such a domino effect in 2008, when banking was concentrated into far larger units. Ironically, then the cry was 'too big to fail', so Galbraith's hypothesis in this respect needs qualification or amendment. Governments and central bankers, in strong contrast to the case in the 1930s, moved quickly to bail out this generation's failing banks, with the curious exception of Lehman Brothers and the more understandable case of the three overstretched banks in Iceland. (There the Prime Minister advised his constituents to again take to the seas in pursuit of fish.)

And in distant Australia

As an Australian, it is satisfying to report that in that small outpost of Anglo-American culture, a generally more innovative set of policies were followed. As in America, tariffs were raised, quotas and absolute prohibitions on trade were imposed and banks were told to limit provision of foreign currency, further restricting imports. But in contrast to America, there was a massive currency depreciation, led by the privately owned Bank of NSW that followed (and reinforced) market forces in defiance of the Commonwealth (government-owned) Bank. There was a centrally mandated wage cut of 10%, which is said by Schedvin to have endorsed market forces rather than led them, but which helped overcome the downward rigidity of wages that created problems elsewhere. The cut in labour costs added to currency depreciation to make exports more competitive and helped local business in its competition with imports.

But in other fields conservative forces prevailed. The government-owned Commonwealth bank, which had both commercial and policy arms, refused to cut interest rates, and Australia had its own conservative objection to easy fiscal policy. Schedvin outlines three approaches that were debated fiercely. Maintain deficit spending at same rate as in 1930-31, adding a modest amount for unemployment relief and help for distressed wheat farmers, financed by extension of bank credit. Default of government loans, allowing diversion of spending to assist the unemployed. Immediately contract government spending to balance government budgets and avoid the 'devastation of chronic inflation'.

The economics profession has not, in my opinion, 'nailed' a definitive explanation of the causes of the Great Depression. I would be surprised if a series of interconnected models of economies with allowance for strong wealth, confidence and policy effects, especially the imposition of tariffs and quotas and conservative monetary and fiscal policies, in each nation, could not simulate a Great Depression after a major shock to wealth and confidence. So far as I am aware such a test has not been conducted and I offer this as a challenge for some suitably qualified economist.

'Rational examination of these alternatives', says Schedvin, 'was, however, buried beneath a dense layer of prejudice, personal conflict, doctrinal rigidity and antediluvian economics'.[16] The political parties fought it out. Debt default was ruled out, mainly because of fear that future borrowing would be impossible, but with a conservative sense that default would be wrong. The governing Labor Party was hopelessly divided and its proposal for moderate deficit expansion was defeated by a coalition of conservative politicians (who held a majority in the Senate) and the 'monetary authorities', effectively the Commonwealth bank. There was a controversial visit from Sir Otto ('the rotter') Niemeyer of the UK Treasury, also a director of the Bank of England, to encourage the colonials to do the right thing – which was tighten belts and pay the interest on the British debt.

Do the differences in policy explain why Australia recovered from the Great Depression faster than the United States? This is a big question but, so far as I can judge, it was Australia's currency depreciation and wage cut, reflecting market forces more decisively than in the USA where there was also very considerable business unhappiness with President Roosevelt's administration. Schedvin points out that, by the end of the 1930s, Australia had achieved 'a substantial withdrawal from the international economy' with a larger manufacturing sector and a growing tertiary sector. In addition 'There were many other economic, political, institutional and social changes that flowed, directly or indirectly, from the searing experience of mass unemployment, widespread bankruptcy, disastrous commodity prices, political turmoil and social upheaval'.[17]

What has been learned?

Galbraith concluded quite accurately that a bout of mad speculation was again possible. 'No one can doubt that the American people remain susceptible to the speculative mood ...' The US Fed's modern ability to impose high margin requirements would, if implemented, limit speculation and make the inevitable correction less damaging. The Securities and Exchange Commission is a bar, 'one hopes effective', to large-scale market manipulation ...'[18]

The long-serving Chairman of the US Federal Reserve board, Alan Greenspan, was unwilling to act to stop the bubble which his own easy-money policy had created. One can speculate that this was precisely because of the point made repeatedly by Galbraith: 'Action to break up a boom must always be weighed against the chance that it will cause unemployment at a politically inopportune moment'. And 'the immediate death not only has the disadvantage of being immediate but of identifying the executioner'.[19]

So in the early 2000s there remained in America, and I suggest elsewhere, a consensus against trying to prevent bubbles arising in asset markets. Instead the modern focus, at the political level certainly, is on job creation. Galbraith says that 'The avoidance of depression and the prevention of unemployment have become for the politician the most critical of all questions of public policy'.[20]

And so it was in the wake of the Crash of 2007-08. Interest rates were cut almost to zero, 'quantitative easing' (swapping private assets for cash), financial sector bailouts and fiscal expansion were all adopted with an almost religious fervour. The contrast with policy in the 1930s could hardly be sharper. How effective it will prove to be it is too soon to say, and we shall return in a later discussion to the issues involved in this vital subject.

9

The Age of Aquarius; oil crisis, inflation and unemployment

The 1960s was a time of revolution. Mostly it was a revolution of young people in western democracies against the old folks and their old ways. Drugs, sex and rock'n'roll was the rallying cry of the revolutionaries, and the time was called by some the Age of Aquarius. But there was the beginnings of a revolution in economics also.

The Age of Aquarius saw two developments that created considerable misery for many working people but also great confusion for politicians and officials. The first troubling development was the rise of inflation. The second was the unexpected rise of unemployment. The ugly word 'stagflation' was coined to describe the unusual combination of stagnation and inflation.

I note in passing that this chapter discusses a crisis of capitalism of which I was a part, both in experiencing its consequences and helping to sort out the correct diagnosis. As a result, I am relying on personal experience far more than the classic sources that I have necessarily used in discussing previous crises

Misery is inevitable in any economy as inflation erodes the value of people's investments, raises their costs of living and makes contracts difficult to adjust and in some cases impossible to enforce. Then as unemployment rises (as it inevitably does) misery is redoubled and in extreme cases redoubled again both for people who lose their jobs and for people who fear losing their jobs.

Confusion also afflicts politicians and people working in central

US & Australian Inflation - From 1960

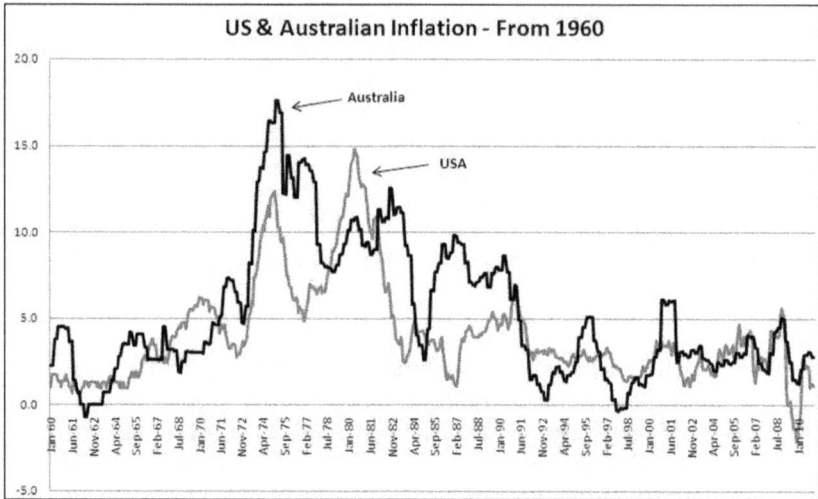

USA & Australian Unemployment Rate (%) - From 1960

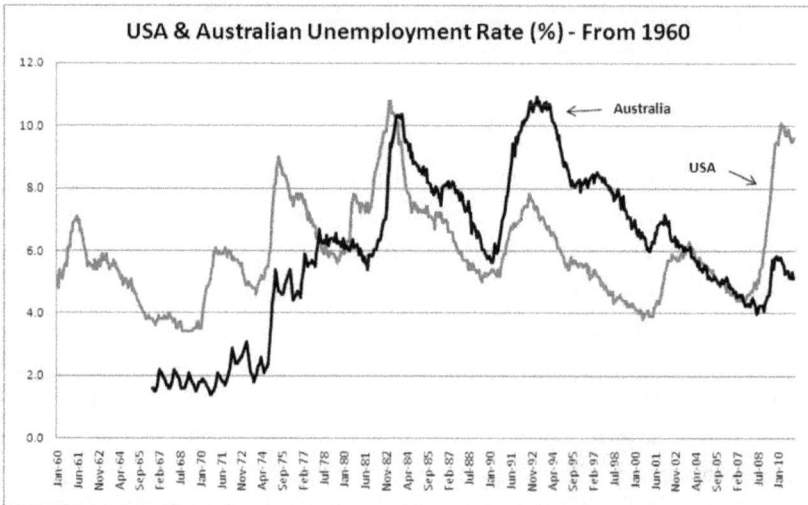

banks and departments of finance. The initial inflation of the late 1960s was due to global causes but showed up in different ways in different nations. This meant a considerable period of misdiagnosis, confusion and mutual recrimination between advisors and politicians. When unemployment rose with inflation, confusion was redoubled as prevailing theories denied this could happen. Low unemployment led to inflation, so the theory stated, and high unemployment reduced or eliminated inflation. There was a curve, called the 'Phillips curve', that described a presumed 'trade-off' between inflation and unemployment.

Armed with a simple Phillips curve, a specialised bureaucrat – we might say 'econocrat' – could advise the levels of inflation consistent with particular levels of unemployment, and a politician could pick the point on the curve that gave him the best chance of being re-elected. But, with the break-down of the simplest 'Phillips curve', economic policy became far less certain and the resulting mistakes mostly made things worse.

The breakthrough came from clever people from the Universities of Manchester, Rochester and Chicago and other similar institutions. The key point was that inflation depends on the expected level of inflation as well as the rate of unemployment. (There are multiple interactions between inflation, expected inflation and the rate of unemployment, which itself reflects the net result of the whole multitude of economic events and disturbances, and in what follows I am summarising all of those interactions in the simple model that was popular in the 1970s. I also note that 'inflation' as defined here is more precisely described as 'goods and services inflation'. In a later chapter I shall distinguish between 'goods and services inflation' and 'asset inflation'.)

Based on his monumental research with Anna J Schwartz on US monetary history from 1867 to 1960, Milton Friedman later concluded that 'Inflation is always and everywhere a monetary phenomenon in the sense that it is and can be produced only by a more rapid increase in the quantity of money than in output. ... A steady rate of monetary growth at a moderate level can provide a framework under which a country can have little inflation and much growth. It will not produce perfect stability; it will not produce heaven on earth; but it can make an important contribution to a stable economic society'.[1]

When inflation started to accelerate in the late 1960s it was against a background of stable inflationary expectations. Economic stimulus reduced unemployment but inflationary expectations were hardly changed. There was stimulus aplenty. In the US economy, President Johnson prosecuted the war against the insurgent Vietnamese and also introduced massive 'Great Society' welfare spending. Stimulus reduced the rate of unemployment and raised the rate of inflation. Initially, the economic parameters behaved according to the simple 'Phillips curve'.

Gradually inflationary expectations rose as the traditional remedy for rising inflation – a credit squeeze – was either applied only weakly or was ineffective. Inflation led to inflationary expectations and both rose largely independent of the state of the economy as summarised by the rate of unemployment. This was the basic reason for the demise of the simple Phillips curve. (I note in passing that my first published paper in economics presented measures of inflationary expectations for Australia and statistical explanations that depended on past inflation and growth of the money supply.)

Inflation introduces many costs into an economy – inflation erodes the value of people's assets, raises their cost of living and makes contracts difficult to adjust and in some cases impossible to enforce. Inflation makes planning investments more uncertain for businesses. Depending on the tax system, inflation pushes individuals into higher tax brackets and makes debt more attractive than equity as a source of finance. These and other costs gradually raise the equilibrium rate of unemployment, setting up feedback loops that weakens the simple 'Phillips curve'. Sometimes increased unemployment came quickly when, for example there were wage hikes in excess of inflation so that real wage increases priced workers out of markets. Dramatic and parallel increases of inflation, inflationary expectations and unemployment all went together when the global oil producers' cartel (OPEC) conspired to hike the price of oil, the capitalist world's lifeblood, as part of the great inflation of the 1970s.

In small, open economies, which in the Age of Aquarius included virtually every economy except for the mighty USA, there was a further complication. Exchange rates between currencies were in those days fixed, or changed only gradually as in Australia's failed 'crawling peg', the system now used by China. It is a basic theorem of economics that small open economies with a fixed exchange rate will import the global rate of inflation, and in the late 1960s and early 1970s the global rate of inflation was set by the world's main economic superpower, the USA. The US economy was inflationary and so many other economies imported the USA inflation.

On August 15, 1971 US President Nixon abandoned the dollar's fixed peg to gold, breaking the traditional (but discontinuous) bond of centuries between national currencies and gold. This in effect introduced John Law's failed experiment in France to the world. Now unless the US Federal Reserve Board provided iron discipline in the management of US monetary policy, global inflation would increase to the extent underwritten by the Fed. Since the members of the Fed are appointed by politicians, there was no effective 'anchor' to prevent inflationary expectations and then inflation itself from growing. Not growing without limit, as no responsible central bank could allow that. But we were to learn, like the revolutionaries of the Age of Aquarius, that it was impossible to be a little bit pregnant or to live for long with only moderate inflation.

President Nixon's surprise visit to China in early 1972 was an important milestone in China's rise to become a potential global superpower. It incidentally provided political 'cover' for the Australian opposition leader, Gough Whitlam whose 1971 trip had been politically controversial. (Just as Nixon sent Henry Kissinger ahead of him in 1971, Australia had sent its central bank chief, HC 'Nugget' Coombs, to China in the early 1960s). Now, after 40 years of mostly rapid growth, China is well on the way to becoming the world's largest economy. Its growth has been fuelled by rapid development of low cost manufactured goods which has in recent years been a force holding down global goods and services inflation. China is now discovering, as Australia and many other much smaller economies did before it, that a semi-flexible exchange rate will not protect it from inflation in the global economy. Whether or not China eventually accepts the case for a fully flexible currency will have a large influence of the future dynamics of the global economy.

Back in the early 1970s, not all economists and policy makers in small open economies understood the simple theorem that a fixed or gradually changing exchange rate meant accepting global inflation, which was dominated in those days by American inflation. In many such nations, inflation was blamed on wage increases, described as 'cost-push' inflation. Sometimes the wage rises exceeded the price inflation, providing both another source of rising unemployment – by raising the cost of employing labour – and a further cause of confusion.

This writer had the great good fortune to be working in an enlightened central bank in one such small open economy (Australia) and was able to produce an analytically convincing demonstration of the imported source of Australia's inflation. This earned me the chance to pursue further studies at the London School of Economics and to connect with economists from the Universities of Chicago, Rochester and Manchester where the 'monetarist' analysis of the world's economic problems was emerging.

England, like Australia, initially misdiagnosed the causes of inflation. We young 'monetarists' cheered when Milton Friedman from Chicago explained to the cost-push economists of Cambridge during a televised debate that they needed a theory of inflation that held true more than 30 miles from Cambridge. England in the 1970s was a nation on the brink of economic catastrophe, held to ransom by powerful unions, and misunderstanding of the way a modern economy works was a big part of the problem. It took the election of Margaret Thatcher and her courage in facing down the unions, privatising many activities and constraining the role of government to set Britain on a more prosperous and far less inflationary path.

America was the prime cause of the inflation that so bedevilled the world in that decade. America too found the solution. US Fed chief, Paul Volcker, announced new operating procedures that saw the federal funds rate, which had averaged 11.2% in 1979, raised to a peak of 20% in June 1981. The economy received a 'short sharp shock'. While the US rate of unemployment surged from approximately 6% in 1979 to almost 11% at the end of 1982, and there was much angst, the Volcker recession was short and with inflation eradicated the US economy performed better than most. Inflation, which peaked at

13.5% in 1981, was successfully lowered to 3.2% by 1983. This bold action 'broke the stick of inflation'.

Paul Volcker, a Democrat, was appointed Chairman of the Federal Reserve in August 1979 by President Jimmy Carter and reappointed in 1983 by President Ronald Reagan. He was not again reappointed by President Reagan, supposedly being disinclined to deliver sufficient financial deregulation. He is history's greatest central banker, its most effective inflation fighter.

Other countries took far longer to emulate the USA. As a senior economist at Australia's central bank I concluded 'enough was enough' when Australia's cash interest rates reached similar levels to those in Volcker's USA. The board of the Reserve Bank accepted my advice even though the head of Australia's Treasury, the brilliant and mercurial John Stone, begged to differ. Stone was an econocrat of the old school with anti-inflationary instincts that I fully shared, but it took another decade and a severe Australian recession to finally reduce inflation to appropriately low levels.

Part of the problem was that we lacked the technical conditions for control of inflation. Most importantly, a floating exchange rate was not introduced to Australia until 1983, and when this vital reform was being debated it was opposed by John Stone. Then financial deregulation made the correct measurement of monetary policy (especially the role of 'money supply') uncertain. But the root cause was a desire to fix inflation gradually, without the pain of a short sharp shock. Eventually, a decade after Paul Volcker's brave and successful experiment, Australia also broke the stick of inflation. This was at least partly by accident as the then Deputy-governor, Ian Macfarlane, admitted in the wake of 'the recession we had to have', to quote the then Prime Minister, Paul Keating.[2]

Australia's Treasury Secretary, incidentally, opposed the float of the Australian dollar for (I think) two reasons. First was the complex analytic reason that, with a floating exchange rate, monetary policy is relatively more important than fiscal policy, whereas with a fixed rate it is the other way around. More important, Stone believed, and still believes, that loss of international reserves provides a far bigger stick with which to beat a profligate government than a falling exchange rate. My own view has not changed. It is that a flexible exchange rate is vital if a nation is to control its economy and especially its rate of goods and services inflation, and this is now the generally accepted perspective.

But it is important to recognise that this is not the only respectable view. As already noted, China has not yet accepted this view. And the nations within the European Union do not accept this view; except for the United Kingdom, which has retained its pound sterling, they have all committed to use the Euro. The switch to the Euro raised prices in the weaker countries such as Greece, Spain and Italy and with the debt crisis now afflicting these countries the jury is still out as to whether being nailed to a strong currency will ultimately help or harm these nations.

As we shall discuss in a later chapter, the story becomes more complex when asset inflation is added to goods and services inflation. But common or garden variety of goods and services inflation was the main subject of the Age of Aquarius, and thus of this chapter.

The costs of inflation

Imagine having to take your wages home in a wheelbarrow, and trying to spend them that afternoon before their value drops by a further order of magnitude. That has been the fate of people in failed economies where the 'anchor' either of the gold standard or a professional and competent central bank is missing. Defeated nations after wars often suffer the extreme pain of hyperinflation, as did Germany and Austria after World War I, in 1922-23. Germany's wholesale price index was 100.6 in July 1922, 2785 in January 1923, 194,000 in July 1923 and 726,000,000,000 in November 1923. Modern Zimbabwe is another, horrible, more recent example.

As a young central banker I visited Israel, no doubt more for my benefit than for Israel's. 'What is Australia's rate of inflation?' I was asked after introductions had been effected. 'About 8%' I replied. 'Is that per month or per week?' my interlocutor responded. Israel has, mercifully, fought its way into clearer waters, with consumer price inflation of the order of 4% per annum.

Inflation is the persistent erosion of the value of the monetary standard. Allowing inflation to arise and to persist is tantamount to endorsing theft. In an inflationary economy it should come as no surprise that standards of private and public morality come under pressure.

Inflation forces up rates of interest, saps competitiveness, reduces incentives to save and to invest and, ultimately, puts at risk a country's financial and economic stability. Eliminating inflation requires a national consensus that the costs of inflation are much greater than generally thought. Establishing and maintaining such a consensus is a crucial step in restoring any nation's prosperity.

I wrote in 1990: 'Achieving a climate of price stability is obviously difficult. Twentieth-century experience suggests that changes to current arrangements will be needed. Possibilities include giving existing central banks a stronger, or even binding, charter to fight inflation; reintroducing something akin to the gold standard, but with supply of the relevant standard more rigidly controlled; and introducing a regime of competitive moneys'.[3]

Moral costs of Inflation

The moral costs of inflation are impossible to quantify, even in principle. Inflation is theft and an economy built on inflation is built on deception. In an inflationary economy, those who are good at theft and deception will be rewarded and so more effort will go into sharp practices of one sort or another. The evident decline of standards of morality in some segments of our business community and in aspects of private behaviour can be traced partly to the incentives and distortions created by inflation. The more obviously moral costs of inflation relate to fairness and distribution of wealth and incomes.

Fairness. Inflation involves large and arbitrary redistributions of income. Inflation generally rewards borrowers and cheats owners of assets that yield fixed rates of interest. The classic case is that of the 'widows and orphans' who purchased government bonds to finance wars and whose assets were subsequently wiped out by inflation. But there are more recent examples:

During Australia's wage explosions of 1974 and 1981 wage earners who kept their jobs gained hugely at the expense of owners of capital and those workers who lost their jobs. These tendencies were partially redressed in later years, but the gainers later were mostly not those who were the earlier losers.

Home owners gained massively at the expense of renters throughout the postwar period, as have many others who have gone into debt to finance the purchase of assets.

Borrowers (including governments) gained massively at the expense of lenders when inflation greatly exceeded nominal rates of interest in the 1970s. Once again these tendencies were reversed in the 1980s, but those who gained recently were not necessarily the earlier losers. Moreover, the risk to borrowers increases when nominal interest rates are high, even if 'real' (inflation adjusted) rates are unchanged (which in general they are not – see below).

I venture the judgment that all of these changes to the distribution of income have been larger than any that have resulted from the effects of deliberate policy choice.

Other costs of inflation – growth and stability

Growth. When the value of the national measuring rod changes in an unpredictable manner, sensible long-term planning is impossible. Businesses tilt their activities toward short-term gain and the general business mentality comes to view speculation and paper shuffling as likely to produce larger gains than investment in projects with a long gestation period. Australia suffered increasingly from this tendency in the 1970s and 1980s and it is no coincidence that this was an era of high and variable inflation.

Inflation worms its way into the very structure of interest rates. Typically there is a premium for inflation so that rates are high when inflation is high. With inflation at 2 per cent and interest rates at 7 per cent, long-term investment is much more likely to proceed than when inflation is 8 per cent and interest rates are 18 per cent. This is the most obvious and direct way in which inflation discourages investment and inhibits the growth of a country's productive capacity.

As this example suggests, real rates of interest are higher when inflation is higher. This is in accord with experience and seems mainly to reflect the greater uncertainty premium that inflation builds into nominal rates. Tax deductibility of nominal interest costs for business reinforces this tendency.

Household behaviour is similarly not immune from the uncertainties created by inflation. With the value of future savings cast into doubt by inflation, is it any wonder that consumption is preferred to saving? 'Buy now and beat the price rise' is a common advertising slogan, while the observation 'why save, you only pay tax on the interest' is a frequent complaint by ordinary folk.

A very specific cost of inflation is its direct contribution to the growth of a nation's international debt. Inflation saps the competitive strength of a country's business units. When domestic costs are rising more rapidly than costs in overseas countries, it is progressively cheaper to import rather than to produce locally. When domestic prices are rising more rapidly than prices on overseas markets, it is better to sell locally than to export.

Of course, periodic currency depreciation goes some way to restoring the competitiveness of an inflationary country's business units. But compensation by currency depreciation is a hit-and-miss affair. The extra uncertainty systematically undermines the will to invest to provide export capacity and to compete with imports. It seems far easier to produce for the soft environment of the local market.

The tendency for inflation to contribute to the growth of international debt will not be seen as a cost by those who believe that such debt is not a problem. Even though much of Australia's international debt is in private hands, including those of its banks, I am not among those who are relaxed about its continued growth. This is because continued growth of debt is a result of imbalances between saving and spending and between production and consumption.

If not checked, these imbalances will erode any nation's economic sovereignty. One important aspect of this is the credit risk that arises with the growth of debt. If international lenders lose confidence in a country's economic performance and policies, the value of that nation's currency will plunge and there will be a sizable premium added to the structure of interest rates. While debt continues to grow, this risk will be ever-present.

Inflation also reduces growth by draining resources from the private sector to the government sector. With 'progressive' tax systems, inflation produces an automatic but non-transparent fiscal dividend for governments via the ugly effect known as 'bracket creep'. This increases government outlays, many of which will inevitably be subject to less rigorous standards than those in the private sector. When expenditure decisions are made in an environment of easy funding, it is no wonder that they do not all provide the maximum contribution to national efficiency.

The Austrian school of economists has emphasised both the fraud involved with inflation and the way in which inflation creates 'discoordination' of economic activities by distorting relative prices. Mistaken investment decisions can severely limit a country's growth potential. The American literature has also identified 'shoe-leather costs' (extra trips to the bank) and 'menu costs' (unnecessary printings of menus). The point, of course, is broader than these terms suggest. Variable prices mean that considerable time can be spent by enterprises trying to decide on the appropriate prices for their products, while consumers and workers also spend extra time searching for goods and/or jobs.

All in all, inflation erodes a nation's growth potential in many ways. The problem is to put an explicit cost on these (and other) costs: Is inflation reducing growth of GDP by 0.1 per cent annually, by 1 per cent or 2 per cent? My instinct tells me that the costs are nearer the upper end of this range, but we are in desperate need of expert comprehensive analysis of the question.

Stability. A final cost of inflation is the threat it poses to financial and economic stability. A climate of inflation introduces unnecessary uncertainty into a wide range of decision-making processes. This creates the general possibility of avoidable errors. Inflation at a higher rate than in other countries produces depreciation of the value of the inflating currency on international markets. This depreciation rarely proceeds smoothly but rather involves major lurches. Typically, the currency becomes overvalued for a time and then drops suddenly. Both the upward pressure and the sudden fall are highly disruptive, as we have seen many times in recent years.

Failure to cure inflation involves costs that greatly exceed the costs of the cure. I cannot prove this in a scientific manner but I believe it is provable. Accurate assessment of the costs of inflation is one of the main challenges for the economics profession and especially its central bankers.

Periodic attempts to check inflation also produce disruption. The major credit squeezes of 1961, 1974, 1981 and 1989 imposed costly checks to people's plans. In the postwar period in Australia the periodic credit squeezes necessary in an environment of inflation have not threatened the stability of the financial system as a whole. But in earlier eras, such as the 1890s and the 1930s, and in other places, extensive damage to financial stability has been done by major unexpected changes in asset values.

The Costs of Stopping Inflation

Stopping inflation requires an understanding of the causes of inflation. Economists are agreed that inflation is fundamentally created by growth of demand exceeding growth of the productive capacity of an economy - 'too much money chasing too few goods'. Once it is underway, a host of factors tend to maintain it. There is the 'wage-price spiral': wage increases are based on past price increases and price increases are based on increases in costs, including wage costs.

Inflation at rates in excess of overseas rates causes currency depreciation and this raises the costs of imports. Inflation produces higher interest rates, which raise the cost of capital. Government taxes and charges rise in line with (or in excess of) costs and this in turn adds pressure to prices.

Entrenched inflation becomes widely accommodated. Everyone

acts to protect themselves from it in ways that ensure its continuation. Economists regard inflationary expectations as the main reason for the persistence of inflation. Reversing inflation involves costs. Cutting growth of demand below the growth of productive capacity usually involves lost output (but not when production for export replaces production for domestic consumption).

If inflation is high and/or deeply entrenched, a long period of low growth, even a deep economic depression, may be required to break the inflationary psychology. For example, in 1960-61 in Australia unemployment rate rose from 1.5 per cent to over 3 per cent before inflation fell to zero. In 1974-75 unemployment rose from 2.5 per cent to 6 per cent before inflation was checked (not killed), falling from a peak of around 16 per cent to around 12 per cent. In 1982-83 unemployment rose to over 10 per cent of the workforce, after which inflation declined from around 12 per cent to below 5 per cent.

Clearly the loss of output and the associated human misery were considerable in each of these episodes. Equally clearly, there was political retribution in the wake of each episode. In 1961, the Liberal (conservative) Menzies government almost lost power to Labor. In 1975, the Whitlam Labor government was dismissed in a landslide. In its turn, the Fraser Liberal government was replaced by the Hawke Labor government in late 1982.

But the enduring cost was that inflation was not beaten. After each episode inflation eventually rose again. There is 'no gain without pain', but enduring the pain and then losing the gain is the height of folly. Now US unemployment is again not much below double digit levels and the US Fed is more worried about deflation than inflation. Current experience is more like the traditional case of strong recession than the stagflation of the Age of Aquarius, but it is important that the benefits of low inflation are not put at risk with an excessively easy monetary policy in the attempt to overcome unemployment. Securing high employment with low inflation in the world's leading capitalist nations is one of the great challenges confronting capitalism today.

In the light of persistent failure to eliminate inflation in the 1970s and 1980s, many influential people concluded that the costs of cutting inflation are simply too great. Australian Treasurer Paul Keating was wont to speak of the 'scorched earth policy' of those who wish to get rid of inflation. There are two points to make in reply. The first is the technical point that the costs of inflation are continuing costs. They persist while inflation persists. So in balancing the immediate but temporary costs of eliminating inflation against the continuing and permanent costs of inflation, it may be rational for a country to accept the short-run costs in exchange for the long-run gains. Full analysis of this point would require accurate estimates of all costs with appropriate discounting of the future. Politicians implicitly use a very high rate of discount and so conclude that the costs of stopping inflation are too high.

The second point is that it may be possible to reduce the transitional costs of breaking an inflationary psychology. Instead of using a draconian 'scorched earth' policy, it may be possible to introduce a circuit-breaker of some kind. Incomes policies are sometimes seen as potential circuit-breakers. Paul Volcker's circuit breaker – a well defined change of approach announced by a credible independent central banker – is a more reliable approach. If people believe that monetary policy will be held firm until inflation is squeezed out of the economy, they will quickly adjust downward their inflationary expectations.

Ironically, Paul Keating's 'scorched earth' policy was ultimately used with success in ending Australia's inflation. Although unemployment reached record post-war levels of around 11% of the Australian workforce, the Keating government survived the 1993 election. Perhaps the Liberal (conservative) opposition lacked credibility, or perhaps Australia's voters felt Paul Keating deserved a full term to make his mark. Ironically, Paul Keating's successor in 1996, John Howard, lost office in 2007 with unemployment below 5% for the first time since the Whitlam government, and inflation very low also.

What Is the Balance?

I have strayed into politics, but this seems like as good a guide as any to what works for citizens. Obviously people don't just vote on economic matters, and the theory that there is a maximum time for a modern political party or coalition to govern is hard to dismiss. Clearly, Australia's post-war political history offers no clear guidance on where a politician should focus in seeking to follow President Clinton's dictum 'Its the economy, stupid'. Clearly the combination of high unemployment and high inflation is a political killer, but low inflation combined with low unemployment is no guarantee of political success.

My judgment, however, on behalf of the welfare of the people is firmly in favour of eliminating inflation and this now seems to be generally accepted by economists. The continuing costs of inflation are much larger than generally thought. The judgment of E. Gerald Corrigan, President of the Federal Reserve Bank of New York, in testimony before the US Congress on February 6, 1990, is one that I fully share: 'Virtually every observable facet of economic history – here in the United States and around the world – tells us that high and/or rising rates of inflation are simply incompatible with sustained economic prosperity'.[4]

It is impossible for any country to be genuinely competitive, to achieve and maintain programs of economic reform and to promote the economic welfare of its citizens with an inflation rate consistently higher than its competitors. The inevitable transitional costs of disinflation can be eased by the adoption of a credible anti-inflationary policy by a strong central bank, with Paul Volcker's bold action as exhibit A.

It is also worth quoting the view of my former colleague and fellow inflation fighter, John Phillips, once Deputy Governor of the Reserve Bank of Australia, who concluded: 'In the battle for national advantage, inflation ranks as one of the three or four great scourges. It probably ranks behind greed and apathy, although it is closely related to both ...'[5]

Confidence and inflation

These conclusions are now generally accepted but the experience of the 1960s, 1970s and 1980s shows they need constant reinforcement. The graph shows the performance of the US equity markets in the Age of Aquarius. While most of the second half of the twentieth century saw rising stock prices, the 1960s and 1970s saw US stock prices 'rangebound', with no upward trend. This is surely a compelling, if unscientific, illustration of the costs of inflation and of the confusion and uncertainty that accompanied it in the Age of Aquarius.

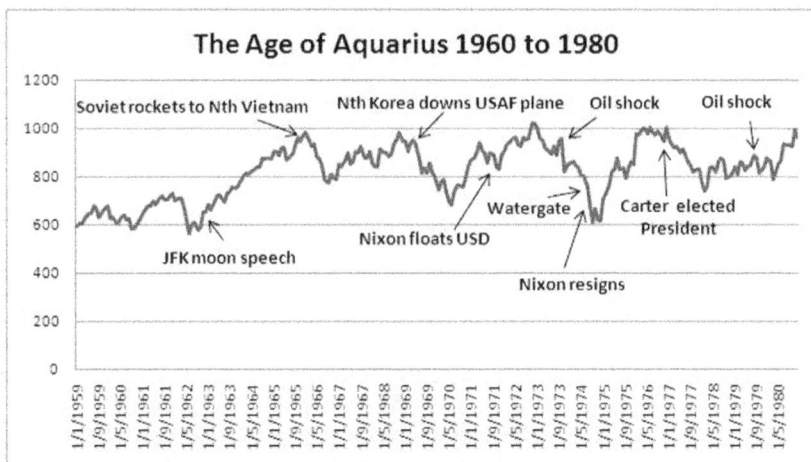

The Age of Aquarius 1960 to 1980

In fact, examination of a range of economic data suggests that the inflation of the Age of Aquarius did great overall damage to the 'developed' nation economies. We well as the substantial increases in the rate of unemployment, one of the most obvious additional pieces of evidence is the substantial reduction of household saving ratios. In the wake of the Global Financial Crisis of 2007-2008, saving ratios have recovered somewhat. Wise governments will do their best to maintain, indeed strengthen, their people's propensity to save. Keeping inflation low, overall stability in goods and services inflation, will be vital.

10

Asian Magic and Western Witchcraft

*Capitalism reached Asia as trade with the European powers.
China was forced to trade after the so-called Opium Wars. Japan
was forcibly opened for trade after many armed incursions.
Some of the 'Tiger' economies of South East Asia were colonised;
others became traders while remaining independent. All of these
nations in modern times have experienced rapid growth – 'Asian
Magic'.*

*The World Wide Web – 'Western Witchcraft' – is a massive
unifying system of global communication that may do more than
any other development to produce a truly global culture. The
so-called 'new economy' market boom was one of the greatest
on record, overall a ninebagger, then sadly followed by an old
economy asset bust.*

The Japanese miracle

In 1852, Commodore Perry of the US navy travelled to Japan in
charge of a squadron of fighting ships in pursuit of a trade treaty. At
Uraga Harbour near Edo (modern Tokyo) in July 1853 he demanded
a trade treaty backed up by a show of naval force. He left a letter from
President Fillimore and returned in February 1854 to find virtually all
the President's demands had been agreed.

Japan joined the modern world when atomic bombs destroyed
Hiroshima and Nagasaki in August 1945. After five days of fierce
internal debate, the Emperor spoke for the first time on radio to
announce his country's surrender. Despite the sneak attack on Pearl

Harbour which brought the United States into World War II, and the ferocity with which the Japanese military fought, the United States decided to treat the conquered nation well.

By way of preparation, the US authorities commissioned a book which has become famous, *The Chrysanthemum and the Sword: Patterns of Japanese Culture*, an influential 1946 study by American anthropologist Ruth Benedict.[1] The aim was to understand and predict the behavior of the Japanese by reference to a series of contradictions in traditional culture. The book was influential in shaping American ideas about Japanese culture during the occupation, and popularized the distinction between guilt cultures and shame cultures. It has become required reading for young people visiting Japan for the first time, as it was for me in 1980.

Led by the example of the Emperor, the Japanese people laid down their arms and cooperated with the occupying force. This force, incidentally included this writer's parents-in-law, who met as army doctor and army nurse and who were stationed quite near to Hiroshima. Sadly, no-one knew to take precautions about the residual radiation and the couple lost three children before my future wife, Elizabeth, was born in 1952.

The American occupation force imposed democracy and a modern capitalist system. With the start of the cold war, Japan was seen as a potentially useful ally and America kick-started a modern industrial economy with large orders of supplies. Cheap labor, a willingness to copy the innovations of others and good planning by the Japanese Ministry of International Trade and Industry (MITI) produced rapid growth of production and standards of living.

In the decades following World War II, Japan implemented stringent tariffs and policies to encourage people to save goodly shares of their incomes. With more money in banks, loans and credit became easier to obtain, and with Japanese exports cheap and imports expensive Japan began running large trade surpluses. The popular beliefs during my childhood were that Japan produced shoddy goods copied from western models with no account of ownership of relevant patents. This allegation is now sometimes made about Chinese industry.

Japan became the 'miracle economy' of its time, and its management techniques were strongly influenced by Dr Edwards Deming, founder of the 'Total Quality' movement. An account of Deming's career includes the following warm accolade: 'The teachings of Dr. Deming affected a quality revolution of gargantuan significance on American manufacturers and consumers. Through his ideas, product quality improved and, thus, popular satisfaction.

'His influential work in Japan – instructing top executives and engineers in quality management – was a driving force behind that nation's economic rise. Dr. Deming contributed directly to Japan's phenomenal export-led growth and its current technological leadership in automobiles, shipbuilding and electronics. The Union of Japanese Science and Engineering (JUSE) saluted its teacher with the institution of the annual Deming Prize for significant achievement in product quality and dependability. In 1960, the Emperor of Japan bestowed on Dr. Deming the Second Order Medal of the Sacred Treasure.'[2]

Japan's exchange rate was widely perceived to be 'undervalued', another current belief about China's yuan. When President Nixon devalued the US dollar against gold in 1971, the Japanese yen was set at ¥308 per US$1, which compares to around 50 cents per US dollar at the start of the twentieth century.

In early 1973, the world's major currencies were allowed to float. Japan's yen floated upwards, despite continued surpluses on trade account, with setbacks during the oil crises of the Age of Aquarius. The yen failed to rise in value even though current account surpluses returned in the early 1980s and grew quickly, leading to allegations of heavy market intervention by the Bank of Japan, allegations directed at the People's Bank of China now.

The Plaza Accord of 1985 concluded that the US dollar was overvalued and, therefore, that the yen and other currencies were undervalued – another analogy with current (or future) developments with respect to the yuan. The Plaza agreement, and subsequent market pressures, led to a rapid rise in the value of the yen. From its average of ¥239 per US$1 in 1985, the yen rose to a peak of ¥128 in 1988, virtually doubling its value relative to the dollar.

With its growing reputation for quality, Japan grew quickly and the

1980s were a time of accelerating boom despite the rising value of the yen. Indeed, strong global demand for Japanese assets as well as goods drove the yen higher in the sort of 'virtuous circle' that also affected the German economy. Speculation was inevitable, particularly in the Tokyo Stock Exchange and the real estate market. The Nikkei stock index rose from its modest (in retrospect) level of 7,000 in the early 1980s to reach its all-time high of almost 39,000 on December 29, 1989. This level represented an increase of 5.57 times in six and-a-half years. Banks had granted increasingly risky loans, many of which were backed by shares in Japan's great manufacturing and trading companies, a practice banned in the Anglozone nations.

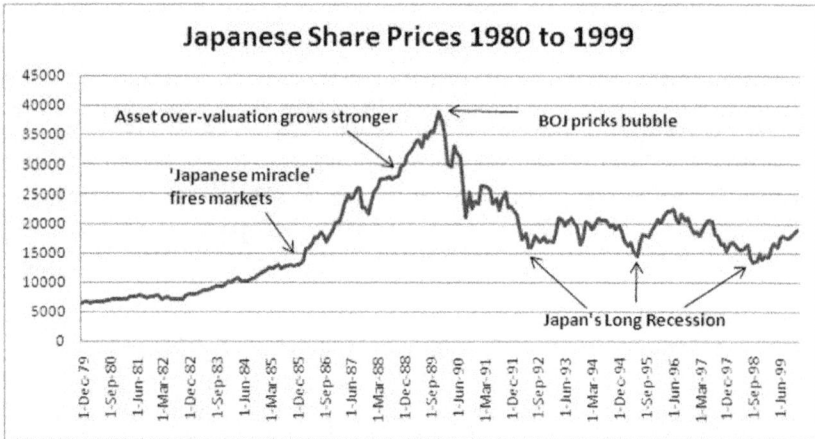

The share price boom is illustrated in the graph. There is little doubt this was a genuine bubble, and the paper wealth created was literally unbelievable. Land prices also rocketed up, and were highest in Tokyo's Ginza district in 1989, with choice properties fetching over 100 million yen (approximately one million US dollars) per square meter ($93,000 per square foot). Prices were only marginally less in other large business districts of Tokyo. As noted earlier, the Australian government sold half of its Tokyo embassy plot in the late 1980s and booked a profit of hundreds of millions of dollars, even after building a new compound that includes 40 staff apartments.

It was the Bank of Japan that pricked Japan's great asset bubble by raising interest rates, though there was an undoubted widespread concern that the bubble must burst. The end of the bubble triggered a substantial share price crash and the so-called 'long recession', a period of economic stagnation that has lingered for two decades.[3] I share what I think is a widespread view is that propping up the Japanese banking system created 'zombie banks' with 'zombie clients' as bad debts were not written off quickly and ruthlessly, and in many cases poor accounting standards ratified the overvaluations. Failure to deal with the consequences of asset deflation left many banks and industrial corporations living a twilight existence.

This is yet another case where smart people could judge that the boom could not go on forever. It is worth remembering that one does not go broke taking a profit. Also that when stock prices are looking too good to be true (on whatever disciplined basis) reality is about to break in, as it was in Japan as the final year of the great boom.

The easy credit that helped create and engorge the real estate bubble continued to be a problem for several years to come and, as late as 1997, banks were still making loans that had a low probability of being repaid. Loan officers and investment staff had a hard time finding anything to invest in that would return a profit. They would sometimes resort to depositing their block of investment cash as ordinary deposits in a competing bank, which would bring howls of complaint from that bank's loan officers and investment staff. Correcting the credit problem became even more difficult as the government began to subsidize failing banks and businesses, creating many so-called 'zombie businesses'. Eventually a carry trade developed in which money was borrowed from Japan, invested for returns elsewhere and then the Japanese were paid back, with a nice profit for the trader.

Richard Koo, Chief Economist of Nomura Securities, has introduced the concept of a 'balance sheet recession' to explain Japan's long recession in a provocative book called *The Holy Grail of Macroeconomics. Lessons from Japan's Great Recession.*[4] Mainstream (academic) economists are somewhat condescending about Koo's book, but in this writer's opinion it deserves taking seriously.

By 2004, prime "A" property in Tokyo's financial districts had slumped dramatically, and Tokyo's residential homes were a fraction of their peak values, but still managed to be listed as the most expensive in the world until being surpassed in the late 2000s by Moscow and other cities. Tens of trillions of dollars of paper wealth was wiped out with the combined collapse of the Tokyo stock and real estate markets. Only in 2007 had property prices again begun to rise; however, they began to fall again in late 2008 in the wake of the Global Financial Crisis of 2007-08.

The time after the bubble's collapse, which after an initial share decline occurred gradually rather than suddenly, is known as the 'lost decade or end of the century' in Japan. In October 2008 the Nikkei 225 stock index reached a 26-year low of 6994.90, despite interest rates at zero.

Japan is suffering now from more than the effects of a major financial disturbance. As concluded by Garnaut and Song in 2004: 'Japan, Taiwan, Singapore and Hong Kong have completed the process of moving rapidly to the world's frontiers of productivity and incomes'. Highly relevant for the next discussion, incidentally: 'Korea is nearing the frontiers. Malaysia and Thailand are moving closer, having been interrupted for a few years by the financial crisis'.[5] Japan has a rapidly aging population and is likely to suffer in many ways from resulting lack of dynamism. Politics seem to be a prime example of the latter affliction, with a succession of elderly Prime Ministers presiding for short periods over an undynamic economy, with no apparent appetite for radical reforms that might create another period of strong growth. (No, this is not a Wikileak revelation, though one supposes that it could be.)

The lessons of Japanese experience are both general and particular. By all means investors should ride the asset boom, but sell (or at least reduce holdings) when commonsense suggests a correction is inevitable. Bankers should clean out their bad debts and recapitalise after a correction. Banks should never hold shares in industrial enterprises and crony capitalism is to be avoided. Pension off the older generation and put good young people in their place. All easier said than done but the alternative is to wither slowly on the vine.

The Asian crisis, 1997-98

The next 'miracle economies', called 'Tiger' economies, were the fast growing nations of South East Asia.

During the 1990s until 1997, Asia attracted a large share of the total capital inflow to developing countries. The economies of Southeast Asia in particular maintained high interest rates attractive to foreign investors looking for high rates of return. In what was a self-reinforcing process large inflows of money boosted asset prices. In the late 1980s and early 1990s the economies of Thailand, Malaysia, Indonesia, Singapore, and South Korea experienced GDP growth rates in the range of 8-12% per annum. These were the latest poster-boys of international finance. High growth was funded by rapidly growing debts, both in absolute terms and relative to overall GDP.

This writer was part of a group that took serious American investors to South East Asia in the middle nineties. Our pitch was to remind the fund managers of the self-reinforcing process when American pension fund managers were first allowed to buy equities. Growing demand drove up the price of equities and helped those funds investing in equities to prosper, meaning they received greater inflows and purchased more equities. Similar logic applied when American investors first began to buy European equities. The third great tide, we argued, was going to be created by the equities of Asian nations. I do recall us also saying that 'high returns mean high risk', which was just as well.

The Asian financial crisis began in June 1997. As the graph of Singaporean share prices suggests, however, continuing growth of debt had created concerns from 1993, creating a rare 'sunlit upland', albeit one with uneasy dips and spikes. Another dampening event was the massive float of Singapore Telecom in October 1993.

The first domino to fall was Thailand, with the collapse of the Thai baht. The Thai government made the entirely conservative decision to float its currency, the baht, cutting its peg to the American dollar, after exhaustive efforts to support it in the face of a severe financial over-extension that was in part driven by escalating real estate prices. The capital flowing into Thailand created debts to foreign investors that made the country effectively bankrupt even before the collapse of its currency. As the crisis spread, most of Southeast Asia and Japan experienced slumping currencies, devalued equities and other assets, and a precipitous rise in private debt.

Overseas debt-to-GDP ratios rose substantially in the four large ASEAN economies in 1993–96, then increased beyond 180% during the worst of the crisis. The graph shows the course of Singaporean shares, but similar pictures can be constructed for other ASEAN nations. The initial decline in the Straits Times index is associated with the sharp rise in American interest rates in 1995. Like the British Bank Rate in the nineteenth century, a rise in the US Federal Funds Rate cannot fail to have international effects, especially for developing nations relying on massive inflows of capital. Also relevant in all the 'tiger' economies was downward revisions to the anticipated profitability of investment which was adversely impacted by concerns at growing debt-to-GDP ratios, a rising US dollar and higher interest rates.

Although most of the governments of South East Asia had seemingly sound fiscal policies, the International Monetary Fund (IMF) implemented a $40 billion program to stabilize the currencies of South Korea, Thailand, and Indonesia, economies particularly hard hit by the crisis. The efforts to stem a potential global economic crisis did little to stabilize the domestic situation in Indonesia, however. After 30 years in power, President Suharto was forced to step down on 21 May 1998 in the wake of widespread rioting that followed sharp increases in the prices of goods and services caused by a drastic devaluation of the rupiah. The effects of the crisis lingered through 1998.

In the Philippines growth dropped to virtually zero in 1998. Only Singapore and Taiwan proved relatively insulated from the shock, but both suffered serious hits in passing, the former more so due to its size and geographical location between Malaysia and Indonesia. By 1999, however, there were clear signs that the economies of Asia were beginning to recover.

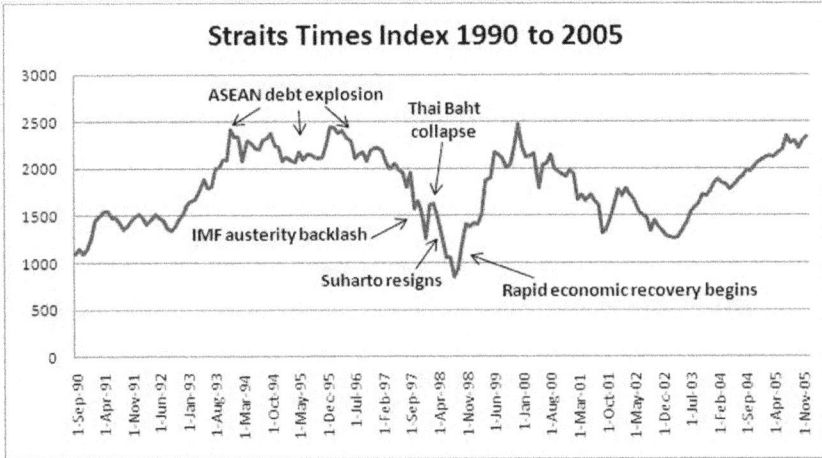

Straits Times Index 1990 to 2005

The Russian bear

The Soviet Union lost the cold war but its consolation was to become a capitalist nation, albeit one that was widely influenced by mafia-style gangsters. Here was a new frontier for brave people who understood the Russian character and language, or could afford advisors who did; advisors who could be paid enough to be trusted. Capitalist Russia was the next domino to fall. Declining productivity, an artificially high fixed exchange rate between the rouble and foreign currencies and a chronic budget deficit (including the cost of war in Chechnya) aided the fall.

Two external shocks hit hard the Russian economy in the late nineties. The first was the Asian financial crisis already discussed. This crisis initiated declines in demand for crude oil and nonferrous metals. Their prices fell, and that weakened Russia's exports and drained foreign exchange reserves. The political crisis came to a head in March 1998 when Russian president Boris Yeltsin suddenly dismissed his Prime Minister and the entire cabinet. The growth of internal loans could only be provided at the expense of the inflow of foreign speculative capital, which was attracted by very high interest rates.

A $22.6 billion International Monetary Fund and World Bank financial package was approved to support reforms and stabilize

Russia's financial markets by swapping an enormous volume of the quickly maturing short-term government bills into long-term Eurobonds. (It was later revealed that a sizeable chunk of this package was stolen when it arrived.) The rescue bid had begun, and experts were urging the government to abandon its continued support for the rouble, when on May 12, 1998 coal miners went on strike over unpaid wages, blocking the Trans-Siberian Railway. By August 1, 1998 there were approximately $12.5 billion in unpaid wages owed to Russian workers. On August 14 the exchange rate of the Russian rouble to the US dollar was still 6.29. Despite the bailout, July monthly interest payments on Russia's debt rose to a figure 40% greater than its monthly tax collections.

At the time, Russia employed a 'floating peg' policy toward the rouble. This is a typical precursor to a full float of a nation's currency, and means that the central bank at any given time is committed that the rouble-to-dollar (or RUR/USD) exchange rate would stay within a particular range. If the rouble threatened to devalue outside of that range (or 'band'), the central bank would intervene by spending foreign reserves to buy roubles. For instance, during approximately the one year prior to the crisis, the Russian central bank committed to maintain a band of 5.3 to 7.1 RUR/USD meaning that it would buy roubles if the market exchange rate threatened to exceed 7.1 roubles per dollar.

The inability of the Russian government to implement a coherent set of economic reforms led to a severe erosion of investor confidence and a chain-reaction that was effectively a run on the central bank. Investors abandoned the market by selling roubles and Russian assets generally, which put strong downward pressure on the rouble. This forced the central bank to spend its foreign reserves to defend the rouble, which in turn further eroded investor confidence and undermined the currency. It is estimated that between October 1, 1997 and August 17, 1998, the central bank expended approximately $27 billion of its U.S. dollar reserves to maintain the floating peg.

On August 13, 1998, the Russian stock, bond, and currency markets collapsed as a result of investor fears that the government would devalue the rouble and default on domestic debt, or both.

Annual yields on rouble denominated bonds were more than 200 percent. The stock market had to be closed for 35 minutes as prices plummeted. When the market closed, it was down 65 percent with a small number of shares actually traded. From January to August the stock market had lost more than 75% of its value, 39% in the month of May alone.

On September 2 the Central Bank of the Russian Federation abandoned the 'floating peg' policy and floated the rouble – a move that was long overdue and helped to stabilise the economy. By September 21 the exchange rate had reached 21 roubles to the US dollar, meaning it had lost two thirds of its value of less than a month earlier, a measure that far more accurately indicated the place of the Russian economy in the global pecking order.

The high-flying hedge fund, Long Term Capital Management (LTCM), failed due to the adverse effects of the Russian collapse. The fund's direct exposure to Russian assets was not great, but it was a fact that many of the banks that LTCM had invested in that was the main problem, exacerbated by the sort of rumours that lead to runs on banks. My own interpretation, mentioned in Chapter 2, is that the technical analysis carried out by LTCM used a particular run of past data that failed to allow for the particular manner in which the crisis played out. Russia defaulted on rouble denominated debt rather than simply inflating it away (as people assumed it would) and closed its foreign exchange market meaning investors could not get their money out at any price. In effect, the 'surprises' were not matters factored into the risk management models used by the fund.

The bankers of New York, encouraged by the New York Fed, in fairly short order organised a bailout in the belief that the failure of LTCM would wreak havoc in the financial system. Within a fairly short time the recapitalised entity was making a profit and repaying capital injected during the crisis. Presumably, the banks who bailed out LTCM made a handsome profit. This writer knows a fund manager specialising in Russian debt who was hit hard at the same time but whose parent bank enabled him to ride out the storm, probably due to the understanding that a fire-sale of the assets made no sense. After due consideration the fund manager was allowed to resign and take the business with him for a tiny consideration. Like the bankers of New York, this fund manager became rich beyond most dreams of avarice when Russian assets recovered their buoyancy. He is now a living embodiment of the theorem that it is an ill wind that fails to produce winners as well as losers.[6]

The Shanghai stock market bubble

The formation of the International Settlement (foreign concession areas) in Shanghai was a result of the Treaty of Nanking of 1842 (which ended the First Opium War). While the Chinese people can rightly feel aggrieved at the behaviour of European capitalists at this time, one compensation was the development of foreign trade in China and of the foreign communities in Shanghai, Macau, Hong Kong and other western enclaves. The market for securities trading in Shanghai began in the late 1860s. The first shares list appeared in June 1866 and by then Shanghai's International Settlement had developed the conditions conducive to the emergence of a share market: several banks, a legal framework for joint-stock companies and interest in diversification among the established trading houses (although the trading houses themselves remained partnerships).

In 1891 during the global boom in mining shares, foreign businessmen founded the Shanghai Sharebrokers' Association headquartered in Shanghai as China's first stock exchange. In 1904 the Association applied for registration in Hong Kong under the provision of the Companies ordinance and was renamed as the 'Shanghai Stock Exchange'. The supply of securities came primarily from local companies

Various commercial developments were overshadowed by industrial shares after the Treaty of Shimonoseki of 1895, which permitted Japan, and by extension other nations which had treaties with China, to establish factories in Shanghai and other treaty ports. Rubber plantations became the staple of stock trading from the second decade of the 20th century.

By the 1930s, Shanghai had emerged as the financial centre of the Far East, where both Chinese and foreign investors could trade stocks, debentures, government bonds, and futures. The operation of the Shanghai Stock Exchange came to an abrupt halt after Japanese troops occupied the Shanghai International Settlement on December 8, 1941. In 1946, Shanghai Stock Exchange resumed its operations before closing again 3 years later in 1949, after the Communist revolution.

After the Cultural Revolution and Deng Xiaoping's rise to power, China was re-opened to the outside world. During the 1980s, China's securities market evolved in tandem with the country's economic reforms and the development of China's socialist market economy. On 26 November 1990, the Shanghai Stock Exchange was re-established and operations began a few weeks later on 19 December. Trade was quiet enough at first, and was negatively impacted by the Asian financial crisis and the SARS epidemic.

Inevitably, however, a 'stock market frenzy' arose as speculative traders rushed into the market, making the Shanghai stock exchange temporarily the world's second largest in terms of turnover. The Shanghai Composite index reached an all-time high of 6,124 points on October 16, 2007, representing a sixfold rise from the low point in April 2005. The benchmark index ended 2008 down a record 70% mainly due to the impact of the Global Financial Crisis. The 'sixbagger' rise in the Shanghai index during the boom was several times the equivalent rise in the comparable US index. Those global fund managers who found a way to invest in the Shanghai index in 2005 and take profits in 2007 (this writer did not) will dine out on the story for many years.

This boom and bust might be thought of as a hearty 'welcome to the capitalist world' for China except for the fact that the Hong Kong stock exchange has for decades been one of the world's most volatile. As someone once said, the Hong Kong market is a serious rival to betting on the horses. Still, great volatility implies great opportunity as well as great risk. The Shanghai sharemarket is possibly the wildest legal and organised market in the world today, certainly no place for the faint-hearted.

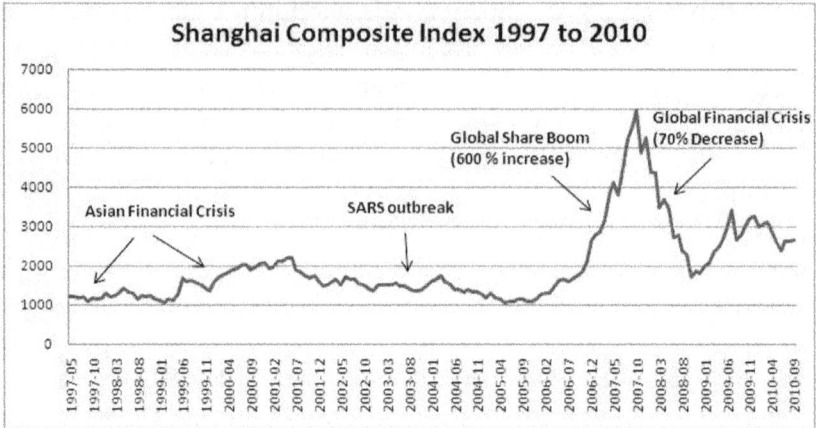

Western Witchcraft: the 'new economy' (dotcom) boom

It is a short jump from 'new territories', or 'reclaimed territories' (in the case of Russian and Chinese markets) to 'new inventions'. Our chapter on 'The Age of Innovation' showed the great energy unleashed by the invention of the railway, the steam ship, the great ocean-spanning cables, new chemicals, new methods of production and new methods of energy production all utilised in developing new territories.

In the late twentieth century came a new method of communication, the Internet, that has already revolutionised many aspects of modern life. It also sparked a market boom with the unique characteristic that potential earnings became all but irrelevant in the definition of value. The Internet, or World Wide Web (hence the www at the front of most Internet addresses) are different concepts for specialists but blur into one for simple users. It has introduced new ways of communicating, provided ready access to information (not all of the same reliability) and new ways to buy or sell just about everything. In writing this book, my personal computer linked to the world wide web was invaluable – filling gaps in my knowledge, finding who were the authors I should read, where books could be purchased quickly and efficiently and actually getting my hands on the books themselves.

Some general material is available here[7], but much, much more is there for the taking if you simply type 'world wide web history' into your favourite search engine. The following material, lightly edited, is presented for those who like their information in a more conventional format, or who still enjoy reading material on paper. My publisher plans to provide an electronic version of this book in due course, but the first edition is for old-fashioned types, which group includes this author. (The links in the web version are suppressed here, but the relevant web addresses are given in the 'Bibliography' section and the links will be available in the e-version.)

1999-2001: 'Dot-com' boom and bust

Low interest rates in 1998–99 encouraged new companies and helped establish a general air of optimism. Although a number of new entrepreneurs had realistic plans and administrative ability, most of them lacked these characteristics but were able to sell their ideas to investors because of the novelty of the dot-com concept. The recent movie, *The Social Network*, provides an interesting partly fictional account the rise of Mr Zukerberg's *Facebook*. Look for the character driven out by rapid growth and the arrival of hardened start-up warriors; the wellsprings of creativity; and the adaptation and survival of the Zukerberg character. In my experience, these are proto-typical features of the start-up business.

The dot-com boom is similar to a number of other technology-inspired booms of the past including railroads in the 1840s, automobiles in the early 20th century, radio in the 1920s, television in the 1940s, transistor electronics in the 1950s, computer time-sharing in the 1960s, and home computers and biotechnology in the early 1980s. The NASDAQ composite index went from 500 (to pick a round number) in 1991 to more than 4500, a ninebagger.

Individual stocks were far more spectacular. The average that comprises 'the index' includes the dogs (or 'woofers' in the argot) that disappear without trace as well as the success stories. I venture to suggest that Amazon, Apple, Google, eBay and the social networking sites have changed the world just as much as those earlier successful inventions. They have also delivered wonderful returns to people

smart enough to invest in their shares

Apple listed in 1984 at a price just over $USD 22 ($3 after adjusting for stock splits). It reached a peak of $32.58 in early 2000 and has

NASDAQ Composite Index 1990 to 2005

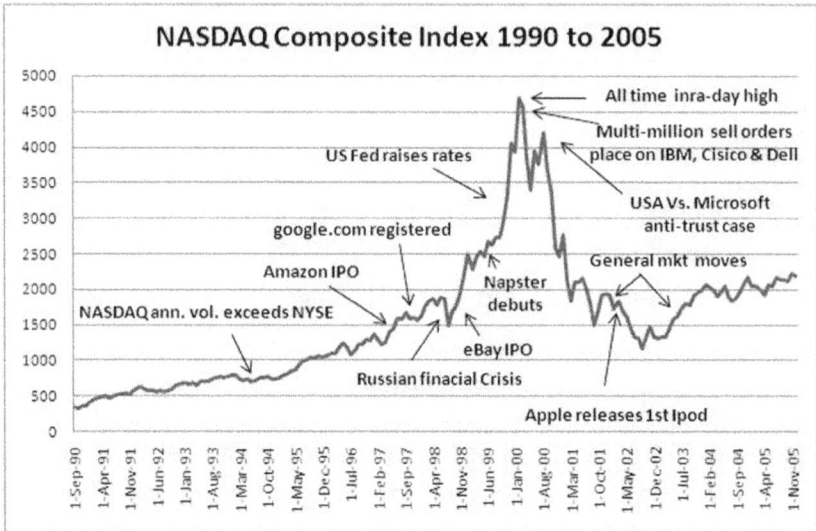

since traded up to an all-time high of $325 in December 2010. This is indeed a multibagger, around 100 times if the data is calculated correctly.

Microsoft listed in 1986 and hit a peak of $USD 47 in late December 1999. After a big correction, the stock has since range traded between $15 and $35 (these numbers are all adjusted for stock splits).

Google listed in 2004 at just over $USD 100 (in adjusted terms) and reached a peak of almost $742 in November 2007. After falling to just under $260 in November 2008, Google recovered to almost $618 in October 2010.

Amazon listed in 1997 at $USD 18 (equivalent to $1.73 after adjustment) and reached a peak of $106.70 in December 1999, a low of just under $10 in September 2001 and has since recovered to a stunning $183 in December 2010. By any measure this is a 100-bagger and one greatly regrets not having owned any of these now-iconic new economy stocks.

The general new economy bubble burst in 2000, and many dot-com startups went out of business after burning through their seed capital and in some cases further funding and failing to become profitable. But as the previous paragraphs record, the best of these companies survived to thrive mightily in the early 21st century. Many companies which began as online retailers blossomed and became highly profitable. More conventional retailers found online merchandising to be a profitable additional source of revenue. While Amazon has branched into many areas, even conventional booksellers now have substantial online sales activities

After the bursting of the dot-com bubble, telecommunications companies had a great deal of overcapacity as many internet business clients went bust. With ongoing investment in local cell infrastructure, this kept connectivity charges low, and helped to make high-speed internet connectivity more affordable. Sadly, Australia failed to fully to share in this experience.

Online music and movies are almost as popular with the young as the social networking sites. Piracy is a massive problem not yet solved, and the root cause is that those who surf the net believe deeply that content should be free. 'Freedom' does not just mean avoidance of payment. People who live in authoritarian countries have learned how to avoid internet censorship, and people everywhere are learning that even previously secret diplomatic documents may show up via Wikileaks or some similar venture. As already noted, Wendy Boswell is an emerging historian of the World Wide Web and provides some useful history here.

In Australia the effect of this form of freedom was seen to great good effect with the website called 'Crikey! especially when it was still edited by its founder Stephen Mayne. Readers are encouraged to send their inside stories from government, corporations or just 'heard in the pub'. Even the Henry Thornton site, mentioned in the preface, has occasionally had the benefit of serious stories from sources who wish to be anonymous for various reasons. After all, this was a feature of early American democracy when the founding fathers wrote their pamphlets.[8]

While some online entertainment and news outlets failed when their seed capital ran out, others persisted and eventually became economically self-sufficient. Traditional media outlets (newspaper publishers, broadcasters and cablecasters in particular) also found the Web to be a useful and (so far marginal) profitable additional channel for content distribution. The unanswered question is whether people will pay a subscription as well as put up with advertising on their screens. Major organisations like Newscorp are grappling with this question right now.

Charles Schwab was a bricks-and-motor financial services firm that became an online financial services firm.[9] Now there are a host of online broking firms, management systems for share portfolios, or sets of funds and investment newsletters. Will the World Wide Web ever become conscious and begin offering independent investment advice or just answering back? 'Just possibly' seems to be the answer.

The holiday period in Australia in 2010 was the first time that conventional retailers expressed serious concern at the inroads from online commerce. Now they are demanding that overseas organizations such as Amazon be required to add Australia's 10% goods and services tax (GST) to their prices. As consumers, Australians will object strenuously to this initiative, and we shall be able to get goods passed on to friends in America (or elsewhere) and reposted, which will in fact be a cheaper solution as Amazon's freight rates to Australia are rather steep.

Web 2.0

Beginning in 2002, new ideas for sharing and exchanging content ad hoc, such as Weblogs ('blogs') and other innovations, rapidly gained acceptance on the Web. This new model for information exchange, primarily featuring DIY user-edited and generated websites, was called 'Web 2.0'. Some believe it will be followed by the full realization of a Semantic Web.

This writer must confess the high degree to which 'machines talking to people' encourage annoyance if not rage as he tries to navigate through a complex maze of question (by the machine) and answer (by the person), when all that the person needs to do is to talk to another person who knows what he or she is saying and who speaks good English. (Australia's 'customer service' helplines are increasingly staffed by people in distant places whose first language is not English.)

Internet-based user-edited ventures such as Wikipedia and its sister projects proved revolutionary in allowing persons to be providers as well as consumers of content. In 2005, three ex-PayPal employees formed a video viewing website called YouTube. Only a year later, YouTube became the most quickly popularized website in history, and started a new concept of user-submitted content in major events, as in the CNN-YouTube Presidential Debates in the United States.

The popularity of YouTube and similar services, combined with the increasing availability and affordability of high-speed connections, has made video content far more common on all kinds of websites. Many video-content hosting and creation sites provide an easy means for their videos to be embedded on third party websites without payment or permission.

This combination of more user-created or edited content, and easy means of sharing content, such as via RSS widgets and video embedding, has led to many sites with a typical 'Web 2.0' feel. They have articles with embedded video, user-submitted comments below the article, and RSS boxes to the side, listing some of the latest articles from other sites. Press reports in late 2010 suggest that online retailers now are somehow trawling the social network sites to get clues about potential customers' preferences and interests.

Web 2.0 has found a place in the global English lexicon. On June 10th, 2009 the *Global Language Monitor* declared it to be the one-millionth English word.'[10]

Asian Magic or Western Witchcraft?

The Asian miracle economies, including Russia, have fully participated in the boom and bust that is characteristic of capitalist experience. The events of this chapter fit into a global picture of overlapping and increasingly frequent major market bubbles followed by busts.

Professional investors and hedge fund managers like the legendary George Soros – the man who broke the British pound - have both the expertise and the resources to follow the action and to make massive profits (or losses) by betting on the booms and the busts.

Whether this is a good thing, a bad thing or just part of the background static is for elected leaders eventually to decide. From a purely economic point of view, we should perhaps recall JM Keynes' comments about the risk of enterprise becoming the 'bubble on a whirlpool of speculation'.[11]

But the last word should go to Edwin Lefevre (AKA Jesse Livermore) whose classic book Reminscences of a Stock Operator should be read by all who decide to get involved in equity markets, whether Western or Eastern. 'Among the hazards of speculation, the happening of the unexpected – I might even say of the unexpectable – ranks high. There are certain chances that the most prudent is justified in taking – chances that he must take if he is to be more than a mercantile mollusk'.[12]

11

How Capitalism Works, and its weaknesses

From Adam Smith's invisible hand to Keynes' and Minsky's economies in crisis to Friedman's monetary theory of inflation and beyond, we provide our layperson's view of how it all works. Complexity is unavoidable with billions of participants, trillions of markets and uncountable numbers of transactions every day but one conclusion is clear – economies are prone to periods of boom and bust.

Adam Smith famously wrote of the role of the invisible hand[1] in coordinating through market forces the myriad decisions of businessmen and women, governments and households – who in their economic activities may be consumers, welfare recipients, workers or entrepreneurs. Like the invisible particles (or strings) of modern physics, the forces connecting them are hidden and will be understood only after careful experiment, observation and theorising. We need to accept that economics is more complicated because individual participants may respond after rational or even irrational thought, unlike (presumably) the particles (or strings) of modern physics.

Put simply, economics is a social science. In reality, many of the assumptions of economic theory are not met except in the broadest sense. So we must advance with some caution.

Any adequate portrayal of the modern economy must recognise demand and supply in a myriad of markets both within countries for non-traded goods and services (a vanishing set) and between countries, which ultimately means globally. Expectations of the players are important but hard to understand or allow for, and confidence of key participants is vital but difficult to influence except negatively.

There are differences in the speed with which markets clear. The global markets for oil and gold are two fast clearing markets. (But oil near US$150 per barrel in 2007 was an odd equilibrium, well above any sensible long-term price.) Labour markets in nations where trade unions are still powerful or provision of information is still imperfect or where people are deeply conservative in holding on to previous norms in pay demands are slow to reach a sustainable equilibrium.

It is the assumption about market clearing that most clearly divides economists interested in macroeconomic theory, modelling or policy. Neo-classical economists deny any market fails to clear but consider assumptions of imperfect information or mistaken expectations to justify lagged adjustment. But there is a school of economics – based on simple facts - that asserts that economies develop irrational financial instability, with runaway asset and credit inflation followed by a reaction that leaves many resources unemployed or underemployed.

Manifestly, when a modern nation, like the USA, can have a third of its workforce unemployed or underemployed, as it was during the Great Depression of the 1930s, and up to a quarter during other great crises of capitalism, there is some imperfection that prevents labour markets from clearing. It was John Maynard Keynes in his *General Theory of Employment, Interest and Money*, written during the Great Depression, who grappled most significantly with this question. He said: 'The outstanding faults of the economic society in which we live are its failure to provide for full employment and its arbitrary and inequitable distribution of wealth and incomes'.[2]

I must confess to being greatly irritated when 'conservatives' shout 'shame' whenever someone mentions Keynes. He was indubitably grappling with the biggest questions, and his efforts have not yet been bettered.

Keynes concluded it was a shortage of 'aggregate demand' that was the prime cause of depression. 'Aggregate demand' is made up of the whole myriad of demand components recognised in simple 'Keynesian' models – demand for consumption goods by domestic households, for investment goods by domestic businesses, for exports by foreigners, demand for resources by governments, demand for labour by governments and businesses (some of which may need to be met from abroad in the open economy case), etc, etc. There are many classes of goods and services in each category, and aggregation (necessary in models) is fraught with conceptual difficulties.

The supply side is just as various. Consumption goods are mostly produced by domestic or overseas businesses; machinery and other capital goods are produced by different firms here and abroad; and labour is supplied by households. The technical conditions of supply are heavily influenced (in the longer term) by 'technical progress', itself influenced by spending (by governments or businesses) on research and development (R&D) and the availability of certain types of specialised humans called entrepreneurs. Easier to produce but equally necessary are supplies of appropriately trained engineers, geologists, accountants, venture capitalists and even economists.

Post-Keynesian economists, notably Hyman Minsky[3], have grappled with the dynamics of boom and bust, including the role of central banks and governments attempting to stabilise what he sees as an inherently unstable economy. My (possibly simplified) understanding of Minsky's work emphasises two key points. Rather than reaching 'equilibrium'(as classical economics assumes) we should think instead of periods of 'tranquility' during which the seeds of the next mania are sown. Gradually either conventional financiers ('banks') loosen their standards for granting credit or investors find new (less reliable) sources of finance. Increased demand for assets is fuelled by increased supplies of credit until, in some cases at least, asset booms turn to bubbles that are followed by quite sudden reversals. Once asset values have plunged, many investors will be left with debts well in excess of the new, depressed, asset values and bankruptcy of both investors and their financiers is likely.

Modern governments try, mostly unsuccessfully, to limit booms and clean up afterwards. Higher interest rates imposed by central banks have typically been regarded as inappropriate because of the uncertainty about whether or not the central bank is dealing with a 'boom' or a 'bubble'. As we saw in Chapter 4, there is a quasi-religious aspect to this debate. From the point of view of a rational central banker, leaning into a situation of sharply rising asset prices makes sense whether or not it is dealing with either a strong boom or a bubble. 'Asset inflation' is a far more neutral description, though less colourful.

'Leaning into' an asset inflation should include issuing warnings, like the US Fed in the late 1920s, raising interest rates under official control and perhaps also imposing higher reserve ratios on lending institutions, or tightening rules limiting lending on margin. The trouble is, when investors are at their most enthusiastic, warnings may be ignored and higher interest rates may fail to stem the enthusiasm. And innovative financiers and even more innovative investors are likely to evade any type of braking device.

Reduced or extra spending by governments (or changes to rates of tax) will help to stabilise goods and labour markets. If there is risk of failure of financiers, at least those regarded as 'too big to fail', governments typically also seek to organise rescue packages involving forgiveness of debts, or injections of capital, ideally in return for equity in the struggling financiers. Bailout whether of investors or bankers creates 'moral hazard' and is likely to lead to greater over-lending and overspending on assets during the next boom.

A nation's tax policies by influencing incentives will influence supply and demand in every market to an extent not well understood. I recall a graph from the talk of an American economist that strongly suggested that it was only when the US capital gains tax was reduced to 20% that the US venture capital industry really took off.

We all know that correlation does not imply causation, but there is plenty of anecdotal evidence that reducing the top rate of income tax well below 50% will encourage the supply of effort by certain highly skilled humans. The logic behind this view is attributed to Arthur Laffer who observed during a restaurant meal that when the tax rate is above 50% it will make sense to put more effort into evading or avoiding tax than into earning more money. Perhaps the chief impact is on such people's country of residence, because the most productive people are highly mobile internationally and likely to resent paying relatively large shares of their incomes to feed those they see as unproductive public officials or welfare recipients.

Overshadowing all of this is the fact that the state of confidence plays an enormous role in modern economies – the influence that Keynes called 'animal spirits' and which seems also to be a key part of Minsky's work. Even when I was a student of economics almost 50 years ago at Melbourne University, our teachers recognised that 'expansionary' policy actions that reduced the confidence of households and business would tend to be self-defeating.

Writing as he did at a time of great depression, Keynes did no more than provide a speculative chapter on inflation. His comments were entirely sensible, focussing on the effect of fully employed resources on the rate of inflation. His analysis of inflation was in the great Humean tradition that there are '100 canals' for adjustment that we do not understand. But one fact stands out – that as an economy approaches full employment it will tend to generate inflation rather than additional output.

Milton Friedman popularised a very simple one good, one asset (money) model of a closed economy. This can be summarised in the famous 'quantity theory' equation relating the supply of money, its 'velocity of circulation' (how often each unit of money is turned over), the price of the single good and its quantity. This equation is best understood as a statement of long-term equilibrium. Allowing for variations in velocity of circulation and in the production of the single good during the adjustment process, the statements in the preceding paragraph hold in the long run when velocity and production have returned to their assumed steady state levels (or rates of growth).[4]

The philosopher David Hume in his only essay on economics wrote of the adjustment process in a way I found entirely convincing. I wrote in 1976: 'Hume stressed the tendency for the balance of payments to equalise "somehow" the supply of money with the demand for money. Hume was agnostic about the possibility of understanding in detail the "hundred canals" whereby excess money flowed out of small open economies but was not agnostic that this would occur. An analogy can be drawn with the proposition that, in a Friedmanite closed economy, doubling the money stock will, eventually and approximately, double the price level'.[5]

In the twentieth century, giant econometric models were built capturing the allegedly stable relationships between the four variables in the quantity theory equation, often using many other variables believed (with some statistical justification) to be influenced by and influencing in turn the four fundamental variables. This was the attempt to identify Hume's "hundred canals" and must at best be described as less than fully convincing, though econometric models have been used with some success in predicting future economic developments and analysing potential policy changes.

Of course it has been recognised that the price and quantity of a single good are not meant to represent single things but rather are weighted average of many prices and their associated products and services. So long as special factors do not impact on individual prices or products, the one-good, one-asset model may be used in 'first approximation' mode. Economic dynamics can be introduced as ad hoc lags or with the assumption that money is a 'buffer stock'. The buffer stock formulation was the contribution of two Canadian graduate students in the late 1950s.[6]

The analysis of open economies took time to sort out, and until this occurred there was more heat than light. As an undergraduate I studied Australia's 'monetary history', inspired by the monumental work of Friedman and Schwartz. I worked out that for the small open economy that was Australia, money was 'demand determined' and the price level was determined by global prices – fumbling my way toward what became the standard case of an open economy with fixed exchange rate.

In the 1970s, this author and a colleague, Henryk Kierzkowski, applied the Archibald and Lipsey analysis to the standard model of trade with two goods – one traded and the other non-traded – and money as a single asset. With a fixed exchange rate, excess money first created a current account deficit and gave a temporary stimulus to economic activity. Eventually, however, the current account deficit eliminated the excess money or if, during the adjustment process the currency was devalued, the economy could end up with a higher price level in proportion to the devaluation.[7]

In this (still highly simplified) model, consumption is defined as equal to income minus a proportion of the gap between the demand for money and real money balances. This gap we called called 'monetary disequilibrium' and in dynamic models whose parameters were estimated with British and Australian data this construct helped explain adjustment of consumption and domestic prices – the latter effect only becoming relevant in the flexible exchange rate regime after the final abandonment of the gold standard. Again, in this case, the equilibrium outcomes did not stretch the basic approach of the one good one asset model, or rather its open economy, fixed exchange rate version, though it did initially generate a lot more heat than light as the debate developed in academic and central banking circles.

This author has tried to find simple ways to introduce a non-monetary asset into this model so as to capture the essential ideas of Minsky but, as the work of Minsky's followers shows, the mathematics quickly become very complicated. The essential role of asset and credit booms and busts in the modern economy shows the importance of pursuing this line of inquiry.

In the late 1990s and early 2000s, a major change to the structure of global capitalism began to be important. The emerging economic superstates of China and India began to influence the western nations by their provision of cheap goods. This requires an obvious application of a two-good, one asset (money) model. In the world of 'dominant China', expanding the global money supply might not raise the prices of manufactured goods charged by China at all, or the relevant adjustment might take many years. With manufactured prices fixed, presumably the prices of other goods would be the main item to adjust, meaning goods not imported from China. In countries other than China, non-traded goods would experience inflation until a new equilibrium was established.

If we introduce a second asset, call it 'bonds', or 'shares', or 'non-monetary capital', its price will also rise in a world where the manufacturing goods price is fixed and money expands. Now we have the possibility of non-monetary asset inflation. In a world of loose monetary policy there will be both asset and non-traded product inflation. Following Minsky, it is necessary to recognise that periods of 'tranquility' will be followed by periods of financier created money, prolonging asset booms and in some cases creating asset bubbles that are followed either by government bailout or recession leading in some cases to depression.

In the real world there are many countries, almost all producing their own money, many, many products and assets other than money for each country, and there are degrees of flexibility between the currencies of each nation. If the money supply of the dominant economy (still that of the USA) whose money serves as a global currency is expanded this will make the prices of non-money assets and non-traded good rise. Ultimately, of course, China's manufacturing prices need to rise also, or China's currency has to rise, but at a time of great structural development of China this development may take years if not decades.

Whether, with manufacturing prices fixed, non-traded goods inflation or non-money asset inflation rises more in response to increasing US money is an empirical matter. Suppose, however, that the USA suffers a domestic recession so that non-traded goods inflation is low or zero. Then rising money supply may only increase non-money asset prices.

When analysts write of 'global imbalances' they are usually writing about an incomplete adjustment in which one country or group of countries have an external deficit (or a falling exchange rate), and another country has an external surplus (or a rising exchange rate) with incomplete price adjustment. The great modern example has the USA and other developed economies in deficit and China and similar nations in surplus.

If, to take a different case, goods inflation is slow to adjust to monetary contraction, the same approach predicts asset deflation. When the British Chancellor of the Exchequer, Winston Churchill, returned the UK to the gold standard at the 1925 overvalued pre-World-War-I value, Britain became an entrenched deficit nation with domestic prices (including wage costs) too high to allow full employment. Asset prices, goods prices and wages all fell while unemployment rose.

My point is that, if prices of a great many goods and services are held down by structural change or by effects of recession or depression, asset inflation will take the place of product inflation in response to expansion of money. This is part of the story of the global economy in the two thousands. Since China did not allow its exchange rate to float upwards, eventually it began to suffer goods inflation and global asset inflation lost some of its strength, and became for a time severe asset deflation. Then the US Fed stepped in and restored monetary expansion.

Explanations based on the occurrence of inflation when an economy was 'approaching full employment' was a model with some persistence, a name – the 'Phillips curve' – and a degree of empirical support from statistical analysis. In the troubled 1970s, however, inflation rocketed up in parallel with unemployment, in contrast with the standard approach that predicted that rising unemployment would end inflation.

Two explanations were offered by economists for the 'stagflation' of the 1970s. The first was that the oil price shock directly impacted on consumers' and business budgets and reduced aggregate demand – hence rising unemployment with rising inflation. The other was that consumers and businesses came to expect inflation and the generally expected rate of inflation got built into a whole range of prices and wages. In this approach the (poorly understood but powerful) direct costs of inflation stunted output and thus employment. Both explanations probably reflected some aspects of reality, but I am aware of no fully convincing attempts to differentiate between the theories.

Milton Friedman famously said 'Inflation is always and everywhere a monetary phenomenon'. He also championed the notion of a 'natural' (equilibrium) level of unemployment, equivalent to the assumption of fixed levels of product (or constant growth of product) in equilibrium. As I have argued, Friedman's view includes a simple long-term relationship between the amount of money in an economy and the price level, or between money growth and the rate of inflation. Strictly speaking, this is a requirement for equilibrium (or, 'tranquility') in a range of economic models, with a high degree of empirical verification.

'Money' is defined in different ways at different times – Cowrie shells in certain Pacific Island communities, gold coins in ancient Rome and in many nations in the nineteenth century, bank notes and bank deposits (or electronic marks in computer files) in the modern world. For most of history, 'money' was defined as some rare and valuable commodity – hence the 'gold standard'. When the gold standard proved too confining purchasing power was guaranteed by powerful central banks or governments – a twentieth century approach that has allowed hyperinflation in some nations, endemic but moderate inflation in other nations and, in recent decades with goods and services inflations contained by new economy developments, massive asset inflation.

Refinements of the simple 'monetary' analysis of the gold standard are needed to cope with John Law's invention – credit money created by banks. In the days of the gold standard a surplus nation gained gold and a deficit country lost gold and central banks reduced or raised interest rates to hasten adjustment in both countries. As we saw in Chapter 6, in the nineteenth century, the Bank of England following the rules of the gold standard went with an economy of regular fluctuations but no destabilising, long-drawn out booms and busts. A country that ran out of gold was unable to pay for imports, which resulted in high interest rates and powerful downward adjustment of living standards. (Within a gold standard nation, individual banks would run out of money, and would reduce loans and raise their lending rates well before they ran out of gold, or they would go broke).

The gold standard was finally abandoned by the Nixon government in the United States in 1971. This was regarded as allowing easier adjustment than the tighter domestic policies (to reduce inflation) that would have been required if the gold standard were to be maintained. Hard money economists saw this as abandoning a useful 'anchor' for inflation, and encouraging widespread resort to inflationary finance. The results, analysed in Chapter 9, showed that this was no fanciful theory.

In strict logic, of course, rigidly controlled printing of paper money might be a better anchor than gold, whose supply was subject to the vagaries of supply and non-monetary uses – for jewellery and dentistry, for example. The trouble is that most governments suffer the same temptation as the French Regent in John Law's time – if printing paper money overcomes shortages of gold and encourages trade, printing even more must be better, right? Wrong, of course, printing too much money produces inflation. Inflation is legalised theft and has many insidious negative effects on business and households.[8]

Banks are like miniature countries under the gold standard. Prudence requires them to keep sufficient reserves – gold in times past, paper money or access to a borrowing facility in modern times. Kindleberger's classic book on *Manias, Panics and Crashes* discusses the financial crises of several centuries.[9] Like Minsky, Kindleberger emphasises a tendency in periods of optimism for credit to expand to meet the demands of trade, especially trade in assets. When optimism turns to

So how can people prevent governments from robbing them by inflation? People must insist that limits be put on growth of the money supply. There have been unsuccessful attempts to impose a relevant constitutional amendment in the USA. The latest attempt involves giving independent central banks a mandate to contain inflation. This has worked for some nations, including Australia, when buttressed by downward 'new economy' pressure on goods and services inflation. The US Fed has, however, chosen to provide additional stimulus twice in the past decade – once under Chairman Greenspan when official rediscount rates fell almost to zero in the wake of the crash of the internet boom and again under Chairman Bernanke during the Global Financial Crisis.

euphoria, credit can become very flexible indeed, even including the invention of new forms of credit such a bills of exchange in the nineteenth century, borrowing from the central bank by commercial banks to fund share purchases in the 1920s or 'subprime loans' in the early 2000s.

The vast global asset inflation of the late twentieth century went with a great expansion of bank credit as ratios of bank loans (credit) to reserves were progressively eased, usually in the name of 'financial deregulation'. Now there are reforms proposed that require central banks and financial sector regulators to 'lean into the wind' of euphoria. This requires central banks to raise interest rates in a boom and 'prudential regulators' to increase reserve ratios and implement other forms of what the economist James Tobin called 'sand in the gears of finance' to destroy or moderate an asset bubble. Whether this approach will work is uncertain. What seems more certain is that central banks and 'prudential regulators' like the US Federal Reserve Board, The Bank of England, Australia's Reserve Bank and Australia's Prudential Regulatory Agency have in future booms to do their best to reduce euphoria and to be seen to be doing their best.

It is a principle of modern management that organisations, like individuals who wish to keep their jobs, must be seen to be doing their best, even if what is believed to be for the best varies over the decades. In his book about the great asset bubble of the 1920s, discussed in Chapter 8, J.K. Galbraith makes the point that the US Fed did not want to be blamed for stopping the boom. 'Action to break up a boom must always be weighed against the chance that it will cause unemployment at a politically inopportune moment'. And 'the immediate death not only has the disadvantage of being immediate but of identifying the executioner'.[10]

Clearly we are in a period of renewed policy activism. Banks will be more cautious for a decade or two, and regulators more diligent. Governments will be making changes to the rules governing financial market participants. But the lesson of history is that there will be future periods of asset boom fuelled by euphoric investors and imprudent financiers. This has implications for individuals or families that wish to build wealth and protect it, as we shall discuss in the following chapter.

In considering asset markets, money, whether gold or paper or electronic marks in computers, is clearly needed in a modern economy and society. It serves as a store of value, a buffer for some of life's contingencies and allows great economic efficiencies. Niall Ferguson's 2008 book *The Ascent of Money* contains an afterword on 'The descent of money'. Ferguson makes the case that economies that combine all the financial and institutional innovations, including banks, bond markets, stock markets, insurance and property owning democracies have performed better than those with none of these or an incomplete set.[11]

Yet the road of a fully monetised economy is not a smooth one. Instead there are frequent roller coaster rides of 'ups and downs, bubbles and busts, manias and panics, shocks and crashes'.[12] A good economic history, such as Kindleberger's epic, reads like a description of a day at a modern theme park, to continue the analogy, with many exciting rides on offer, some too scary for anyone but adolescent males. And gun traders in modern investment banks or hedge funds look and act like adolescent males in most aspects of their lives, or so it often seems to any reasonably mature observer.

Despite systematic attempts to build and protect wealth, the irregular but frequent 'ups and downs' of economic activity and markets mean one's financial life is full of uncertainty in a deep sense that distinguishes it from risk. Accurate prediction is literally impossible, as any account of the effect of the wars of the capitalist era makes abundantly clear. Yet there are examples where clear headed and ruthless financiers profited by financing both sides of major wars, and there is Lord Rothschild's reputed dictum that 'the time to buy is when the blood is running in the streets'.

There are also plenty of examples of people who profit from playing the markets is a similarly ruthless and dispassionate manner. One general belief of equity investors is that equity markets tend to predict economic fluctuations – with share price corrections predicting more recessions than ever eventuate. Bond dealers know from long experience that inflation, or fear of inflation, will raise interest rates and reduce the values of bond portfolios. Currency traders know that inflation in one country if not halted will lead to severe falls in that country's exchange rate, but if that country's central bank is 'responsible' inflation will normally lead to higher interest rates in that country and a stronger currency. Thus people who are able correctly to analyse the course of economic fluctuations may be able to make money from investing in the dazzling modern arrays of financial instruments.

A warning is appropriate at this point, as some of the best economists, as judged by common consent or the award of Nobel Prizes, were able to lose great fortunes by badly misreading choppy markets. Keynes lost a great fortune and then recovered a great fortune, reportedly using borrowed money to get started again. Many investors lost a lot of money in 1987 by failing to predict the crash, while others protected their 'long equity' position early and only just hung on until the crash occurred. This writer's experience includes falling for an old trick of assuming that Australia's central bank would do what analysis said it *ought* to do.

Economists are quite good at predicting long-run outcomes but especially bad at correctly predicting the timing of events, especially it seems the timing of events in financial markets. The Nobel Prize winning economists who created the Long Term Credit Management (LTCM) hedge fund made fortunes for a time then lost the lot when financial conditions appeared that were apparently impossible for their models to predict. This was partly because these bright but naive men used a short run of history in developing their models, the sort of silly mistake that this book is dedicated to discouraging.

Those of us who lived through the Global Financial Crisis of 2007-08, and in particular the global financial freeze of 2008 have been privileged to have been involved in one of the great crises of capitalism. Broadly 'Keynesian' policies of great fiscal expansion and zero official rates of interest were implemented with enthusiasm. Whether these policies will succeed in limiting the damage is uncertain at the time of writing this book. There are plausible concerns about the possibility of sovereign debt defaults, further bank failures, a 'lost decade' like that in Japan in the 1990s (extending well into the 2000s) and extreme market volatility doing great damage to the financial wealth of a generation.

The father of fractal geometry, Benoit Mandelbrot, in 2004 wrote with Richard Hudson a book called *The (mis)Behaviour of Markets*.[13] Mandelbrot points out that asset markets do not move in classically random patterns (assumed in much of the economics and finance literature) but rather in 'great vaulting leaps' (to use Galbraith's description). Mandelbrot agrees with those he calls 'orthodox economists' that stock prices are 'probably' not usefully predictable. He argues that his approach can protect wealth but not enhance it.

Exciting and promising though this work is, I must beg to differ. Movements in great vaulting leaps lead stock prices closer to or more often away from sustainable levels. As others have shown, asset prices often overshoot equilibrium levels. Provided an investor is highly disciplined on decisions to buy or sell, there is wealth to be created by active management of asset portfolios.

This is the implied position of most economic historians. History strongly supports the proposition that major financial crises are followed by major fiscal crises says Niall Ferguson in a 2009 article 'An Empire at Risk'.[14] 'On average,' write Carmen Reinhart and Kenneth Rogoff in their book, *This Time Is Different*, 'government debt rises by 86 percent during the three years following a banking crisis'.[15] Financial crises create debt explosions, usually producing either a debt default (when the debt is in a foreign currency), or a bout of high inflation. The history of all the great European empires is replete with such episodes. Indeed, concludes Ferguson, serial default and high inflation have tended to be the surest symptom of imperial decline.

The U.S. is unlikely to default on its debt, meaning the choice it is facing is serious fiscal consolidation or the Fed printing money – buying newly minted Treasury bonds in exchange for even more newly minted greenbacks – followed by the familiar story of rising inflation and declining real-debt burdens. It's a scenario many investors around the world fear. That is why they have been selling dollars and buying gold and other commodities. More recently, global bond rates have been rising, more evidence of inflationary expectations.

Inflation seems to some people – including members of the Federal Reserve Board – a low probability now, with U.S. unemployment close to 10 percent, weak labour unions, huge quantities of unused capacity in global manufacturing and people's expectations of inflation not too unstable, so far as can be judged from survey data. But inflation is often seen as the least costly way to escape from excessive debt, so this possibility seems likely to me.

Another possibility is a rise in the 'real' (inflation adjusted) interest rate, one definition of which is an actual interest rate minus inflation. This can happen in one of three ways: the nominal interest rate rises and inflation stays the same; the nominal rate stays the same and inflation falls; or – the worst case – the nominal interest rate rises and inflation falls.

There are a number of past cases (e.g., France in the 1930s, Japan recently) when nominal rates have risen even at a time of deflation. Foreign investors might ask for a higher nominal return on U.S. Treasuries to compensate them for the weakening dollar. And inflation might keep falling, to the surprise of most forecasters.

Whether rising real interest rates is worse than a burst of inflation depends on the precise circumstances. For a heavily indebted government and an even more heavily indebted public, rising real interest rates mean an increasingly heavy debt-service burden. The relatively short duration (maturity) of most of America's current debts mean that large debts have to be refinanced each year. That means any rise in interest rates would quickly hurt government, business and household budgets.

Even without rising real interest rates, large deficits mean rising debt service payments. There is also in the 'developed' capitalist nations immense pressure to spend more on health and education, and to meet unfunded public service pension payments. Like debt service payments these payments are virtually certain to keep rising in the USA, short of some Thatcherite revolution. To avoid default, it is typically spending on defence that has to be cut, as already assumed in the USA's forward budget estimates.

'This is how empires decline' says Ferguson. It begins with a debt explosion. It ends with an inexorable reduction in the resources available for the armed forces. US voters presumably realise this and the US leaders have soon to produce a credible plan to restore the federal budget to balance over the next five to 10 years. If it does not there is a real danger that a debt crisis will seriously weaken American power.

There are many precedents, as Ferguson points out. Habsburg Spain defaulted on all or part of its debt 14 times between 1557 and 1696 and also succumbed to inflation due to a surfeit of New World treasure. Prerevolutionary France was spending 62 percent of royal revenue on debt service by 1788. The Ottoman Empire saw interest payments and amortization rise from 15 percent of the budget in 1860 to 50 percent in 1875. By the interwar years, interest payments were consuming 44 percent of the British budget, making it intensely difficult to re-arm in the face of the new German threat. Following World War II the UK had lost most of its overseas assets and its time as a great power was over. This is what Ferguson calls 'the fatal arithmetic of imperial decline'.[16]

Yet even if outcomes damaging to many people come to pass there will be some people who are brave enough, or lucky enough to create great wealth for themselves and their families. It has sometimes been said that the economic system is like a biological system or even a geological system. Companies and individuals and families rise and fall, there are innovations (like mutations) which bring great success and some changes (or failure to change) that lead to the death of whole species. Evolution in economics is partly directed by entrepreneurs, governments and officials, but these entities suffer similar uncertainties that mean most decisions have at best a moderate probability of achieving the intended effect.

It might be thought that mankind has learned the lessons of the great wars and great depression and developed the tools and disciplines necessary to avoid both wars and unsustainable booms and busts, but we are entitled to be skeptical. Indeed, great skepticism is probably an essential survival trait.

We know economies exhibit fluctuations, including booms and busts, but we are better at explaining the fluctuations after the event than we are at predicting outcomes. We are aware that the modern world has many global linkages and also many frictions, bringing great benefits and great threats. Adam Smith's invisible hand guides and coordinates the global economy in all its glorious complexity and uncertainty but it is its very invisibility that makes economic prediction and prescription an imperfect art.

The twentieth century included the two worst wars and the greatest global depression so far experienced. After a period of strong growth with low inflation the world experienced damaging goods and services inflation in the 1970s extending in some nations to the 1980s. Again there was a period of lower volatility, known as the 'Great moderation'. The 1990s and 2000s have been a time of asset inflation followed by deflation. If this is evidence of a trend to greater economic and geopolitical instability we have cause for great concern, as it is difficult to imagine a *more* tumultuous century that did not put the capitalist philosophy at great risk.

The experience covered in this book, and the more detailed studies available elsewhere, strongly suggests that wars and unsustainable financial booms followed by collapse are part of the human condition. Wars involve such destruction and misery that they can only be regarded as the last resort of any sane leader. We must however be agnostic about whether generally faster communications in a globalised world of necessity leads to greater volatility of economic life, and indeed we cannot be certain that economic and market volatility is on balance good or bad. Smart people will, however, be prepared to minimise financial losses and create new wealth from inevitable, unavoidable volatility.

12

The messages of boom and bust

Boom and bust are inherent features of capitalism. The tendency to episodes of over-confidence, even mania, is present in many people, maybe especially the most creative. The message of history is that occasionally, perhaps under modern conditions more frequently, there is a tendency to episodes of collective optimism or even mania. This can create politicians who embark on great projects, or go to war, or attempt both tasks at the same time. Companies similarly can pursue impossible dreams, and occasionally ordinary people as investors back such companies in what becomes an asset bubble. Sometimes the dream is realised, creating great wealth.

Episodes of collective over-optimism or mania always end in a crisis in which great damage is done to whole economies, and to many individuals and families. There is thus an understandable desire among governments to head off such episodes so as to prevent the costly aftermath. After all, periods of costly correction may coincide with elections, and governments are likely to be judged responsible, even if only in part, and will be punished at the polls.

This is the ideology of modern democratic governments in capitalist nations, but I believe it to be wrong. It is wrong for at least two powerful reasons. The first is that it may not be possible, probably is not possible, to prevent episodes of economic euphoria. Trying to do the impossible is a recipe for failure. Attempts to do the impossible may be heroic but are seldom sensible, and do little for a government's reputation with its voters.

The second reason to question current beliefs is that periods of boom lead to great achievements, and the inevitable crash punishes most of the dishonest and the incompetent players. Stifling the booms will remove or reduce the possibility of great achievements. This will damage the inherent dynamism of capitalism. Clearly, however, society can and should have in place mechanisms to help the more or less innocent bystanders. A civilised nation must not stand by and watch people starving to death, or forced to entertain criminal acts to feed themselves and their families. Welfare is costly, and its presence blunts incentives, so there is a careful balance needed here. Some economists, including this writer, believe incentives have already been blunted too much in modern capitalist societies by high rates of tax and welfare payments.

As alternative forms of economic organisation demonstrate, there is a very real risk of strangling the golden goose that is a dynamic capitalist economy. The Bolshevik revolution in Russia replaced one corrupt system of government with another. Russian communism, with its great promise of 'From each according to his ability, to each according to his needs', failed to make the Russian people prosperous, though it may have united the proletariat in its misery. It was the best part of a century before capitalism made a halting return to Russia, and then in the form of what some have called gangster-capitalism.

China and some other Asian nations also made a great mess of the economy under the more thorough-going forms of collectivism, notably so under the rule of the Great Helmsman, Mao Zedong. The communist ideal has great attractions to some personalities but the very visible hand of the bureaucrat and central planner has consistently failed to deliver the returns of capitalism's invisible hand. Now modern China, with central planning for some matters but a capitalist economy in many others, is perhaps the world's most dynamic economy. Like Singapore and other Asian nations, modern China has shown that authoritarian capitalism works. Whether authoritarian capitalism – considerable freedom in the economic sphere, lack of real freedom in the political sphere – can persist for decades or even centuries is one of the great modern mysteries.

Whether democracy is robust enough to cope with rapidly changing global economic, environmental and geopolitical developments is yet to be proved. There is a view that increasing complexity may create gridlock in democratic nations. But an authoritarian government, like an autocratic corporate leader, is perhaps more likely to produce a wrong answer quickly.

In this chapter we focus on what should and can be done to cope with the general tendency to financial boom and bust, leading in extreme cases to bubbles followed by depression.

Lessons for governments

Current policy is piling an Everest of new government debt on existing mountains of private debt. Ben Bernanke has repeated Alan Greenspan's mistake in taking US cash rates to record lows, and 'quantitative easing' (= printing money) adds massive monetary policy ease. If, as I expect, this leads to massive inflation in due course, this will pose a great challenge to capitalism. Inflation did great damage to the capitalist economies in the Age of Aquarius, as shown in Chapter 9, and the damage will be greater if there is another similar episode.

Building economic activity on mountains of debt is also fraught with risk. Debt needs to be serviced, and government debt has produced many problems in the history of capitalism. Excessive government debt was the root cause of the twin bubbles of 1720, and excessive government debt is always 'cured' by inflation, outright default or a vast squeeze on services, including spending on defence leading to the decline of a debt laden nation's ability to defend itself or protect its other interests. Excessive private debt makes companies fragile and at risk of bankruptcy, and puts individuals and families at risk of needing to embrace a greatly straitened way of life. Private debt is a tangible sign of people or corporations spending in excess of earnings, and reducing debt reverses this process.

All governments need to devise and implement robust systems of overall financial regulation. 'Robust' encompasses stability policy that insists on financial institutions with capital adequate for conceivable emergencies. Required capital ratios should flex with the economy in predictable ways. Stable and well understood macroeconomics policies are required and should include fiscal arrangements that also provide some degree of 'automatic stabilisation'. Welfare policy should help protect the poorest people from absolute destitution in the inevitable overall economic downturns or in the case of personal financial catastrophe. 'Progressive' tax systems and comprehensive welfare arrangements add up to 'automatic stabilisers', at least as long as a government's credit rating remains good and until incentives are blunted.

A set of rules that appeal to this writer are to have government with only a limited set of tasks, encompassing defence of the realm, maintenance of law and order, underpinning basic systems (by subsidising private charities) to provide healthcare, food and shelter for those who cannot fend for themselves and providing good education for children whose parents cannot do so for them. This means planning for taxes that cover the average cost of government over the course of normal economic fluctuations. If, as seems appropriate to this writer, society opts for a modestly 'progressive' system of taxes, the tax system should impose higher taxes on people with the highest incomes (or wealth if society prefers to tax wealth rather than income). But too much 'progressivity' in income or wealth taxes will damage incentives to work and to save, so care needs to be taken in the choice of the tax scales.

The interrelated issues of debt mountains and inflation require urgent and serious attention by the governments of capitalist nations. The leading nations need also to give serious attention to the global financial framework.

Modern capitalist nations, it seems to me, have gone much too far along a consumerist road. The prevailing ideology of economists is 'maximisation of lifetime consumption', so the consumerist bias has some powerful backing. This capitalist bias is creating vast differences in saving patterns between 'developed' and 'developing' nations, and this is the source of great opportunity for swings in currency values (if exchange rates are flexible) or in ownership of assets in the high saving nations and growth of international debt owed by the low saving nations. Current imbalances among the family of nations are unsustainable and it would be useful to develop a more coherent economic policy framework. To this writer, a modified ideology for developed nations with explicit weight on 'acquisition of knowledge' and away from simple consumerism would be a good start.

One specific change to present general tax arrangements would be for developed nations in particular to place greater weight on consumption taxes and less weight on income or wealth taxes. This would tend to limit consumption in the developed nations, and thus help to harmonise the fiscal imbalances already discussed. It would also provide a tax that would help to even out the ebbs and flows of economic activity, as a semi-automatic increase in consumption taxes in booms and decreases in downturns would provide a more efficient economic moderating mechanism than current income and wealth taxes. I am not seeking a way to iron out fluctuations altogether, because of the benefit of times of economic boom or even euphoria. Rather I am proposing a more effective automatic stabiliser, one that would more strongly test the reality of booms and reduce the severity of busts.

Governments also have a legitimate role in devising and maintaining sensible rules about various features of the financial system. The first such feature should be doing whatever can be done to encourage prudent and ethical behaviour by financial institutions and financial salespeople. I do not go so far as simply advocating the old rule of *caveat emptor* – let the buyer beware – thought this approach is tempting to people, like me, of a libertarian inclination. This said, it would be helpful to include courses on the essence of modern finance in school programs, courses that teach people to beware of conmen and that if something looks too good to be true it probably is. Naturally, proven fraud must be punished, and that is a feature of regulatory systems that need constant attention. But as Charles MacKay said in his book already cited in Chapter 5: 'Nobody seemed to imagine that the nation itself was as culpable as the South-Sea company. Nobody blamed the credulity and avarice of the people, - the degrading lust of gain, which had swallowed up every nobler quality of the national character, or the infatuation which had made the multitude run their heads with such frantic eagerness into the net held out for them by scheming projectors'.

Rules should require financial institutions to hold sufficient capital to provide real discouragement to practices that too easily allow, indeed encourage, funding of asset booms. Some form of dynamic capital ratio regime is desirable, with required reserves as a ratio to assets rising as a boom gathers strength. Again, the aim is not to stop an asset boom, but to make sure it has been properly tested and is not being engorged by a diet of easy money.

This writer is happy to stand with Paul Volcker in calling for the return of the Glass-Steagall law in the United States, and equivalent rules elsewhere. Such laws separate financial institutions into 'commercial banks' which are closely regulated may have government-backed deposit insurance and 'investment banks' that are lightly regulated but with no government guarantees. It is also desirable to use anti-monopoly laws to attack the problem of institutions that are seen to be 'too big to fail', thought with global financial institutions this probably requires at least international coordination through one or other of the relevant international financial organisations. Clearly, regular stress-testing of bank balance sheets is highly desirable and one expects this to be done with global outcomes in mind.

It is far harder to anticipate and to provide similar resistance to new forms of finance. But, as we have seen, new forms of finance, including the now infamous securitised sub-prime loans, are part of the landscape of boom and bust. The trick is to find ways of preventing the generals of financial regulation from fighting the last war but one. Listening with respect to outsiders is one technique that might be suggested to senior regulators, perhaps reminding them that it is the grain of sand that produces the pearl. Firing or requiring the resignation of a regulator who has failed is of course applying a classic capitalist technique to encourage the others and should probably be used more often than it has been.

This writer believes that, in a sufficiently serious crisis, it is desirable for large financial institutions that are at risk of failing to be rescued by relevant governments. This is controversial. The standard objection to bailout is that it encourages what economists call 'moral hazard'. If financiers develop foolish management practices leading to failure, but are rescued, they (or their successors) have little incentive to behave more sensibly in future. Extreme free market economists say allowing failed financial enterprises to go broke will remove this moral hazard and make for a more robust, sustainable financial system. The trouble is, if failed financial enterprises are big enough to create a serious, potentially global, depression, avoidance of this will dominate thinking in any real crisis.

President George Bush said while announcing his bailout plan during the Global Financial Crisis: 'I'm a strong believer in free enterprise, so my natural instinct is to oppose government intervention. I believe companies that make bad decisions should be allowed to go out of business. Under normal circumstances, I would have followed this course. But these are not normal circumstances. The market is not functioning properly. There has been a widespread loss of confidence, and major sectors of America's financial system are at risk of shutting down.

'The government's top economic experts warn that, without immediate action by Congress, America could slip into a financial panic and a distressing scenario would unfold'.[1] This could be put more simply. This writer recalls seeing President Bush saying on global television something like 'I didn't want to do this, but they told me there would be a great depression if I didn't'.

The trouble with not providing bailout has been seen many times before. To take just two examples covered in this book, the inability of the Victorian colonial government to bail out the financiers in Melbourne in the 1890s meant many sound banks as well as unsound financial institutions were forced to shut their doors, making the downturn far worse than it might have been. The US government's inability or unwillingness to save the myriad of US banks was also a material factor in making the Great Depression of the 1930s far worse than it might have been, as current US Fed Chief Ben Bernanke's own research shows.

In the current Global Financial Crisis, the risks of declining to bailout a major financier were seen in the case of Lehman Brothers.

This unlovely organisation no doubt deserved to fail, but its failure produced a situation of massive financial gridlock that caused the world of finance to wobble on its axis, and could well have turned a nasty downturn into another Great Depression. There is still risk of such an outcome, focussed on the twin issues of global inflation and sovereign debt default, so we need to be crystal clear that bailout is necessary – with provisos.

Governments bailing out companies 'too big to fail' should take equity in the failed enterprise so that taxpayers have a chance of recovering their investment. The rules should also provide for the dismissal with minimum or no compensation for the most senior executives and board members as soon as replacements are installed. This requires that unequivocal failure – defined as requiring taxpayers' funding – is like proven fraud as a case for dismissal without the usual protections of contract law. These two rules should help to overcome the so-called 'moral hazard' implicit in bailout with no real sanctions.

Governments also have an interest in the design of incentive plans for executives in major financial institutions. How this should be implemented and enforced is worthy of debate, but I am confident that rules are desirable that encourage executives to take a long-term view of the profitability and viability of the financial institutions that they manage. Similar rules may benefit other corporations also but the mooted change is vitally important for the health of a nation's financial system. Indeed, in the cases of major global banks and other financial institutions, it is vital for the health of the global economy.

Principles that are highly desirable include the following: bonuses go into a trust that is not paid out until some time, say five years, after the executive retires; clawback allowed indeed required on some pro rata basis if losses are made, so that executives cannot benefit from taking large risks and being rewarded only for success, with no penalty for failure; bonuses earned in this way might be taxed when received at the normal capital gains rate.

This writer agrees with Keynes that excessive inequality is one of the great threats to capitalism. Hard thought needs to be given to what to do about this. Possibly salaries that are more than some widely agreed substantial multiple of average wages in society might attract a rate of income tax – say 50% – well above the normal highest rate, which I would set at 30%. I do not believe that this would greatly reduce the supply of senior executives. And a steady intellectual diet of Hayek will help officials and people to adjust to the smaller government sector implied by a top income tax rate of 30%.[2]

A far bigger question is whether a different monetary regime is needed. Many writers have concluded that the gold standard worked well during the dynamic nineteenth century. The trouble is that this regime was hostage to the chance of major discoveries of gold even though such discoveries did tend to occur in what might be called a counter-cyclical manner. This matter is discussed in the next section.

A related point deserves equally careful thought. When the Global Financial Crisis of 2007-08 struck, there was a widespread sense of panic, including among the leaders of the world's greatest nations. There was no real alternative to bailing out the major American banks, just as the European community will not be able to avoid bailing out the finances of its weaker members or its banks should these dominoes begin to topple. Changing the rules to minimize the chance of future failure of financial institutions 'too big to fail' is, of course, a necessary and worthwhile task, as is establishing the protocols for such bailouts in future.

The bottom line is that serious policy instability has been added to an inherently fragile global economy. Large discretionary lurches in policy settings confuses households and businesses and disrupts planning by private individuals and institutions. The world needs substantially less policy discretion and more stable, well understood policy rules. Failure to implement such rules-based policy regimes is perhaps the greatest future risk to capitalism.

However, the discretionary use of extreme monetary and fiscal stimulus is a different matter altogether. Two years ago, governments everywhere were urgently devising ways to stimulate their economies. It was a matter of full speed ahead and damn the torpedos. Now those same governments are more or less desperately seeking to devise ways to claw back excessive budget deficits and contain growth of government debt and interest payment on that debt. Could these governments not foresee the swing from concern at possible depression to concern at excessive debt?

As global inflation continues to build, similar questions will confront monetary policy.

Lessons for central banks

The principles inherent in the lessons for government apply here also. Inflation targeting seems to be working as well as any system tried in recent years, and is a prime example of a stable, well understood, rules-based policy. I discuss first changes to the apparently simple approach of inflation targeting. Then, as foreshadowed, I consider the monetary regime more generally.

I observe that 'inflation targeting' is generally defined as 'goods and services inflation targeting'. Mostly the target is a consumer price index in 'underlying' form, after omitting low or high outlying prices. Because monetary policy famously deals with long and variable lags, central banks are inevitably drawn into basing today's monetary policy on the rate of inflation expected in 12 to eighteen month's time. This leads central banks to consider a whole set of economic variables, including growth of output and jobs in relation to what the bank staff believe to be the sustainable rates of growth.

'Inflation targeting' as usually defined omits various forms of asset inflation. The long-serving Chairman of the US Fed, Alan Greenspan, said he did not believe in trying to respond to asset booms or even bubbles, being content to clean up the mess (by cutting official cash rates) after the boom or bubble had burst. Although I have not had the benefit of discussion with insiders on this matter, I gather from reports that Chairman Bernanke has a more eclectic view of this matter, as he should.

In my view, central banks should lean into asset booms in the spirit of providing stern resistance without attempting to crush such booms. Rather there should be some tendency to higher interest rates over and above what is needed to stabilise 'goods and services inflation'. As already noted, there is some logic in a 'Taylor rule' as a guide to the setting of interest rates, and the refinement of adding an asset inflation term is worth considering.

For a small open economy with a flexible exchange rate it will be more prudent to focus on the prices of property and other domestic assets, eg Tulips if in Holland in 1636, property if in Melbourne in the 1880s, and so on. Shares are the quintessential global product – with share prices everywhere heavily influenced by Wall Street. It would be an act of futility for the central bank of small open economies like Australia or Sweden to focus on trying to stop share prices from rising if there was a boom in American share prices. It would be far better to persuade the US Fed to lean into the boom and do everyone a favour.

This logic leads inexorably to some form of global monetary policy. As China becomes more powerful, there is a steadily strengthening case for it to adopt a properly flexible exchange rate if the current monetary policy 'architecture' is retained. When this is achieved, and as China's capital market become more important, there will be a stronger and stronger case for coordination of Chinese and American fiscal and monetary policies. Agreed domestic inflation targets (including asset inflation) for both major economic superpowers would ultimately lead to similar monetary policies and this might also lead share prices to behave more sensibly. But if it were felt by the central banks of China and the USA – meeting as the 'Group of 2' (G2) - that there was danger of a share price bubble developing in either Wall Street in New York or on the Bund in Shanghai, monetary policy in both places could be tightened somewhat more than the amount suggested by each nations' goods and services inflation targeting regime.

But is there a better system than monetary policy based on inflation targeting via the instrument of 'official' cash rates in a myriad of individual countries, which is the current mainstream approach? One should at least consider a modern version of the gold standard. In place of a standard based on gold, one could imagine a commodity standard including pre-set weightings of gold, silver, platinum, copper, aluminium and even uranium. There would be a preset annual growth (say 5%) of the overall commodity bundle produced by an agency such as the International Monetary Fund (IMF). The IMF would be responsible for acquiring the commodity bundle on a more or less continuous basis and feeding it to central banks in proportions based on each nations' real GDP. Whether such a commodity bundle would reside in the IMF's vaults is an important technical matter that I will leave to those better qualified to answer.

This idea is not, of course, original, but rather is closely related to Keynes' *Bancor*. *Bancor* is the name of the supranational currency that John Maynard Keynes proposed in the years 1940-42 and which the United Kingdom suggested for introduction after the Second World War. This 'supranational currency' would, Keynes argued, be used in international trade as a unit of account within a multilateral barter clearing system – the *International Clearing Union* – which would also have to be newly formed. This British proposal for a supranational currency could not prevail against the interests of the United States, which at the Bretton Woods conference established the U.S. dollar as the world's key currency.

Since the outbreak of the Global Financial Crisis in 2007-08 Keynes' proposal is winning adherents: In a speech delivered in March 2009 entitled *Reform the International Monetary System*, Zhou Xiaochuan, the governor of the People's Bank of China called Keynes' BANCOR approach 'farsighted' and proposed the adoption of IMF SDRs as a global reserve currency. He argued that a national currency was unsuitable as a global reserve currency because of the difficulty faced by reserve currency issuers in trying to simultaneously achieve their domestic monetary policy goals and meet other countries' demand for reserve currency.[3] A similar analysis can be found in the Report of the United Nation's 'Experts on reforms of the international monetary and financial system'[4] as well as in a recent International Monetary Fund's 'Reserve Accumulation and International Monetary Stability'.[5]

There are two essential differences between current arrangements and a BANCOR system based on a bundle of commodities or SDRs. Setting cash rates country by country, even by similar Taylor rules in pursuit of a common target for goods and services inflation, de-emphasises 'quantity of money' targets. Setting and implementing a global 'base money' target would de-emphasise interest rate targets. It is not at this time possible to decide which system might prove most robust, but clearly both need to be analysed carefully. Along with rules for containment of bank lending, either a quantity focus or an effective interest rate focus is needed if capitalism is to minimise unhelpful financial system instability.

My more conservative friends will fear a global quantity-based monetary system is a 'socialist plot', the same point they make about plans to control greenhouse gas emissions. While the head of the global central bank would wield considerable power, he would serve only at the pleasure of his political masters, although with a fixed term or terms. He would have a clear mandate to control inflation. The primary target would be goods and services inflation, with asset inflation as an important secondary target to be varied as the world gained experience of the proposed new system. Nations could retain their own currencies if they wished, although sensible leaders would link these currencies to the global currency. Devaluation of national currencies would be possible,

The modern capitalist world is sitting uneasily between two radically different systems of monetary policy. The 'discretion' allowed with flexible Taylor Rule methods of setting interest rates in each nation contributes to the 'imbalances' that so bedevil global economic development. Moving to a global system of base money control, administered by a global monetary authority independent of political government, is the logical alternative to the current system. It may take a very damaging outbreak of inflationary global boom and bust for this idea to be taken seriously.

though serial devaluers would find it increasingly necessary to prepare contracts in a strong currency, which might increasingly be the global currency.[6]

Lessons for investors

Financial instability is unlikely to be eliminated from capitalism and as I have argued this is in any case undesirable. Sizable financial fluctuations came within the ten year 'trade cycle' of the nineteenth century, with large-scale bank failures in some countries, including frontier societies such as Australia and the United States. The first half of the twentieth century saw massive financial instability associated with war and the boom and bust of the roaring twenties and the depressed thirties. There is evidence of more frequent episodes of financial and economic instability following the relatively steady decades of the 1950s and 1960s.

The conclusion is inescapable: no individual or family seeking to build or protect wealth should be a passive investor in the face of the financial instability of the modern capitalist world. Yet one of the mantras of financial institutions who want to manage other people's money is 'time in the market beats market timing'.

Since it provides the clearest example of the whole span of history we have examined, I repeat the graph summarising US share prices in the Roaring Twenties and the Great Depression. Leaving money passively to allow the magic of time and compound interest is a possible strategy, but surely far from the best strategy.

The graph shows the peak & trough pattern typical of episodes of financial boom and bust and also the potential of a more active strategy. Consider the consequences of a 'buy and hold' strategy for US equity investors from 1925 to 1939. Broadly, speaking, the US industrial index started at an index value of 150 in 1925 and ended 15 years later at 150, on the eve of World War II. To be sure, there

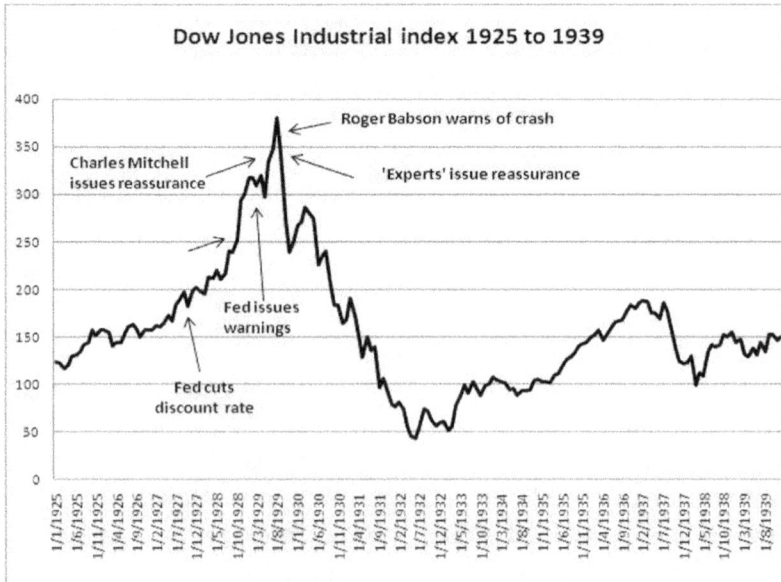

Dow Jones Industrial index 1925 to 1939

were dividends not counted in the data presented here, equivalent to returns on a bank deposit. Given the risks of violent swings in the value of a share portfolio, it might perhaps have been better to have left one's money in a bank, so long as depositors were confident that their bank would not fail. If one doubts this proposition, money under the bed is another possibility, so long as home security is tight and one trusts ones government not to devalue the currency through inflation.

There are risks, of course, in simply getting out of bed in the morning. Suppose one is sufficiently brave to build and hold a share portfolio. Then consider the potential benefit of selling shares somewhere along the rising part of the graph – say at an average of 300 (well short of the peak of 380) – and buying back into the market somewhere on the way down, at an average of 100, say, well short of the absolute low of 42. An active investor might have sold again at around 150 in 1935 and again bought back in somewhere in the subsequent downturn, but the main wealth creation and protection would have taken place between 1925 and 1931.

Of course, the 'time in the market' men will say that an active investor might have brought shares at 300, or even 350 and not sold until forced to do so sometime in late 1931 at 100, but it would have taken considerable misplaced ingenuity to get things so wrong. My point is that any person who is committed to active management of a share portfolio but with the self-discipline only to make significant transactions when share prices are clearly out of kilter with average performance will be able to do far better than a rigid policy of 'buy and hold' or 'time in the market beats market timing'.

Great discipline is needed to wait for the really big movements. A person with such a task can spend time buying and selling assets such as shares in individual companies or, better still, cattle or wheat. This will develop a feel for asset markets and provide practice in coming to judgments in the face of the inevitable uncertainties and surprises delivered by asset markets.

What do I mean by share prices 'clearly out of kilter'? For an index like that in the graph, the obvious benchmark is the long run growth of that index. Over 200 years, the US industrial index used in this graph shows modest annual compound growth. Allowing for this upward tilt in the graph would lead an active investor to sell a bit later and buy back in a bit sooner. The point, however, is to have a disciplined strategy that forces one to sell as the market rises well above the long run average and to buy when markets are well below the long run average.

Sophisticated investors will use more complicated methods than deviation from a long-term average, such as price-earnings ratios, Elliot wave theories and perhaps the phases of the moon or even its alignment with the planets. All such measures have their supporters and complications, and to my way of thinking simplicity is best in such matters. But the main point is to have a firmly rooted discipline for buying or selling, based on deep knowledge of the history of booms and busts. Discipline and deep historical knowledge will provide protection against being caught in the coils of either greed or fear, and help one to avoid panic at all costs.

Even an investor who prefers to buy only specific stocks should be able to benefit from trading the big fluctuations, selling when the stock is becoming expensive and buying when it is cheap, provided of course that he or she concludes that the company whose stock he/she buying is likely to survive. I am old enough to remember making a decision to buy News Corporation stock at $3 per share. Then the only question was 'will News Corporation survive?' An extremely cautious investor, (or a wildly risk-loving investor whose total wealth was in News Corporation stock) might not be prepared to back the survival hypothesis, but that is why investment professionals tend to hold a well diversified portfolio of stocks, or to play an index.

Of course, the oppositive problem may be more difficult. Some of the best examples come from the new economy (dotcom) boom. When to sell Apple, Amazon, Google or Microsoft, or indeed to hang on for decades, is not obvious. 'It is hard to go broke taking a profit', is not a bad rule as is the practice of taking profits gradually in a rising market. It can be observed that this is a good problem to have.

The graph on page 263 provides some perspective on Wall Street's bubble years, which are far from being over. The new economy bubble of the late 1990s and the peak reached in October 2007 were both

The Bubble Years - Dow Jones Index

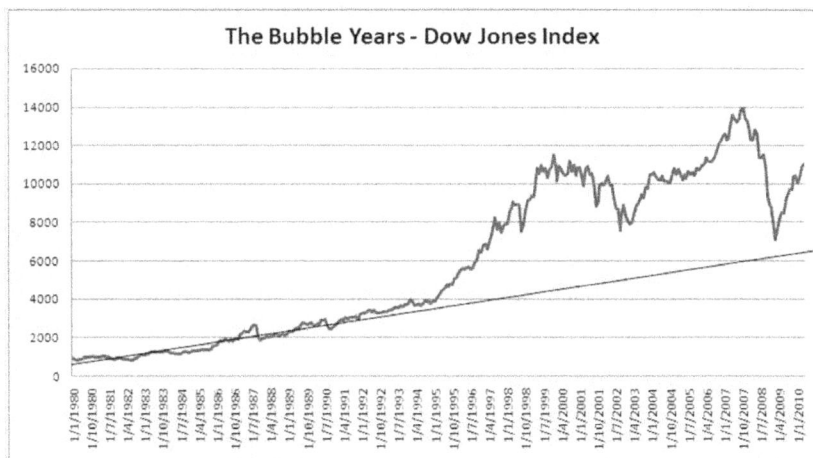

so far above the long-run trend that the mythical Australian known as 'blind Freddie' could have guessed that a correction was inevitable. Indeed, blind Freddie would have more likely been tempted to sell out far too soon rather than hanging about too long.

Once the bank bailouts were completed in September 2008 and fiscal and monetary policy were set easy just about everywhere, the fact that the index in late 2008 was close to its long-run trend line might have tempted blind Freddie to re-enter the market. At the time of writing that re-entry would be looking good.

Of course, gazing at graphs like this is far from all that a canny investor must do. There are many indicators of confidence or its converse. Increasingly too there are published surveys of investors' opinions about the future, although whether such surveys are best used as reinforcing or contrary indicators is a moot point. ('The time to sell is when the lift-drivers are urging one to buy'.) There is no substitute for systematic analysis of as long a period of market action in its historical context as possible.

Assembling the relevant data and historical analysis is no mean task, and requires serious effort and substantial resource input. Any institution or family that cannot make the substantial investment in training and time both studying history and working in front of screens conveying data and news should delegate the task of building and protecting wealth to someone who can do so. Someone completely trustworthy.

Summary: Conclusions and messages

General conclusions
1. Capitalism, whilst imperfect, is the best way to organise economic affairs to maximise human welfare.
2. Crises are an inevitable part of capitalism.
3. Crises provide both danger and opportunity .
4. Crises bring benefits as well as costs, and benefits very likely outweigh costs, except in the case of wars or great depressions.
5. Crises are infrequent, although perhaps becoming more frequent.

Messages for politicians
1. Study the history of capitalism's crises.
2. Do not assume financial boom and bust are necessarily bad.
3. Think carefully before implementing regulations tending to strangle the golden goose that is capitalism.
4. Always prefer market-based solutions to regulatory challenges over political or bureaucratic diktat.
5. Make regulatory systems simple, clear, stable and well-understood.

Messages for financial system regulators, including central banks
1. Inflation is still the best target for central banks.
2. Inflation must be defined broadly to include asset inflation.
3. Monetary policy (and banking regulation) should 'lean into' asset inflation to test if it is based on substance or mere froth and bubble.
4. With increasing globalisation, considerable thought needs to be given to global monetary policy and global financial system regulation.
5. Global monetary policy probably needs to be based on steady growth of a broad-based commodity standard, like Keynes' *Bancor*, rather than a variety of Taylor rules for varying interest rates country by country. This question needs serious analysis.

Messages for investors
1. Get informed; study the history of capitalism's crises.
2. Get serious; a family wishing to build or protect wealth needs dedicated financial expertise and a long view.
3. Be brave; play the markets to maximise your net worth; and that of your family or clients.
4. Be smart; you will not go broke making a profit.
5. Have fun; winners are grinners.

13

Future Crises of Capitalism

In the twenty-first century capitalism will face challenges from rival ideologies, from great natural disasters and the possible but uncertain effects of climate change, whether a side effect of human development or part of the natural rhythm of planet earth. But most predictable are episodes of boom and bust, including future financial crises. Such episodes are a feature of capitalism, and cannot be eradicated without destroying capitalism's vital essence – strangling the golden goose that is capitalism. I suggest ways to suppress the madder episodes of boom to reduce the severity of subsequent busts.

In the absence of some great catastrophe, the future will be like the past, only more so. There will be the same challenges, the same risks and the same opportunities, but the technology will be more effective. Sailing ships and cannons are one way to make war; stealth bombers and nuclear weapons, engineered diseases and robot warriors are far more deadly methods altogether. The success of capitalism has given mankind the capacity to change fundamentally the course of its own history, and in extremis to end the progress of human civilisation. Weapons of mass destruction and climate change are two prime candidates.

Coal fires, thick fogs, horse manure and open drains once made London an unhealthy place in which to live and work. Now London is healthier while the aquifers of Asia are drying up, greenhouse gas emissions and/or 'natural' cycles may be changing the global climate, and economic development is producing vast degradations of environments and loss of biodiversity. If allowed to operate with prices on carbon and other agents of pollution, market forces will stem adverse environmental developments. In many ways, the world's great cities are far more pleasant places to live than in the wilderness and, in any case, free and prosperous people can choose their own mix of both.

Religious ideologies dominated the world of man for aeons. Rationalist science-based capitalism battled religion for centuries and has largely reached an accommodation with religion except for fundamentalists of all varieties. Some other cultures, like modern Confucianism, have adopted the capitalist way of generating wealth, and may be less handicapped by old ideologies. Whether this produces convergence or conflict is one of the great questions of the twenty-first century. It will only be answered by the evolving future.

There are different approaches within notionally capitalist nations. Compare Frenchmen rioting over a two year increase in the age at which they can claim a pension with Americans emigrating to Australia, where demand for labor is great. Compare even America's welfare systems with China's far harsher welfare regime, if it exists at all. Ultimately capitalism is about competition, and the up-and-coming nations usually compete harder than the ancient regimes. The result is convergence, but this takes many decades, even centuries.

The Islamic civilisations kept rational ideas alive during the West's dark ages and provided the base for the emergence of modern science and the market economy in and after the Renaissance. Today there is a struggle between modernity and fundamentalism through the Christian, Islamic and Judaic worlds. The challenge of fundamental Islam will very likely produce more terror attacks on the capitalist heartland, and modern technology has the potential to make some of these attacks truly horrific.

Winston Churchill in his fine book *The Story of the Malakand Field Force*, whose preface was signed off in the Cavalry Barracks, Bangalore, on 30th December 1897, said that, as a general proposition, 'silver makes a better weapon than steel'. This is the basic case for slow and steady progress in defeating Islamic fundamentalism, but the victims of terror attacks are entitled to insist that their leaders strike back with overwhelming force, as they have. In both camps, technologies of defence and retribution are being developed with all possible speed.

At a more micro level, Muslim minorities are producing cultural tensions wherever they settle. The relevant behaviours include the imposition of ridiculous prohibitions on women, young men clumping into aggressive groups causing trouble in the streets or on the beaches and Imams preaching inflammatory sermons in mosques. Serious backlash is possible in this area also, and every nation is entitled to insist that newcomers abide by existing laws and cultural mores. Sadly, Australia is one nation that fails to insist on this requirement.

Likely trends and their implications

As already stated, one certainty is that capitalism will experience future episodes of financial boom and bust, encouraging or suppressing whatever other challenges are faced by capitalist civilisation. Asset prices will again boom, banks and other sources of finance will accommodate the boom and in some cases turn it into a bubble. Boom or bubble, the music has to stop and this will leave investors and companies, governments and central banks, to pick up the pieces.

As Tolstoy said of families, every asset boom is alike; every financial bust is unhappy in its own way. The statistical pattern of asset prices will be the familiar b+b shape seen throughout history, but the causes and consequences are likely to vary according to the regulations of capitalism. This writer fears that the current rules and practices of financial governance will generate instability that will surprise most observers. We shall return to this fundamental matter following a discussion of other trends and some possible surprises.

The rise and urbanisation of China is likely to continue, with China becoming the world's largest economy (in absolute terms) before too long. Whether China can become the world's richest (in per capita terms) any time soon must be doubted as its current growth model depends on massive numbers of poorly paid workers. If current trends persist, China will however eventually become a dominant global superpower. Again we shall see two superpowers, three if India maintains its current progress.

China has long been an inventive civilisation. The Chinese people have demonstrated the art of business for a couple of thousand years and their leaders must be vastly amused at the grossly inept financial management illustrated in the recent past in the West. With the USA, UK and most of Europe deeply in debt, China and India, with Japan and Germany, are doing most of the saving, and are heading down the path to own us all.

Although nothing travels in straight lines forever, whether we all like it or not the western world of finance is going to dance to a different tune. It is not going to be bagpipes in Edinburgh or a fiddle in New York or Boston, or an oompha band at the German Beer Festival. The new lords of finance may prefer an Erhu, or perhaps a Banhu, or a Ruan and a Guan, traditional Chinese instruments, or else symphonies played in Shanghai. The western governments and central banks will have to learn to deal fairly and skilfully with the governments of China, India, Russia, Brazil and other rapidly developing economic powers.

It is possible, even likely, that the American economy will continue to decline over time as ever more jobs and industries are allowed to die because they can be replaced by imports. Faced with a deeply uncomfortable fiscal situation, the USA may revert to its traditional isolationist position, enabling it to improve its budgetary position and strengthen its ability to defend itself, invest in less polluting energy sources and the health of its peoples. The new focus of the American government and the largest global mining companies may be on drilling for oil in Alaska or even winning the race to exploit prospective planets and asteroids as new sources of high value resources.

In such a world, America's allies, including Australia, could no longer rely on America's strategic support. Depending on the attitude of Japan, Korea, Indonesia and China, there may be circumstances with immense consequences for Australia's ability to remain independent without greatly increased focus on defence. Such a focus would require a substantial rethink of aspects of Australian culture, and would come at great cost to our ability to invest in areas such as health, education, infrastructure and social welfare. The cost of remaining independent may include adopting a more selfish, tough, market oriented society and a more ruthless attitude to refugees and other disadvantaged people living elsewhere.

Despite the relative decline of the western nations, the world's population is likely to become older, better educated and, with notable exceptions, more prosperous. These are the trends, which depend on continued free trade and the absence of severe adverse shocks. There will be new pressures on government and private budgets as older people transition from paid work to leisure or unpaid work, fall ill and require expensive, but technically feasible, treatments.

Birth rates will drop and in some countries or regions – especially Japan and Europe – there will be unused and potentially decaying infrastructure. This will provide vast opportunities for people to move to underpopulated countries or regions, but such movement will risk creating or exacerbating serious ethnic and cultural conflicts.

The future world will feature expensive oil, raw materials, food and clean water. There will be increased tension between important cultural and ethnic groups. The internet will become more important, and subject to many more forms of sabotage. Governments will continue to attempt internet censorship despite huge opposition from the masses. There is a risk that giant bureaucracies are built to administer the censorship which will nevertheless constantly be broken by ever younger school children who are too clever for lumbering bureaucrats.

Democracy will come under pressure because of China's economic and military success, because of the massive complexity of so many problems and in particular because so many democratic nations have huge debts which limit the freedom of their governments to act. More and more decisions will be made by corporations, which are inherently undemocratic entities and focussed on profits ahead of customers, workers or the environment. Past revolutions, political or corporate, have been reactions to circumstances people did not accept, and there will be surprises – not all will be pleasant.

Governments may lose power relative to their peoples and to agile businesses. National regulatory agencies will become less effective as globalisation develops growing impetus – as the man on the Clapham omnibus said 'you ain't seen nothing yet'. Young, internet savvy people are already gaining the ascendency in business and society in general. The declining power of western governments, and perhaps also powers of authoritarian governments, will make transactions, especially transactions in cyberspace, both more frequent and far harder to prohibit. Effectively, cyberspace is already the new Wild West, with 'let the buyer beware' as its mantra. Will there be effective resistance to this or will capitalism be reworked in a generally freer form?

The world will become a tougher, more competitive and environmentally less pleasant place. Wealthy people will retreat to personal cocoons protected by elaborate and costly security arrangements; others will take their chances in 'free zones'. Environmentalism may undergo a massive loss of credibility as the 'sky is falling' approach of so many environmental zealots is perceived by the broad mass of people to be false or greatly overstated. Apocalyptic environmentalism will be replaced by concern for sensible use of resources and general cleanliness of cities and the environment. If governments do not act to frustrate market solutions, Adam Smith's invisible hand will provide some rewards for clean air and water, pleasant environments and affordable medical treatment for the nine billion people expected to be alive in 2050. But the biggest environmental issues require collective action, if they require any action – it is a matter of what economists call 'externalities'.

Much depends on whether or not concerns raised by current mainstream science about drastic environmental damage are correct or not. If the climate skeptics are right all will be well with current 'business as usual'. If the mainstream climate worriers are correct, we shall all be struggling to adapt and there will be serious damage to live with or repair. Some regions will become more productive, some far less so, and there will be many, many millions of environmental refugees. This will present massive challenges for wealthy, culturally isolated nations like Australia.

Looking ahead, there will be no absolute shortage of oil or of other resources. However, it seems highly unlikely that energy sources, like oil shale and tar sand, will meet demand fast enough to stop the oil price soaring. Lithium batteries and gas are possibilities but the rate of penetration will be slow. Natural gas will fill considerable demands. Soaring energy prices will adversely affect all people and will throw many governments into disarray. Energy producing nations, like Australia, will become richer, but at a cost to their non-energy, non-resource producing sectors. For many nations nuclear power generation will be seen as the cheapest clean energy option. By mid-century the world should know if nuclear fusion is a viable energy source, and if it is there will be unlimited cheap energy.

Countries which can feed themselves may start worrying about the future and limit sales of food on the open market as powerful nations and companies start to lock in food supplies for themselves by use of deals and threats. Small scale crises and wars are likely to erupt over the issue. Food prices will rise sharply and many poor people will continue to suffer hunger and disease. Objection to genetically modified organisms (GMOs) will fade as the realisation dawns that this is the only way to feed nine billion people. Similar developments may help solve health problems – e.g., spare parts grown in genetically modified animals.

Food producing nations will need increasingly to protect their productive capacities, including water, disease free herds and crops and markets. Spending on defence, broadly defined, will need to be greatly increased, especially if America reverts to isolation, as already discussed. This will reduce investment in the sources of prosperity, and slow the path of capitalist development.

There will be increased emphasis on new technologies put to work – 'innovation'. Already there is massive investment to discover and bring to market (or keep secret within government) new technologies in the USA, China and progressive smaller developed nations. In many areas there will be a race to develop technologies to solve problems caused by environmental degradation, increasingly expensive raw materials, food, clean water and energy.

Savvy technologists will become more highly respected and

remunerated. Nations whose budgetary problems or culture puts a low value on innovation will fall behind in their standards of living and ability to defend themselves. Australia should be better able to afford an innovative culture than most, but its culture needs to change to be more welcoming of technically based innovation if it is to compete in the most important race of all. Currently, Australia's main political parties just do not get this point.

The world is currently a two-speed economy, with China and other 'developing' nations growing rapidly and most of the 'developed' nations struggling. Australia sits between these two groups as the fastest growing rich nation. To some extent the current situation is natural, as less developed nations can learn from and emulate current leaders. But, as we see now, vast parts of the world growing at different rates and with different cultures creates 'imbalances'. The chief cultural difference is that developed nations have become very consumerist in orientation, with lifestyles based on consuming ahead of the ability to earn, a lifestyle funded by debt and with valuable assets increasingly owned by the developing nations that still save and invest a large proportion of their (far lower) incomes.

It is a great historical irony that communist China is capitalist America's banker. How this major imbalance plays out is impossible to predict, but common sense suggests the Americans need to save more and the Chinese need to spend more, and for some time this could take the form of greater investment and faster catch-up to the frontiers of capitalism. Furthermore, with current technologies the global environment will be under great strain as Chinese and Indian consumption rises. There are changes proposed to the international policy 'architecture' to reduce and better manage divergent economic trends. Whether sensible changes will be implemented is still uncertain.

And in distant Australia ...

Australia is a classic 'two-speed' economy. It is one of few countries raising interest rates that are in effect waging war against small businesses, or at least those with no direct connection to what is happening in the great mining provinces in the Pilbara or in the NSW and Queensland coalfields or the Northern Australian gas fields. Rising interest rates are pushing up the Australian dollar, which in turn is driving up imports and damaging many small exporters outside the resource sector. Without far wiser economic management than currently on offer, Australia's two-speed economy is likely to experience a standard boom and bust disaster that will lead to widespread job losses and business failures as interest rates and the Australian dollar rise.

The poor are always with us

The continued existence of poverty in the midst of plenty is a great weakness of capitalism. History and current experience, as in Robert Mugabe's Zimbabwe, shows that when whole nations are sunk in poverty it is most often due to incompetent and corrupt leadership. Ultimately either the leadership will change or people will vote with their feet. There are many examples of economic and political refugees already in the modern world, and many scenarios where the numbers in this group will expand to the point where they become a serious inconvenience to citizens of free, prosperous capitalist nations.

The current global resources boom cannot last forever. Australia needs to save a greater proportion of its current windfall than it is currently doing. There should be increased investment in infrastructure and education and in promoting innovation. More controversially, after paying off its modest government debt, Australia should steadily build a war chest of global bluechip assets only 2% of which should be Australian companies. As a country alone and friendless in the Asian region we need to double annual spending on defence.

Extreme poverty within nations that are already free and prosperous is a standing rebuke to the capitalist system. Extreme libertarians in those countries argue that people are free to choose their own future and that opportunity abounds for those equipped to see opportunity and grasp its potential. At the very least, this argument suggests the need for leaders to do their utmost to provide children of the poor with a good education.

How much further to go to level the playing field of opportunity is controversial. Should children of indigenous parents be sent to grow up in the homes of recent immigrants, as with Australia's 'stolen generation'? Should parents in poverty stricken communities, with clear evidence of alcoholism and drug dependence, gratuitous violence and child abuse be bribed to change their behaviour, or should the full force of the law be applied at great emotional and fiscal cost? Australia's recent 'intervention' in poor, mostly indigenous, communities in northern Australia tried both bribery (albeit compulsory bribery) and the force of law with mixed results.

Concern for the disadvantaged is a constant and commendable theme in capitalist nations, although the degree of concern wavers and wobbles and overall is deficient in many people's minds. But private philanthropy is limited unless backed by very generous tax incentives, quite possibly because most people believe that in paying high taxes they are doing all that should be required to help others. Evidence of enormous rewards going to managers of financial companies that required taxpayer support in the current crisis is a feature of modern capitalism that weakens the will to help others among the group that Australians call 'battlers'.

Should corporations run the world?

The development of corporatism is another great challenge to modern capitalism. Corporatism in my sense is a term to describe politics dominated by the interests of business corporations, and in particular large monopolistic corporations that develop predatory attitudes to their customers. It cannot be denied that corporations are inherently undemocratic organisations, and that the increasing power of corporations is a threat to democracy. It is standard practice for corporations to donate large amounts to major political parties, and people who do this expect at least access to elected leaders but usually an agenda to be implemented that is in no sense the will of the majority of voters.

The key point is that a modern corporate CEO is effectively

an absolute monarch. A successful CEO is narrowly focussed on maximising shareholder value, or he will be replaced by the Board of Directors, equivalent perhaps to the Roman Senate. Democratic values of freedom, respect for the individual, diversity of thought and action may be acknowledged in a corporate charter but in practice these commendable aims are strongly subservient to the narrowly economic aim of maximising shareholder value.

There are idealists who argue that the best corporations embrace 'empowerment' of individuals, the use of self-managed teams and the free interplay of individual views among employers who are also valued shareholders. There may be a few examples of such organisations (for example among the knowledge intensive industries of Silicon Valley), but far more common is a strong degree of uniformity imposed by an autocratic, rigid central bureaucratic elite. Sadly, at this stage of business evolution, autocratic and rigid centralisation is more conducive to maximising shareholder value than democratic debate and decision making.

Almost by definition, the larger the company the greater the power of its Chief Executive. So as globalisation takes hold, fewer and fewer CEOs each wield more and more power and receive bigger and bigger rewards. There are virtually no checks on this process, provided the CEO is producing the goods for shareholders and is not detected breaking the law.

This process is directly damaging to democracy. Whilst corporations have always been inherently antidemocratic, the inexorable move to fewer but larger corporations involves increasing threats to the freedom of individuals. Where there are many corporations, someone who finds a particular corporate regime oppressive can readily change his or her employer. When there are fewer corporations there is less choice, and in addition fierce economic competition leaves less room for diversity of corporate style.

The regulatory pendulum

The classic policy response to monopoly power of corporations is anti-trust legislation. Globalisation is being led by ever larger corporations and there is no global agency charged with preventing the establishment of global monopolies. Nor do I recommend that we try to establish such an agency. Rather I think the trend to ever larger international companies will be resisted as part of the inevitable backlash against what is perceived by many people as an overly laissez faire business structure. Especially in the field of finance, many voters see laissez-faire capitalism as a major contributor to the Global Financial Crisis and its consequences.

Just as there are discernable movements in the great seesaw of confidence in capitalist economies, there is a regulatory pendulum. Led by Britain in the eighteenth century, the world embarked on the path to free trade. By the early twentieth century there was free movement of goods, capital and people in much of the capitalist world. This first golden age of capitalism ended with the assassin's bullet at Sarajevo. The two world wars and the Great Depression created 'protection all round' – tariffs and quotas on imports of goods, exchange controls on capital flows and many new borders being guarded closely in Europe in particular, as well as the iron curtain separating Communism and Capitalism.

The story of the past sixty years has included massive economic deregulation, and the finance industries have been at the forefront. The formation of the European Union (EU) has introduced free trade in goods and services within Europe, and successive rounds of global trade liberalisation has freed global trade in goods and services with the prominent exception of agricultural products. Capital controls have also been relaxed and currencies floated, in this case with the prominent exception of China. People have been freest to move within the EU. However, all developed nations are still trying to restrict the inflow of people despite increasingly porous borders. Just as water finds its own level, disadvantaged or persecuted people have a massive incentive to move to freer and more prosperous nations, and the leading capitalist nations need the cheap labor they provide for tasks that their citizens are reluctant to do at any price. These basic economic forces bedevil attempts to prevent the free movement of peoples, and some economists would seek to replace current bureaucratic rationing devices by some pricing mechanism – selling places in prosperous nations to those willing to pay the highest price.

> *How far this pendulum swings is highly uncertain, but the task for economists as I see it is to devise protections against the madder forms of free market finance while retaining the basic dynamism of free markets with a global focus.*

I am inclined to the view that the regulatory pendulum will now swing away from the laissez-faire world that developed in the late twentieth century. Individual nations will not wish to cede control to a global agency and the only answer to perceived exploitation by massive, undemocratic global corporations will be the reintroduction or reinforcement of forms of protection for consumers and workers in individual countries.

The challenge to 'Keynesian' economics

Is unemployment of 10 percent tolerable, with an equivalent number underemployed? This question is answered by most people with a resounding 'no'. But *how* to improve such a situation is far from settled. Indeed, at the time of writing, the UK government is conducting austerity programs that involve slashing jobs in the public service while US officials are trying to kick-start their economy with every form of stimulus known to man. The best that can be said about this disconnect is that it will provide a test of two starkly different approaches. My money is on the British experiment, since it forces British people to confront the basic underpinnings of economic success – thrift, hard work and smart ways to do things.

Financial crises have arisen in the past with communication by horseback and sailing ship and deals struck in coffee shops. Now global communication at almost the speed of light, computers capable of initiating an almost infinite number of trades and large numbers of smart people trading with the aid of sophisticated systems greatly increase both opportunities and risks. Financial instability is growing in magnitude and occurring more often.

The Bank of England in the past manipulated its Bank Rate following the laws of the global gold standard to produce stability in an age of great innovation, with massive development of new lands and new industries. The gold standard as practiced in the nineteenth century was focussed on what economists called 'external balance', in practice as represented by the state of each nation's gold reserves. One problem, as noted in Chapter 6, is the dependence of this standard on intermittent discoveries of gold. Another is the fact that the stock of gold in a nation's vaults is a lagging indicator. In principle, a gold standard or a broader commodity standard could

During the recent global crisis, the US government felt compelled to bail out many of its major financial institutions and the US Fed set interest rates close to zero and printed money at an unprecedented rate. Fiscal stimulus has been applied everywhere and the result is budget deficits in many western nations 'as far as the eye can see'. There is widespread concern at the possibility of sovereign debt default, and the historian Niall Ferguson has written persuasively about the decline of empire due to extreme fiscal imbalance.

work with inflation within a nation (or globally), as its principal target. Such an approach could allow for the fact that changes in the degree of tightness of monetary policy affects inflation with a lag and so it is future inflation (a 'leading indicator') that is an appropriate target for monetary policy.

Some modest suggestions for reforming global capitalism

Clearly the USA and other western nations need to adopt policies that encourage hard work, thrift and innovation so as to develop economic fundamentals more in line with those of China and other developing nations. That means higher consumption taxes and lower rates of tax on employment, income, capital gains and wealth.

It might also be desirable from a global perspective for developing nations to make some changes in the opposite direction to tax rates but I very much doubt that these nations will wish to forego the benefits of their fast growth which is fuelled in part by the existing structure of taxes. Overall, my vote is for a faster growing world as that will provide the wherewithal to solve the endemic problems of poverty and inequality as well as the 'diabolical' problems of climate change, pollution and destruction of environments.

Innovation requires serious money to be spent on Research and Development (R&D) and 'commercialisation', which involves getting new technology to market. Increased spending on R&D should include spending by publicly funded research institutes (including the leading universities) as well as business, which in turn requires tax incentives as well as competitively awarded grants. I am familiar with these funding mechanisms in Australia, including our highly successful 'Cooperative Research Centre' (CRC) Program, whose advisory board I chaired for five years from 2005. Despite great (and proven) success, the budget of this and other programs to encourage innovation in Australia has been cut by the current Labor government.

Global monetary policy must become more conservative and more coordinated. The currently conventional way to do this would be for the USA to restore a neutral monetary policy with official cash rates of a modest positive value, rather than the unsustainable near zero rates adopted during the panic phase of the current financial crisis. In addition, China would adopt a fully flexible exchange rate, allowing it to run a sufficiently tight monetary policy to stop its rising inflationary problem. Currently, China is suffering inflation that if not stopped will turn a low nominal exchange rate into a high 'real' exchange rate.

But, as I have argued in Chapter 12, management of global monetary policy requires a major rethink to decide whether what is needed is a global base money regime allowing steady growth of a new commodity standard or a greatly extended SDR standard administered by an independent global agency of some sort. A reformed International Monetary Fund (IMF) might be given this task, but only when voting rights of its members are altered to more closely accord with the importance of major countries or groups of countries. With these and other reforms, the IMF would be given the task of liquidity management, including the possibility of intervention to provide funds for solvent financial institutions suffering in a general liquidity crisis.

Backed by this global base money standard, and provision for global liquidity management, individual national currencies might be made legal tender everywhere, achieving an old dream of serious competition in the provision of money. The US dollar is a de facto global currency but with the US economy in serious trouble and running loose monetary policy, the US has forfeited the right to own the global monetary policy regime. With a truly global base money regime, countries that used it to underpin their domestic monetary policy would gain the same sort of respect that is accorded nations that provide the rule of law, respect for property rights (including patent law) and a strong education for all children.

Financial regulation needs a new approach also. The idea of a global financial regulator is just too horrible to contemplate. An existing global body, such as the Bank for International Settlements (BIS) with runs on the board, should continue to provide ongoing analysis of economic conditions and prospects (in competition with other international agencies including the IMF) but also take the lead in recommending global standards for financial regulations, using or adapting the ideas outlined in Chapter 12.

In particular, the world needs again to separate 'banks' and 'investment banks', and to provide and enforce restrictions on the size of financial institutions so that no individual institution is 'too big to fail'. It is not possible to prevent entirely new ways for financial institutions to get into trouble, or for the introduction of new types of financial instruments, and one arm of a reformed BIS should monitor, analyse and publicise financial innovations, having the courage to criticise innovations that it felt were dangerous. There is a potential role for retired bankers to sit on the boards of major international and domestic regulatory agencies – poachers turned gamekeepers are better placed to spot the activities of young poachers than life-long bureaucrats.

However, it is not size of individual financial institutions alone that determines the risks to the global financial system. After all, it was the failure of many small banks in the 1930s, and the failure of a small number of large 'financial institutions' in the 2000s that made the subsequent economic crisis so serious in the first case and so worrying in the latter case, notwithstanding the widespread bailouts. Basic banking should be like public utilities providing water, electricity, gas and other essentials of modern communities. No harm in such entities being privately owned but, if they are, tight public supervision and regulation is needed. Management by risk averse people is required, prudent reserve ratios should be enforced and customers' deposits should be guaranteed.

Investment banks, hedge funds and other speculative financial ventures should not have their customers' assets guaranteed, should be subject to lighter regulation, ideally no regulation, than basic banks and all this should be widely explained and publicised. However, because of the risk of contagion, it is not possible to move to this ideal system quickly, if at all. Bailout may occasionally be required but when this occurs the government should take equity so that taxpayers have some chance of recovering the costs of the bailout and executives should lose accumulated bonuses on a pro rata basis, if necessary setting aside relevant employment contracts. Draconian? Yes, but otherwise moral hazard will run wild, as it was perceived to do during and after the Global Financial Crisis of 2007-08.

As already discussed, new forms of 'automatic stabilisers' are desirable to improve the working of fiscal policy. This approach needs also to be extended to financial system regulation with the aim of testing and to some extent limiting overly expansive lending during booms and to encourage new lending after the bust has occurred. Heads of the major international agencies, central banks and national financial regulators should be more prepared to speak out about the perils of 'irrational exuberance' when they judge that optimism is reaching the stage where too many silly decisions are likely to be made.

The capitalist world, perhaps especially the world of finance, needs to solve the problem of inequality. Ideally, those who could command extraordinarily large remuneration would impose self restraint, or give large amounts to charity. (Believe it or not, this writer knows people who actually do this.) But if this does not become the norm, society needs to decide whether to enforce a degree of restraint by punitive taxation. There is also a role to be played by rules or tax policies applied to incentive plans to promote long-term thinking in business, including financial business.

Despite its obvious imperfections, capitalism is by far the best way to order the world's economic affairs. I can believe with the extreme libertarians that predatory capitalism with few if any restraints would produce the fastest possible growth of the sort of goods and services valued most highly in currently advanced capitalist economies. But the side effects would be immense, and would include even greater inequality, larger swings in the seesaw of boom and bust and even greater environmental damage. I cannot prove this, but close encounters with many leading capitalists have convinced me this will be the case.

So I feel certain that sensible regulations, of the sort discussed here, are needed if capitalism is to survive and prosper.

The risk of financial instability out of control, due to over-ambitious attempts to control boom and bust

The killjoys and wowsers are always with us. I have argued that boom and bust are part of the natural order of capitalism, requiring wise management rather than prohibition. Econocrats and politicians will continue trying to control financial instability, with an obvious risk of strangling the golden goose that is capitalism. Overkill is more likely to happen if existing methods of managing economies spin out of control. This in my view is the greatest risk facing modern capitalism.

The immediate risk is that sluggish recovery in most 'developed' nations will fade as stimulus is withdrawn. At best, fiscal and monetary authorities face a difficult and tricky balancing act. Withdraw stimulus too quickly and business and household confidence weakens. The swing from near universal agreement on the need for substantial monetary and fiscal stimulus when the global crisis struck to the present (late 2010) concern at the growth of government debt piled on the substantial private debt built up in Western nations since the dawning of the Age of Aquarius is truly worrying. Could officials and other opinion leaders not anticipate this risk and reduce it by moderating their natural desire to 'do something'? Or have the current generation of officials and politicians developed the same short-termism they criticise in private bankers and other businessmen?

The apparent change of focus from fiscal stimulus to restraint can only be unhelpful for the confidence of households and firms, and without confidence there can be no lasting recovery. There has not so far been a similar broad swing in thinking about monetary policy, although some nations, including Australia, China and India, have begun to raise official cash rates. But US official cash rates almost zero and the Fed's use of substantial 'quantitative easing' will fuel global inflationary expectations, and the substantial rise in the price of gold and other commodities is one sign that there is more than a whiff of inflation in the air. A build up of inflationary expectations would further erode confidence of business and households. Confidence would be further damaged by a lurch from extreme ease in monetary policy to restraint, so a calm and well explained transition is needed in the nations with currently excessive monetary ease.

We must all hope that stimulus will be withdrawn at just the right speed; the 'Goldilocks' solution. But if not, the global economy may lapse into erratic behaviour, bouncing between an inflationary ceiling and a recessed floor, with authorities pulling policy levers that are not reliably connected to the outcomes that matter: jobs, growth and steady confidence.

With even the wisest possible gradual tightening of policy in a 'Goldilocks' world, a renewed shock might further weaken confidence. Worse still, another adverse shock may be beyond the power of further fiscal expansion or renewed monetary ease to remediate.

The debt problems of the weaker European nations and European banks have been one focus of concern. The European banks could yet be hiding large potentially bad debts and a single large failure could unleash a cascade of further failures. One must doubt if the international and Eurozone agencies could summon the will or the resources to prevent a cascade of bank failures. Such a shock would end the tepid recovery of the western nations, lay the basis for Eurozone depression and send policy back into the melting pot.

And what if the other 'imbalances' between the developed West and the developing East fail to be resolved? The United Nations Climate Change Conference in Copenhagen in late 2009 exposed damaging geopolitical fault lines and created a challenge to political correctness. How fair is it for the West, so far responsible for most of the excess emissions of greenhouse gasses, to insist the developing East curtail development to make a serious contribution to overall elimination of emissions?

Even if nations at Copenhagen had achieved agreement to adopt the deep emission cuts that most scientists believe are needed to prevent serious global warming, who would have policed this agreement and at what cost to economic growth? Scientists and economists have not convinced us all of the answers to three questions:

1) is there a problem;
2) what are the likely costs and consequences of business as usual; and
3) what are the likely costs and consequences of action to limit emissions?

The elites who conduct debates on such matters show little desire to convince their opponents and the general public. There will be no concerted global action until general agreement is reached. This is one reason that Australia's climate change advisor, Ross Garnaut, describes the climate change issue as 'diabolical'.

Even if a harmonious and not too costly agreement between East and West is eventually achieved on climate change, that will not solve the problem of great current economic 'imbalances'. China must learn to spend more and the US to spend less. Furthermore, a rising Chinese exchange rate is necessary if this is to happen with the least amount of friction. But China wants its industries to remain competitive and is discreetly reducing its holdings of US government paper while acquiring other western nations' assets (including Australian resource companies). At the time of writing, China is struggling to control inflation and Premier Wen has warned of the risk of a bubble economy. It seems China's leadership team has studied the history of capitalism.

The biggest threat to modern capitalism in my view is the possibility of instability caused by policy swings: expansion; recovery; asset inflation; goods inflation; policy tightens; economy falls back; recession starting the whole process anew. Such outcomes would destabilise the beliefs of the econocrats in major countries, as well as their political masters. It would also present a severe blow to the confidence of households and firms, and confidence is a vital part of the capitalist way.

Individual economies, and the global economy, need stable, well understood policies that are varied to a large extent by predictable rules and automatic changes in a stabilising direction. This is not the present situation, and many changes are needed if we are to devise a more robust and sustainable system of global financial governance.

Au revoir

Despite the manifest challenges, I am optimistic about the future of capitalism. It has proven to be a mighty engine for growth and prosperity. Capitalism tends to reward people who contribute most to society – the wealthy cowboys of finance excepted, perhaps – and Adam Smith's invisible hand allocates resources to their best uses far better than any system of centralised command and control. The capitalist system of governance is by its nature consistent with democracy and encourages freedom, which after food, shelter and sex is perhaps mankind's greatest need.

New forms of renewable energy, including the long-awaited development of workable fusion reactors will eventually provide unlimited cheap energy. Cheaper methods of water purification and a vast cultural change in favour of conserving water and other natural resources will solve looming shortages and create a sustainable global economy. Cultural change in favour of more inexpensive pursuits like reading, writing, painting, playing and composing music, developing and playing games and away from massive consumption of 'things' would make many current global challenges far easier to solve.

The world is full of inventive people who desire to create the future rather than predicting it or planning to cope with it. There are vast underutilised human resources languishing in poor countries and in countries and companies that do not fully value the contribution of women.

Despite the risks and dangers, modern capitalism is well placed to deal with people who would seek to destroy the capitalist way of life, principally by showing them there is a better way to live but also by vigorously defending our way of life. Capitalism has dealt with recurrent episodes of financial boom and bust, past challenges to a clean and safe environment and endemic war and revolution. The freedom that goes with a democratic, capitalist regime helps to make people resourceful, flexible and strong.

This is our greatest guarantee of continued growth and prosperity in a volatile, overcrowded and polluted world. The challenges of dealing with shocks and disturbances will provide many satisfying tasks for the rising generation. As someone said, capitalism is crisis. That is its chief weakness, but also its greatest strength, since in crisis lies opportunity.

Endnotes

1. The Crash of 2007-08, as it seemed at the time

1. The author of this book has been writing a daily blog under the *nom de plume* of Henry Thornton for more than a decade. As indicated, considerable material in this chapter comes from "Henry's Blog".
2. Skidelsky, *Keynes. The Return of the Master*, 5.
3. As we say in Australia, blind Freddie could see that Greenspan had made a mess of monetary policy when he cut the Federal Funds rate to a totally unsustainable 1%. The most scientific exposition of Greenspan's big monetary policy mistake is in John B Taylor's 2009 book, *Getting off Track. How Governments Actions and Interventions Caused, Prolonged, and worsened the Financial Crisis*.
4. Skidelsky, op. cit., 8.
5. Galbraith, *The Great Crash. 1929*, 24.
6. The Raff Report, 29 May, 2007.
7. Henry's Blog, 13 July, 2007.
8. Henry Thornton , "Asset Inflation Conundrum", 5 June, 2007.
9. Henry's "Lexington", 23 July, 2007.
10. Martin Wolf, "Fear makes its welcome return", 16 August, 2007.
11. Henry's Blog, 27 September, 2007.
12. Eoin Callan and Jeremy Grant, "Trouble in credit market won't go away soon: Paulson", 13, September, 2007.
13. International Monetary Fund, Article IV Consultation with Australia.
14. Henry's Blog, 1 November, 2007.
15. Henry's Blog, 24 December, 2007.
16. Henry's Blog, 18 March, 2008.
17. Henry Thornton, "Should the Reserve Bank Drop Inflation targeting?", 24 April, 2008.
18. Bank for International Settlements, *Annual Report, 2007-08*.
19. Henry's Blog, 12 June, 2008.
20. "The battle of the pockets is joined", *The Economist*, 12 June, 2008.
21. Barry Eichengreen and Kevin H O'Rourke, "A Tale of Two Depressions",

Vox, 6 April, 2009, updated 4 June, 2009 and 8 March, 2010.

22. William Rees-Mogg, "My 80th birthday wish: not to see another Black Monday", 15 July, 2008.

23. Henry's Blog, 18 August, 2008.

24. Skidelsky, op. cit., 8.

25. My account is at Henry's Blog, 25 February, 2010.

26. Skidelsky, op. cit., 10.

27. Galbraith, op. cit., 141.

28. Anatole Kaletsky, "New capitalist model needed: World Economic Forum", 5 February, 2010.

29. Ross Garnaut (with David Llewellyn-Smith), *The Great Crash of 2008*, 224.

2. Capitalism is Crisis; and Crisis is Opportunity

1. Niall Ferguson, *The Ascent of Money*, 4.

2. J.A. Schumpeter, *Capitalism, Socialism and Democracy*, 83.

3. Peter Lynch, *One Up On Wall Street*.

4. Simon, "Three Asset-price bubbles", 12.

5. C.P. Kindleberger and Robert Aliber, *Manias, Panics and Crashes*, 116-117.

6. Wellington's famous comment about Waterloo, from: http://en.wikiquote.org/wiki/Arthur_Wellesley,_1st_Duke_of_Wellington.

7. Ferguson, *Ascent*, 82-87.

8. Geoffrey Blainey, *The Great Seesaw*, 267-269. See also share price graphs in Chapter 6 of this book.

9. Ferguson, *Ascent*, 297.

10. Blainey, *Seesaw*, 269-272.

11. J.M. Keynes, *The Economic Consequences of the Peace*, 11.

12. Keynes, *Consequences*, op. cit., 3.

13. Ferguson, *Ascent*, 299.

14. This writer recalls seeing a man from East Germany say the quoted words on television reports of the event. Similar sentiments are expressed by Li Cunxin in his chapter 18, headed with great irony "The Filthy Capitalist America" in his book *Mao's Last Dancer*.

15. A nice chronology of major events in the global market for oil is provided at *Annual Oil Market Chronology*, http://www.eia.doe.gov/cabs/AOMC/Full.html#a1980.

16. Kindelberger and Aliber, *Manias*, Appendix, 294-303.

17. Ferguson, *Ascent*, 169-175.

18. Kindleberger, ibid.

3. War and Peace and Capitalism; a many stranded rope

1. Keynes, *The Economic Possibilities for our Grandchildren*, 362
2. Kennedy, *The Rise and Fall of the Great Powers*, xvii.
3. Kennedy, op. cit., xviii
4. Blainey, *The Causes of War*, 7.
5. ibid.
6. While he does not, so far as I can judge, argue with Keynes' economic analysis, Paul Johnson in *Modern Times* totally disagrees with Keynes on the influence of the Treaty of Versailles. Indeed, Johnson calls *The Economic Consequences of the Peace* 'one of the most destructive books of the century, which contributed indirectly and in several ways to the future war Keynes himself was so anxious to avert'. (Johnson, *Modern Times*, 30).
7. Keynes, *The Economic Consequences of the Peace*, 9
8. ibid., 15-16.
9. ibid., 19 and 22.
10. ibid., 3.
11. Blainey, op. cit., 9-11.
12. ibid., 10.
13. Smith, *The Wealth of Nations*, 26-27.
14. Blainey, op. cit., p.270. Chapter 17 of Blainey's book is called 'War, Peace and Neutrality'. It sets out in analytic form his conclusions about the causes of war and the circumstances when nations will avoid war.
15. Ferguson, *The War of the World*, xli.

4. Dutch Tulip Mania, 1636; with brief comments on the modern market for art

1. Ferguson, *The Ascent of Money*, 128.
2. ibid., 135.
3. Ferguson, 138.
4. Sheramy Bundrick, Van Gogh's Chair.
5. Charles MacKay's *Memoirs of Extraordinary Popular Delusions and the Madness of Crowds*, 87-89.
6. Plutus (or PLOUTOS) was the god of wealth. In agrarian Greece he was at first associated purely with bounty of rich harvests. Later he came to represent wealth in more general terms. Plutus was a son of Demeter, the goddess of agriculture, He was blinded by Zeus so he would distribute wealth indiscriminately and without favour towards the good or the virtuous.
7. MacKay, op. cit., 90.
8. ibid.
9. Garber, *Famous First Bubbles. The Fundamentals of Early Mania*, 12.

10. Garber, op. cit., 4-9.
11. ibid., 7. I have not personally checked the 1926 edition of Palgrave.
12. ibid., 9. I cannot find this quote in my edition (the fifth) of Kindleberger, who devotes two whole pages to definitions, and it is possible he and co-author Robert Aliber tightened the text in response to criticism from Chicago.
13. John Simon, "Three Australian Asset-price Bubbles", 18.
14. Garber, op. cit., 29 and note 4.
15. Garber, "Tulipmania", p.558.
16. Garber, *Famous First Bubbles*, 83.
17. MacKay, 90-91.
18. Garber, *Famous First Bubbles*, 34.
19. Anne Goldgar, *Tulipmania*, 7.
20. Goldgar, op. cit., 304.
21. Ash, "Fine art and the bubble in money".
22. Rita Reif, "A $27 Million Loan ...".
23. Mirriam Kreinin Souccar, "Art Market Bubble Bursts".
24. ibid.

5. The Twin Crises of 1720; France and England gulled by professionals

1. Charles MacKay, *Memoirs of Extraordinary Popular Delusions and the Madness of Crowds*, 53-60.
2. Larry Neal, "How the Bubbles Began and Ended".
3. Malcolm Balen, *The King, The Crook, and the Gambler*, 11.
4. Joseph Schumpeter, *History of Economic Analysis*, 295.
5. MacKay, op. cit., The material quoted here and in the following four paragraphs is from 6-10.
6. ibid., 14.
7. Balen, op. cit., 60.
8. Both graphs in this chapter are simple versions of those based on the same data collated by Neal and also used by Garber in his book published in 2000. Source is Google Images.
9. Neal, op. cit., 364-365.
10. Balen, op. cit., 73.
11. Quotes in the next six paragraphs are from ibid., 27-34.
12. Balen, op. cit., 65.
13. ibid., 73.
14. Ibid., 83.
15. Neal, op. cit., 402-404.
16. MacKay, op. cit., 23. Remaining quotes, with the exceptions noted, are from MacKay, 27-84.
17. Helen Paul, 'Politicians and public reaction to the South Sea Bubble:

Preaching to the converted' concludes that 'Many of the directors were quietly given back some of their confiscated property'. She asserts that 'The trials were an early example of political spin'. Her forthcoming book on the South Sea Bubble will add further deep insight.

18. See especially Richard Dale et al, 'Financial markets can go mad' and Peter Temin and Hans-Joachim Roth, "Riding the South Sea Bubble". My own research on systems in disequilibrium is summarised in P.D. Jonson, "Money, Prices and Output".

19. Balen, op. cit., 129.

20. MacKay, op. cit., 69.

6. The Age of Innovation spreads the Industrial Revolution

1. Ashton, *Industrial Revolution*, 4-5.

2. Keynes, "Economic Possibilities for Our Grandchildren". *Essays in Persuasion*, 363.

3. This is the major theme of Paul Johnson's *Modern Times*.

4. Ashton, op. cit., Chapter 1, "Introduction", 1-22 is a gem.

5. The Bank Rate data are from Clapham, *The Bank of England. A History, Vol. II, 1797-1914*, Appendix B.

6. These facts, and the colourful anecdotes in the next several paragraphs, are from Chancellor, *The Devil Take the Hindmost* , 103-112.

7. My hypothesis is that this ambivalence comes from deep envy. "Speculators", which means all businesspersons to most parliamentarians, usually earn far more than legislators, many of whom brood about the unfairness of this situation, especially as they usually believe they do a far more important job.

8. Quotes until further notice from Chancellor, op. cit., 129-136.

9. Clapham, Vol. II, op. cit., 205.

10. Blainey, *The Great Seesaw*, 270.

11. Chancellor, op. cit., 155.

12. Geisst, *Wall Street: a history : from its beginnings to the fall of Enron*, 48.

13. Clapham, Vol. II, op. cit., 222-223. In this section I rely mostly on Clapham, with quotes unless otherwise noted from 224-257.

14. Clapham, Vol. II, 258-259, quoting from Bagehot, 1892 ed., 184.

15. Clapham, Vol. II, op. cit., 271.

16. Chancellor, op. cit., 171,173. In this section I rely mostly on Chancellor, with further quotes from 176-185.

17. Clapham, VII, op. cit., 292. Subsequent quotes are from 293-298.

18. An engaging account is presented by Bruner and Carr, *The Panic of 1907*.

19. Schumpeter, *History of Economic Analysis*, 1124.

7. Marvellous Melbourne's Astounding Property boom and Bust; and a short subsequent history of Australia

1. Geoffrey Blainey, *A Land Half-won*, 158. Other sources to cover Australia's recurrent gold and other mineral discoveries are Geoffrey Blainey, *The Rush That Never Ended*, and David Hill, *The Fever that Forever Changed Australia, Gold!*
2. Blainey, op. cit., *A Land Half-won*, 160. For more on the Eureka rebellion, see also Hill, op. cit., Chapter Six, and Richard Butler, *Eureka Stockade*.
3. Blainey, op. cit., *A Land Half-won*, 163-164.
4. ibid, 168.
5. Graeme Davison, *The Rise and Fall of Marvellous Melbourne*.
6. Michael Cannon, *The Land Boomers*, 8.
7. Blainey, op. cit., 216-217.
8. ibid., 281-284.
9. A stump jump plough rides over roots or tree stumps rather than getting stuck in or behind them. Credit goes to the Smith Brothers, Richard Bowyer and Clarence Herbert, working in the South Australian wheat land in the 1870s.
10. Blainey, "A Theory of Mineral Discovery: Australia in the nineteenth Century".
11. Blainey, *A Land Half-won*, op. cit., 296-299.
12. ibid., 296-297. The entire discussion of the great prosperity from 1850 to 1890 relies on Chapter 18 "The Pistons of Prosperity".
13. Cannon, op. cit., 24. Quotes in the following paragraphs are from 24-28.
14. The quotes in this paragraph are from ibid., 30,31.
15. Simon, "Three Australian Asset-price Bubbles", 21 and "Appendix: Historical Data". The graph of Victorian land prices is from various Victorian Year-Books compiled by Simon.
16. ibid., 21 and Silberberg, "Rates of return on Melbourne land investment, 1880-92".
17. This quote and those in the next few paragraphs are from Cannon, op. cit., 31-33.
18. ibid., 56-57.
19. Geoffrey Blainey, *Gold and Paper*, 75.
20. This quote and others in this section are from Cannon, op. cit., Chapter 4, "The hungry 1890s", 42-52 unless otherwise indicated. The historian Geoffrey Blainey points out that the death rate in Victoria was lower in 1892 and 1893 than in each of the previous two years, and lower than in Britain and major European countries in the early 1890s.
21. Blainey, *Gold and Paper*, op. cit., 77.
22. ibid., 85.
23. ibid., 102.
24. Shann, *An Economic History of Australia*, 375.

25. Gerard Henderson, "Avoiding the bubble trouble", 11 March, 2003.
26. Tim Toohey, David Colosimo and Andrew Boak, "A Study of Australian Housing. Uniquely Positioned or a Bubble?", 6 September, 2010.
27. George Meudell, *The Pleasant Career of a Spendthrift*, 288. Cannon's *The Land Boomers* contains a chapter on 'The Meudell Mystery' which those interested in conspiracy theory will find mighty entertaining.

8. The Roaring Twenties and the Great Depression

1. Galbraith, *The Great Crash 1929*, 194.
2. Keynes, *The General Theory of Employment, Interest and Money*, 159.
3. Galbraith, op. cit., 14.
4. Johnson, *Modern Times*, 223.
5. Galbraith, op. cit., 11, 12. In the remainder of this section, quotes unless otherwise identified are from 16-27.
6. ibid., 29. The quotes in the remainder of this section are from 30-42.
7. The Glass-Steagall Act, passed in 1933, mandated the separation of commercial banks from riskier investment banks. This act was abolished in 1999, leading to the creation of far larger banking groups – most 'too big to fail' – whose investment bankers ran amuck. No lesser figure than Paul Volcker has called for this Act's restoration, but this view has, sadly, not prevailed at the time of writing.
8. Galbraith, op. cit., 43. Remaining quotes in this section are from 59-72.
9. ibid., 74. Remaining quotes in this section are from 74-98.
10. Schedvin, *Australia and the Great Depression*, 3, 46.
11. Blainey, *The Great Seesaw*, 278.
12. Galbraith, op. cit., 172.
13. Friedman and Schwartz, *A Monetary History of the United States*, 11.
14. Bernanke, 'Non-Monetary Effects of the Financial Crisis in the Propagation of the Great Depression', Abstract.
15. Ferguson, *The Ascent of Money*, 162-165.
16. Schedvin, op. cit., 9.
17. ibid., Chapter XVI and 378. On the American situation, I have relied in particular on Paul Johnson's, *The History of the American People* and Amity Schlaes, *The Forgotten Man*.
18. Galbraith, op. cit., 188-190.
19. ibid., 190.
20. ibid.

9. The Age of Aquarius; Oil crisis, inflation and unemployment

1. Milton Friedman and Anna J Schwartz, *A Monetary History*. Milton Friedman, *The Counter-Revolution in Monetary Theory* is the source of the famous quote, http://en.wikiquote.org/wiki/Milton_Friedman.
2. Treasurer Keating's claim to be Australia's chief inflation fighter was made in an interview by Paul Cleary in *The Australian* on 29, November, 2010. My comment is in Henry Thornton 'In Accord with a Former Critic'.
3. P.D. Jonson, "Inflation; Its Costs; Its Causes and Its Cure". The material in this chapter comes partly from this article.
4. Gerald E. Corrigan, Statement before the United States House of Representatives Subcommittee on Domestic Monetary Policy, 6 February, 1990.
5. M.J. Phillips, "What price money?" Reserve Bank of Australia, *Bulletin*, March 1990.

10. Asian Magic and Western Witchcraft

1. Ruth Benedict, *The Chrysanthemum and the Sword: Patterns of Japanese Culture*.
2. Extract from Dr. W. Edwards Deming, Skymark.com, http://www.skymark.com/resources/leaders/deming.asp.
3. Niall Ferguson, *Ascent of Money*, 169.
4. Richard Koo, *The Holy Grail of Macroeconomics. Lessons from Japan's Great Recession*.
5. Garnaut and Song, "Truncated Globalisation: the Fate of the Asia Pacific Economies". *See also* Drysdale and Garnaut, "The Pacific: an application of a general theory of economic integration".
6. A lively study of the whole LTCM issue is that by J Downing, "Long Term Capital Management".
7. Wendy Boswell, "History of the Internet", http://websearch.about.com/od/whatistheinternet/a/historyinternet.htm.
8. Paul Jonson, *A History of the American People*, 191-193.
9. Wikipedia, "Charles Schwab Corporation", http://en.wikipedia.org/wiki/Charles_Schwab_Corporation.
10. The Global Language Monitor, "1,000,000th English Word Announced", http://www.languagemonitor.com/news/1000000th-english-word-announced.
11. J.M. Keynes, *General Theory*, 159.
12. Edwin Leferve (AKA Jesse Livermore), *Reminiscences of a Stock Operator*, 188.

11. How Capitalism Works

1. Adam Smith, *An Inquiry into the Nature and Causes of the Wealth of Nations*, 456.
2. J.M. Keynes, *The General Theory of Employment, Interest and Money*, 372.

3. Hyman P. Minsky, *Stabilising an Unstable Economy.*
4. Milton Friedman and Anna J Schwartz, *A Monetary History of the United States 1867-1960*. It is often assumed, as a first approximation, that velocity is constant and the quantity of the single good does not vary much. Ergo, if the money supply is doubled, the price level will (eventually) double. Alternatively, if the rate of growth of the money supply doubles, the rate of growth of prices (inflation) will eventually double.
5. P.D. Jonson, "Money, Prices and Output, an Integrative Essay".
6. Archibald and Lipsey, "Monetary and Value Theory. A Critique of Lange and Patinkin".
7. P.D. Jonson and Henryk I. Kierkowski, "The Balance of Payments, An Analytic Exercise".
8. P.D. Jonson, "'Inflation. Its Causes, *Its Costs and its Cure"*.
9. Charles Kindleberger and Robert Aliber, *Manias, Panics and Crashes.*
10. J.K. Galbraith, *The Great Crash 1929*. 120.
11. Niall Ferguson, *The Ascent of Money.*
12. Larry Neal, "A Shocking View of Economic History", quoted by Ferguson, *Ascent*, 44.
13. Mandelbrot and Hudson, *The (mis)Behaviour of Markets. A Fractal View of Financial Turbulence.*
14. Niall Ferguson, "An Empire at Risk".
15. Carmen Reinhart and Kenneth Rogoff, *This Time Is Different.*
16. Ferguson, *An Empire at Risk*, op. cit., final paragraph.

12. The messages of boom and bust

1. George W Bush, President George W. Bush's speech to the nation on the economic crisis, 25 September, 2008.
2. If inspiration is needed, careful study of Hayek's *The Road to Serfdom* and *The Constitution of Liberty* will be helpful. I spent some time looking for Hayek's views on boom and bust, and the best contribution I found is the chapter on "The Monetary Framework" in the latter work. It is noteworthy that he starts that chapter with Keynes' famous quote about the strategy of debauching the currency by those who wish to overturn the existing basis of society, very relevant for Chapter 9 of this book.
3. Zhou Xiaochuan "Reform the International Monetary System", 23 March, 2009.
4. UN, "Report of the Commission of Experts", 21 September, 2009.
5. IMF, "Reserve Accumulation and International Monetary Stability", 13 April, 2010.
6. In addition to all the books and articles cited previously in this book, I also recommend Roubini and Mihn, *Crisis Economics*. Mr Roubini, widely known as 'Dr Doom', modestly admits to predicting the recent crisis well in advance

of anyone else, giving his suggestions for reform some undoubted street cred. My review of this book is listed in the references below. I also commend the books by Peter Lynch and "Edwin Lefevre".

Bibliography

Ash, Adrian, "Fine art and the bubble in money". *MoneyWeek*, 13 February, 2007, http://www.moneyweek.com/investments/fine-art-and-the-bubble-in-money.aspx.

Archibald, G.C. and Lipsey, R.G. "Monetary and Value Theory. A Critique of Lange and Patinkin". *Review of Economic Studies*, October 1958.

Ashton, T.S. *The Industrial Revolution 1760-1830*. London: Oxford University Press, 1948.

Baghot, W. *Lombard Street. A description of the Money Market*. London: Henry S. King, 1873.

Bank for International Settlements, 78th Annual Report, June 2008, http://www.bis.org/publ/arpdf/ar2008e.htm.

Balen, Malcolm. *The King, the Crook and the Gambler*. London: Fourth Estate, 2004, original publication in Great Britain as *A Very English Deceit*, 2002 and in hardcover as *The Secret History of the South Sea Bubble*, 2003.

Benedict, Ruth. *The Chrysanthemum and the Sword: Patterns of Japanese Culture*. Cleveland: Meridium Books, 1967.

Bernanke, B.S. "Non-Monetary Effects of the Financial Crisis in the Propagation of the Great Depression". *NBER Working Paper #1054*, January 1983.

—. and Blinder, Alan S. "Credit, Money and Aggregate Demand". *American Economic Review*, LXXVIII (2), May 1988, 435-9. Reprinted in David Laidler (ed), *Foundations of Monetary Economics*, Edgar Elgar Publishing Limited, UK, 1999.

Blainey, Geoffrey. *A Land Half-won*. South Melbourne: Macmillan, 1980.

—. *Gold and Paper. A History of the National Bank of Australia*. Melbourne: Macmillan, 1958, (Revised edition, 1983).

—. *The Causes of War*. Melbourne: Sun books, 1973.

—. *The Great Seesaw*. Melbourne: Macmillan, 1998.

298 *Great Crises of Capitalism*

—. *The Rush that Never Ended*. Melbourne: Melbourne University Press, 1963, (Second Edition, 1969).

Bordo, M.D. "The Great Contraction and the Current Crisis: Historical Parallels and Policy Lessons". Shadow Open Market Committee Symposium, 24 April, 2009.

Boswell, Wendy. "History of the Internet". http://websearch.about.com/od/whatistheinternet/a/historyinternet.htm.

Bruner R.F. and Carr, S. D., "The Panic of 1907". *Lessons Learned from the Market's Perfect Storm*. New Jersey: John Wiley, 2007.

Bundrick, Sheramy. "Van Gogh's Chair. The blog of Author & Art Historian Sheramy Bundrick". October 4, 2008, http://vangoghschair.blogspot.com/2008/10/tulip-mania.html.

Bush, George W., "Speech to the nation on the economic crisis". *The New York Times*, 25 September, 2008.

Butler, Richard. *Eureka Stockade*. Sydney: Angus and Robertson, 1983.

Callan, E. and Grant, Jeremy. "Trouble in credit market won't go away soon: Paulson". *The Australian*, September 13, 2007.

Cannon, Michael. *The Land Boomers*. Melbourne: Melbourne University Press, 1966, (Illustrated edition, Thomas Nelson, 1976).

Chancellor, Edward. *The Devil Take the Hindmost. A History of Financial Speculation*, New York: Plume, 2000.

Churchill, Winston. *The Story of the Malakand Field Force*. London: Thomas Nelson & Sons, 1916. For this book Churchill edited his letters from Malakand, originally published in the *Daily Telegraph* in the late nineteenth century. The preface was signed off in the Cavalry Barracks, Bangalore, on 30 December, 1897.

Clapham, Sir John. *The Bank of England. A History, Volume I, 1694-1797*. Cambridge: Cambridge University Press, 1944, (Reprinted 1958).

—, *The Bank of England. A History, Volume II, 1797-1914*. Cambridge: Cambridge University Press, 1944, (Reprinted 1958).

Cleary, Paul. "Keating warns Labor has forgotten lessons of 'recession we had to have'." *The Australian*, November 29, 2010.

Corrigan, G. E., "Statement before the United States House of Representatives Subcommittee on Domestic Monetary Policy". 6 February, 1990.

Cunxin, Li., *Mao's Last Dancer*, Ringwood: Viking, 2003.

Dale, R.S., Johnson, J.E.V. and Tang, L., "Financial Markets can go mad; evidence of irrational behaviour during the South Sea Bubble". *Economic History Review*, LVIII, 2 (2005), 233-271.

Davison, Graeme, *The Rise and Fall of Marvellous Melbourne*, Melbourne University Press, 1978, Reprinted 1988.

Downing, J. "Long Term Capital Management, Study for The Professional Risk Managers". International Association, 2009, http://prmia.org/pdf/Case_Studies/Long_Term_Capital_Management_Shory_version_April_2009.pdf.

Drysdale, Peter and Garnaut, Ross."The Pacific: an application of a general theory of economic integration", in Fred Bergsten and Marcus Noland (eds). *Pacific Dynamism and the International Economic System*. Washington DC: Institute for International Economics, 1993,183-224.

Economist, The. "The battle of the pockets is joined", 12 June, 2008.

Eichengreen, Barry, and O'Rourke, K.H. "A Tale of Two Depressions". *Vox*, 6 April, 2009, updated 4 June, 2009 and 8 March, 2010, http://www.voxeu.org/index.php?q=node/3421.

Ferguson, Niall. *The Ascent of Money. A Financial history of the World*. New York: Penguin books, 2008.

—. *The War of the World. Twentieth-Century Conflict and the Descent of the West*. New York: Penguin, 2006.

—. "An Empire at Risk". Niall Ferguson website, 15 December, 2009, http://www.niallferguson.com/site/FERG/Templates/ArticleItem.aspx?pageid=226.

Friedman, Milton and Anna J Schwartz. *A Monetary History of the United States 1867 to 1960*. Princeton: Princeton University Press, 1963, (9th Paperback Printing, 1993).

Friedman, Milton. *The Counter-Revolution in Monetary Theory, First Wincott Memorial Lecture*. London: IEA, 1970.

Galbraith, John Kenneth. *The Great Crash 1929*. New York: Marriner Books, 2009.

Garber, Peter. "Tulipmania". *Journal of Political Economy*, Vol. 97, no. 3, 1989.

—. *Famous First Bubbles. The Fundamentals of Early Manias*. Cambridge: The MIT Press, 2000.

Garnaut, Ross (with David Llewellyn-Smith). *The Great Crash of 2008*. Melbourne:

Melbourne University Press, 2009.

—. and Ligang Song. "Truncated Globalisation: the Fate of the Asia Pacific Economies", paper for Research School of Pacific and Asian Studies and Asia Pacific School of Economics and Government, the Australian National University, http://rossgarnaut.com.au/Documents/TRUNCATED%20 GLOBALISATION%202004.pdf.

Geisst, Charles. *Wall Street: a history: from its beginnings to the fall of Enron* (Revised Edition). Oxford: Oxford University Press, 2004.

Global Financial Data Inc. https://www.globalfinancialdata.com/Default.aspx.

Goldgar, Anne. *Tulipmania. Money, Honor, and Knowledge in the Dutch Golden Age*. Chicago: University of Chicago Press, 2007.

The Global Language Monitor. "1,000,000 th English Word Announced". http:// www.languagemonitor.com/news/1000000th-english-word-announced.

Helpman, Elhanan. *The Mystery of Economic Growth*. Cambridge Massachusetts: 2004.

Henderson, Gerard. "Avoiding the bubble trouble". *Sydney Morning Herald*, 11 March, 2003.

Henry Thornton, "Asset Inflation Conundrum". 5 June, 2007, http://www. henrythornton.com/article.asp?article_id=4737.

—. "In Accord with a Former Critic", December 7, 2010, http://www. henrythornton.com/article.asp?article_id=6204.

—. "Lord Desai of Immigration". 10 December, 2002, http://www. henrythornton.com/article.asp?article_id=1927.

—. "Should the Reserve Bank Drop Inflation targeting?" 24 April, 2008, http:// www.henrythornton.com/article.asp?article_id=514.

—. 13 July, 2007, http://www.henrythornton.com/blog.asp?blog_id=942.

—. 27 September, 2007, http://www.henrythornton.com/blog.asp?blog_id=1006.

—. 1 November, 2007, http://www.henrythornton.com/blog.asp?blog_id=1034.

—. 24 December, 2007, http://www.henrythornton.com/blog.asp?blog_id=1070.

—. 18 March, 2008, http://www.henrythornton.com/blog.asp?blog_id=1139.

—. 12 June, 2008, http://www.henrythornton.com/blog.asp?blog_id=1213.

—. 18 August, 2008, http://www.henrythornton.com/blog.asp?blog_id=1268.

—. 25 February, 2010, http://www.henrythornton.com/blog.asp?blog_id=1732.

—. 23 July, 2007, http://www.henrythornton.com/article.asp?article_id=4807.

—. 29 May, 2007, http://www.henrythornton.com/article.asp?article_id=4727.

Hill, David. *The Fever that Forever Changed Australia, Gold!*. Melbourne: William Heinemann, 2010.

Hume, David. *Writings on Economics*. Edited and Introduced by Eugene Rotwein. Edinburgh: Nelson, 1955.

International Monetary Fund. "Reserve Accumulation and International Monetary Stability". Prepared by the Strategy, Policy and Review Department, In collaboration with the Finance, Legal, Monetary and Capital Markets, Research and Statistics Departments, and consultation with the Area Departments, Approved by Reza Moghadam, 13 April, 2010, http://www.imf.org/external/np/pp/eng/2010/041310.pdf.

Johnson, Paul. *Modern Times. The World from the Twenties to the Nineties*. New York: Harper Perennial, 1982.

—. *A History of the American People*. London: Weidenfield and Nicholson, 1997, (Revised Edition, New York: Harper, 1999).

Jonson, P.D. "Paul Johnson on Boom and Bust". Henry Thornton.com, 27 December, 2004, http://www.henrythornton.com/article.asp?article_id=2987.

—. "Crisis Economics". Henry Thornton.com, 15 November, 2010, http://www.henrythornton.com/article.asp?article_id=6194.

—. and Henryk I Kierkowski, "The Balance of Payments, An Analytic Exercise". *Manchester School*, June 1975.

—. "Inflation; Its Costs; Its Causes and Its Cure". *Policy*, Winter 1990.

—. "Money, Prices and Output". *Kredit und Kapital*, 1976, reprinted in David Laidler (ed), *Foundations of Monetary Economics*. London: Edgar Elgar Publishing,1999.

—. "Money and Economic Activity in the Open Economy: The United Kingdom, 1880-1970", *Journal of Political Economy*, 1976, vol. 84, no. 5.

—. "Global Warming; Pascal's Wager". Henry Thornton.com, 1 June, 2006, http://www.henrythornton.com/article.asp?article_id=4079.

Kaletsky, A., "New capitalist model needed: World Economic Forum". *The Australian*, 5 February, 2010.

Kelly, Paul. *The end of certainty. The story of the 1980s*. Sydney: Allen & Unwin, 1992.

—. *The march of patriots: the struggle for modern Australia.* Melbourne: Melbourne University Press, 2009.

Kennedy, Paul. *The Rise and Fall of the Great Powers. Economic Change and Military Conflict from 1500 to 2000.* London: Fontana Press, 1989.

Keynes, John Maynard. *Essays in Persuasion,* 1931, New York: Classic House Books, 2009.

—. *The Economic Consequences of the Peace,* New York: Harcourt, 1920.

—. *The General Theory of Employment, Interest and Money* (1936). London: Macmillan, 1973.

Kindleberger, C.P. and Aliber, Robert. *Manias, Panics and Crashes. A History of Financial Crises.* London: John Wiley and Sons, 2005.

Koo, Richard. *The Holy Grail of Macroeconomics. Lessons from Japan's Great Recession.* Singapore: John Wiley & Sons, 2009.

Lefevre, E., (AKA Jesse Livermore). *Reminiscences of a Stock Operator.* New York: George H. Doran Company, 1923. (Vermont: Books of Wall Street Edition, Burlington, 8th Printing, 1987).

Lucas, Robert E. JR. *Lectures on Economic Growth.* Cambridge: Harvard University Press, 2002.

Lynch, Peter with Rothschild, John. *One Up On Wall Street.* New York: Penguin Books, 1990.

MacKay, Charles. *Memoirs of Extraordinary Popular Delusions and the Madness of Crowds,* (first published in two volumes in 1841). London: Routledge, 1892.

Meudell, George. *The Pleasant Career of a Spendthrift,* London: Routledge, 1929.

Minsky, H.P., *Stabilising an Unstable Economy.* New York: McGraw Hill, 2008.

Neal, Larry. "A Shocking View of Economic History". *Journal of Economic History,* 60, 2 (2000), 317-34.

—. "The Banque Royale and the South Sea company: How the Bubbles Began" and "The Bank of England and the South Sea Company: How the Bubbles Ended". *The Rise of Financial capitalism: International capital markets in the Age of Reason,* Cambridge University Press, reprinted in Ross B Emmett, *Great Bubbles Volume 3.* London: Pickering and Chatto, 2008.

Paul, Helen Julia. "Politicians and public reaction to the South Sea Bubble: Preaching to the converted?" *Discussion Paper in Economics and Econometrics*

0923, University of Southampton, December 2009.

——. *The South Sea Bubble: an economic history of its origins and consequences*. London: Routledge, 2011.

Phillips, M.J. "What price money?". Reserve Bank of Australia, *Bulletin*, March 1990.

Rees-Mogg, W., "My 80th birthday wish: not to see another Black Monday." *The Australian*, 15 July, 2008.

Reif, Rita. "A $27 Million Loan by Sotheby's Helped Alan Bond to Buy 'Irises'". *New York Times,* 18 October, 1989.

Reinhart, C.M. and Rogoff, K.S.*This Time is Different. Eight Centuries of Financial Folly*. Princeton: Princeton University Press, 2009.

Ricardo, David. *The Principles of Political Economy and Taxation*, Introduction by Donald Winch. London: Everyman Classics, 1992.

Roubini, Nouriel and Mihm, Stephen. *Crisis Economics. A Crash Course in the Future of Finance*. New York: Penguin, 2010.

Schedvin, C.B., *Australia and the Great Depression*. Sydney: Sydney University Press, 1970 (Reprint, 1988).

Schumpeter, J.A. *Capitalism, Socialism and Democracy*, London: Unwin University Books, 1943, Tenth Impression, 1965.

——. *History of Economic Analysis*. Oxford: Oxford University Press, Inc, 1954, (Eighth printing, 1972).

Shann, Edward. *An Economic History of Australia*. Cambridge: Cambridge University Press, 1930, (Reprinted 1963).

Shlaes, Amity. *The Forgotten Man. A New History of the Great Depression*. New York: Harper Perennial, 2007.

Simon, John. "Three Asset-price Bubbles". Paper for Reserve Bank of Australia Conference on Asset Prices and Monetary Policy, August 2003. http://www.rba.gov.au/publications/confs/2003/simon.pdf.

Silberberg, Ron, "Rates of return on Melbourne land investment, 1880-92". *Economic Record*, 51, 203-217.

Skidelsky, Robert. *Keynes. The Return of the Master.* London: Allen Lane 2009.

Souccar, Miriam Kreinin. "Art Market Bubble Bursts", *Crain's New York Business,* 17

November, 2008, http://www.ekfineart.com/files/Crain's_New_York.pdf.

Sorkin, Andrew Ross. *Too big to fail. Inside the battle to save Wall Street*. London: Allen Lane, 2010.

Smith, Adam. *An Inquiry into the Nature and Causes of the Wealth of Nations*, (First published 1776). Oxford: Clarendon Press, Oxford, 1976.

Taylor, John. *Getting off Track. How Governments Actions and Interventions Caused, Prolonged, and worsened the Financial Crisis*. Stanford: Hoover Institution Press, 2009.

Temin, Peter, and Voth, Hans-Joachim. "Riding the South Sea Bubble". *The American Economic Review*, Vol. 94, No. 5 (Dec. 2004), 1654-1668.

Toohey, Tim, Colosimo, David and Boak, Andrew. "A Study of Australian Housing. Uniquely Positioned or a Bubble?". *Goldman Sachs Research Report*, 6 September, 2010.

Triffin, Robert. *Our International Monetary System: Yesterday, Today and Tomorrow*. New York: Random House, 1968.

United Nations. "Report of the Commission of Experts of the President of the United Nations General Assembly on Reforms of the International Monetary and Financial System", 21 September, 2009, http://www.un.org/ga/econcrisissummit/docs/FinalReport_CoE.pdf.

United States Department of Energy, and successor agencies. "Annual Oil Market Chronology". http://www.eia.doe.gov/cabs/AOMC/Full.html#a1980.

Duke of Wellington, Remark to Thomas Creevey (18 June, 1815), using the word nice in its original sense of "uncertain", about the Battle of Waterloo, as quoted in *Creevey Papers* (1903), by Thomas Creevey, Ch. X, 236. This has also been misquoted as "A damn close-run thing." http://en.wikiquote.org/wiki/Arthur_Wellesley,_1st_Duke_of_Wellington.

Wikipedia. Charles Schwab Corporation, http://en.wikipedia.org/wiki/Charles_Schwab_Corporation.

Wolf, Robert. "Fear makes its welcome return". *The Australian*, 16 August 2007.

Zhou Xiaochuan. "Reform the International Monetary System". People's Bank of China, published in English by USC-US-China Institute, 23 March, 2009, http://china.usc.edu/ShowArticle.aspx?articleID=1597.

Glossary of Terms

ASEAN: stands for the Association of South East Asian Nations. ASEAN is a regional economic and political organisation whose major members include Vietnam, Thailand, Singapore, Malaysia, Indonesia and the Philippines. ASEAN is a trading bloc that allows relatively free trade between member states but maintains tariffs against international imports. ASEAN states retain more economic and political sovereignty than European Union countries and there is no regional currency like the Euro.

Asian Financial Crisis: A regional financial crisis that affected South East Asia and parts of East Asia between 1997 and 1998. The crisis began when investors believed South East Asian nations were borrowing too much. It worsened when the Thai baht collapsed in value followed by the national currencies of Malaysia, Indonesia, the Philippines and South Korea soon followed. The International Monetary Fund intervened and offered bailouts to these countries in exchange for economic and political reforms. South Korea, Thailand and Indonesia accepted IMF bailouts while Malaysia rejected assistance. The Asian Financial Crisis hit many of the emerging Asian Tiger economies and was responsible for Indonesia moving from an authoritarian government to a democracy.

Asian 'Tiger' Economies: Refers to the small Asian countries that achieved rapid growth in the second half of the 20th Century. These countries include South Korea, Hong Kong, Taiwan and Singapore. Each introduced policies similar to those of Japan after World War II that encouraged export driven economic growth by protecting and subsidising exporters. The strategy was highly successful and the Tigers are amongst the richest Asian economies on a per-capita measurement. China and Vietnam have also copied the export driven economic growth model of the Asian Tigers to great success.

Authoritarian Capitalism: Differs from democratic capitalism in that economic freedom exists but political freedoms limited by an authoritarian government. China, Vietnam and Singapore are perhaps the best known authoritarian capitalist states. Each country has a capitalist economic system but under the guise of a one party state that restricts freedom of speech and other personal liberties.

Bank Act: Officially titled the Bank Charter Act of 1844, this act passed by the British parliament empowered the Bank of England to issue notes while restricting the powers of commercial banks. The Act gave the Bank of England a monopoly on printing money but it had to be backed by gold. However, the Act was suspended on several occasions such as in 1847, 1857 and 1866.

Bank of England: the Bank of England was established in 1694 as the central bank of England. It is one of the oldest continuing central banks in the world. The Bank was initially established as a private bank to raise money to rebuild the British navy but over time has become Britain's central bank. It was nationalised in 1946 and made an independent public organisation in 1997. The Bank of England has been involved in much of British economic history, especially during the Industrial Revolution.

Bank Rate: the bank rate is the amount of interest central banks charge on loans to commercial banks. Central banks change the bank rate according to economic conditions. Inflation normally forces bank rates higher, while rates are often lowered to stimulate economic growth in recessions.

British East India Company: Was created as one of Britain's first joint stock companies to extend British trade and empire into Asia. The company was created in 1600 and lasted until 1874. The British East India Company was very similar to its Dutch equivalent with special rights and powers bestowed upon it by the government. The company also ruled India as part of the British Empire from 1757 to 1858.

Capitalism: Capitalism is the modern, now almost universal, system of social, economic and productive organisation. Its features include a dominant role for markets in allocating resources, private production of most goods and services, rational, evidence-based decision making by individuals, businesses and governments (or the appearance of this) and freedom of people to act within a framework provided by a stable, well understood 'rule of law' in what they perceive to be their own interests.

Commonwealth Bank: the biggest commercial bank in Australia. The Commonwealth Bank was created as a federal government bank in 1911 before being privatised in 1991. The Commonwealth Bank is now a listed public company on the Australian Securities Exchange.

Communism: a political and economic system based on state control of the economy. The basic principles of communism are outlined in Karl Marx and Friedrich Engel's *Communist Manifesto*. They saw history as a narrative of class struggle between different groups within society and predicted capitalism would eventually collapse once proletarian workers achieved class consciousness and overthrew the capitalist establishment. The Bolshevik Party created the first self proclaimed communist country when they seized power in a coup in 1917. Although the Soviet Union was founded as a communist country, some communists argue it became Stalinist and was therefore not truly communist.

Corporatism: A possible threat to democratic capitalism as economic power becomes centralised in massive corporations with the ability to influence government policy. Massive corporations can lobby and pressure government policy changes so that they play by a different set of rules to everyone else. For example, American investment banks and carmakers lobbied the federal government for bailouts by arguing they were "too big to fail".

Crisis: Crisis in modern English usage encompasses surprise, uncertainty as to outcomes and the possibility of great damage to important goals.

Democratic Capitalism: A term to describe countries with democratic political systems and capitalist economies. Common features of democratic capitalist states include elected governments, free speech, religious freedom, private property rights, copyright and patent laws and limited government economic intervention. Democratic capitalism ranges from laissez-faire capitalism in the United States to socialised capitalism in Europe. The central difference between the two is democratic capitalism is that there is greater state intervention, higher taxes and provision of public goods in socialised capitalism than in the laisezz-faire form.

Dot-com Bubble: The dot-com bubble was a speculative bubble in internet and technology companies traded on the American NASDAQ market. The bubble peaked in 2000 and burst shortly thereafter. Many dot-com companies went bust because they were simply websites and did nothing profitable. Amazon, eBay, Google and Yahoo all survived the dot-com bubble and emerged as the dominant internet companies.

Dutch East India Company: was established as the world's first stock company in 1602 by the Dutch government. The Dutch East India Company was given a trading monopoly on all commerce between the Cape of Good Hope in Africa and Straits of Magellan. The company was the first to offer investors the opportunity to buy stock and was therefore an important development in the history of corporations and capitalism.

Eureka Rebellion: a rebellion that occurred on the Ballarat goldfields in 1854, the Eureka Rebellion is seen as an important moment in the development of Australian democracy and colonial history. Miners who refused to pay the gold mining license tax built a stockade and fought British soldiers and Victorian police. Twenty eight people died in the firefight and the event was soon immortalised in Australian history. It is argued that the Eureka Rebellion led to the introduction of male suffrage in elections for the Victorian lower house.

European Economic Community: A European trade bloc created in the 1950's that is now part of the European Union. Important member states include Germany, the United Kingdom, France, Italy and Spain. The EEC was established during the Cold War to create a "common market" in Western Europe to encourage trade by lowering tariffs and streamlining regulations. The EEC has expanded since its founding and now comprises nearly all of Western Europe. Although the EEC has made trade freer between members, it still retains extremely high tariffs against foreign countries.

European Union: the European Union is a multinational political and economic organisation in Europe. The EU began as the European Economic Community in the 1950's but has since grown into a regional political and economic bloc. The majority of countries on the European continent and Great Britain are now members of the EU. The EU has its own currency called the Euro, however Great Britain, still has its own national currency.

Externalities: An externality is a cost or benefit from commerce that is not factored into the price of the transaction. A good example of an externality is pollution which is not factored into the price of electricity. Negative externalities such as pollution are often taxed so the price reflects a truer cost.

Florida Land Boom: A real estate bubble in Florida that preceded the Great Crash and Great Depression. The Florida land boom was fuelled by easy money, speculation, property flipping and imperfect knowledge among buyers. The boom ended once regulators started investigating the frenzy and a series of hurricanes hit the region.

Gangster-Capitalism: a phrase used to describe the form of capitalism in post-communist Russia. Russian gangster-capitalism saw the emergence of an elite oligarchy, powerful organised crime syndicates and the failure of political institutions to effectively regulate the economy. Gangster-capitalism resulted in capital flight from Russia, extreme inequality and high unemployment.

Glass-Steagall Act: Officially known as the Banking Act of 1933, Glass-Steagall introduced new federal American financial regulations in response to the stockmarket collapse and bank failures of the Great Depression. The Act established the Federal Deposit Insurance Commission that guaranteed bank deposits and also forced banks to separate savings and investment accounts. Glass-Steagall was effectively repealed in 1999 with new Congressional legislation and some argue this decision allowed new financial speculation to take place that led to the Global Financial Crisis.

Global Financial Crisis: an ongoing international financial crisis that began in the United States in 2007. The root causes of the GFC were sub-prime lending, extremely complex and risky financial speculation and easy credit because of low U.S. interest rates. The U.S. government bailed out major investment banks to the tune of $700 billion and has spent more on stimulus spending to stop unemployment from rising above an already high 10%. Major Western economies, with the exception of Australia, have all been hit hard by the GFC. In contrast, China and India continue to grow and many believe the GFC is the beginning of a new era that will see these two countries surpass the U.S. economy sometime in the future.

Gold Standard: A monetary system where currency is backed by gold. The gold standard was the dominant monetary system before it was replaced by fiat currencies in the 20th Century. America finally abandoned the gold standard in 1971 when President Nixon ended the U.S. dollar's convertibility into gold. All countries now operate with fiat currency that is simply printed by central banks.

Great Crash: The name given to the Wall Street stock market crash of October 1929. The Great Crash saw share prices tumble and marked the beginning of the Great Depression. The crash started on the now infamous Black Tuesday and share prices fell for more than two years.

Great Depression: The name now used used to describe the international economic depression of the 1930's. The Great Depression began in America and soon spread to the rest of the world. Stock market collapses, specifically the infamous Black Tuesday of 1929, poor policy and bank failures caused the Great Depression, but also the international repercussions of the US downturn. State control over the economy increased as a result of the Great Depression with new government regulations, agencies and social security programs.

'Great Society': A defining policy of Lyndon Johnson's Presidency. The Great Society was a liberal agenda that sought to increase federal government funding for health, education, poverty reduction and the arts. The abolition of Jim Crow racial segregation laws and the promotion of civil rights were also important aspects of the Great Society. These policies were introduced while America was fighting the Vietnam War and contributed to inflation and massive budget deficits as the country could not afford the guns of war and butter of the Great Society.

Index: Measure of some collection of items. The consumer price index measures the average price of a collection of items thought to be consumed by households. A share index shows the average price of a bundle of shares.

Industrial Revolution: a technological and economic revolution that spanned the 18th and 19th Centuries. The Industrial Revolution saw the development of new technologies such as steam and coal power, the construction of roads, canals and dams, and rapid economic growth in Europe and North America. Britain was the first country to experience the Industrial Revolution and, combined with its empire, emerged as the world superpower. The United States and Germany soon followed British industrialisation and by the end of the 19th Century rivalled British economic might.

International Monetary Fund: The International Monetary Fund is a multinational financial organisation established as part of the Bretton-Woods system following World War II. The IMF encourages member states to introduce capitalist economic reforms such as privatisation, deregulation, lower taxes and balanced budgets. The IMF is also the international lender of last resort and has bailed out numerous countries including Mexico, Indonesia and more recently Greece. A common criticism of the IMF is that its bailouts are conditional on laissez faire economic reforms that have made many countries in South America and Africa worse off in the long term.

Japan's long recession: the term for Japan's long term recession throughout the 1990's and into the 2000's. The spectacular share price and real estate bubble of the late 1980's burst and started the long recession. The long recession is interesting to economists for two reasons. First, Japan had been the greatest economic success story of the 20th Century until this recession. Japan still has not fully recovered from the long recession to the time of writing. Second, massive stimulus spending from the Japanese government failed to shock the economy back into growth. Many conservative economists cite the failure of stimulus spending and bailouts in Japan as evidence against Global Financial Crisis bailouts in the U.S. and internationally.

Keynesianism: Economic policies commonly associated with John Maynard Keynes, who is seen by some as the greatest economist of the 20th Century. Keynes advocated limited government intervention to mitigate the effects of economic downturns. Keynesian economic policies support public spending to stimulate the economy even if this brings government budgets into deficit. President Franklin Roosevelt followed Keynesian policies in his response to the Great Depression. There has been a resurgence and new interest in Keynesian economics in the aftermath of the Global Financial Crisis that began in 2008.

Long Depression: the Long Depression lasted for much of the 1870's to the 1890's. Most industrialised countries including Britain, Germany and the United States experienced slow growth and high unemployment over this time. The Long Depression was the most severe depression until the Great Depression of the 1930's.

Louisiana Purchase: This was an agreement between the United States and France in 1803 where France agreed to exchange the Louisiana Territory for fifteen million US dollars. The Louisiana Purchase was and remains the greatest real estate purchase in human history. The new Louisiana Territory doubled the territorial size of the United States at the time and was an important step in fulfilling America's "Manifest Destiny". However, one problem of the Louisiana Purchase was that it exacerbated the American debate on slavery in new territories.

Mercantilism: An economic ideology that was prevalent during the era of European Empires. Mercantilism is similar to capitalism in many ways, however the main difference is mercantilism sees international trade as a zero sum game and thus countries want to always export more than they import. Mercantilism favours protectionism over free trade give exporters and domestic firms an advantage over foreign competition. The Mercantilist era ended in the second half of the 19th Century when Britain led much of the world to free trade.

'Miracle Economy': a term used to describe the Australian economy in the late 20th Century. The Australian economy is considered a miracle economy because of its natural endowments in agriculture and minerals and strong economic performance relative to other advanced economies. As we write this book, Australia is riding high on its renewed mining boom having avoided the worst effects of the Global Financial Crisis in the United States and Europe.

Mississippi Bubble: One of the earliest and greatest bubble and bust cases. The French Mississippi Company urged investors to buy shares in the company that was supposedly exploring the then Mississippi territory in North America, among other vast schemes. The Mississippi Company's share price rose from 100 to 10,000 in less than a year and ended in a spectacular bust once investors realised Mississippi was nothing more than a swamp filled with alligators.

Moral Hazard: Is an argument against government bailouts of private industry. According to the moral hazard argument, companies should not be bailed out because this only encourages them to act more recklessly as they believe the government will intervene as they are "too big to fail". Many conservative and libertarian economists opposed the Bush administration's TARP bailout, which bailed out many U.S. financial institutions to the tune of $700 billion, on moral hazard grounds.

Napoleonic Wars: Were a series of European wars fought at the beginning of the 19th Century during Napoleon Bonaparte's reign as Emperor of France. The Napoleonic Wars marked the height of French power in Europe as Napoleon's armies conquered territory into Russia. The French were eventually defeated by the British-Prussian-Russian alliance at the Battle of Waterloo in 1815. The wars are an important in the context of the history of capitalism because speculators, speculators and financiers, such as the Rothschilds, made fortunes out of them.

'New World': Typically refers to countries that were settled by European Empires in the Americas. Spain was the first European power to establish an empire in South America, however Portugal, the Netherlands, France and Britain soon followed suit. The United States prided itself on being part of the 'New World' and not 'Old World' Europe which was seen to be against American ideas of liberty, republicanism and opportunity.

OPEC: Formally known as the Organization of the Petroleum Exporting Countries, OPEC is an international oil cartel comprised of twelve oil-exporting countries. As a cartel, member countries agree to restrict oil exports to increase the international oil price. OPEC members control two thirds of the world's proven oil reserves and account for 33% of world oil exports.

'Philips curve': The theory that assumes there is an inverse correlation between inflation and unemployment. The 'Philips curve' was conventional economic wisdom until the emergence of stagflation in the 1960's and 1970's.

Progressive taxation: An income tax system where the tax rate scales upwards with an individual's income. Those on low incomes pay a lower percentage of their income as tax than wealthy individuals. The majority of countries have progressive tax systems, with Europe being the most progressive. Alternative tax systems to progressive taxation include flat taxation and consumption taxation.

Quantitative Easing: A Central Bank monetary policy where money is printed as a last resort to stimulate economic growth. The U.S. Federal Reserve has adopted this policy in the wake of the Global Financial Crisis and interest rates are virtually zero. It is feared current quantitative easing will create high inflation in the future because the printed money is backed by no tangible asset.

Smoot-Hawley Tariff: A protectionist tariff passed by the American Congress in 1930, Smoot-Hawley is seen to have exacerbated the Great Depression by forcing retaliatory tariffs and reducing international trade. The two authors of the act were Republicans who had been urging President Hoover to increase tariffs.

South Sea Act: A British regulatory law passed in response to the South Sea Bubble. The South Sea Act was intended to prevent the speculation that led to the South Sea Bubble bust. The Act was one of the earliest laws introduced by a capitalist country to discourage extreme speculation.

South Sea Company: The South Sea Company was a British joint stock company that traded in South America during the 18th Century. The company was involved in the transatlantic slave trade and was given a monopoly over British trade in the region. Similar to the Mississippi Bubble, speculation drove the company's share price up until it suddenly burst in 1720.

Stagflation: An economic phenomenon where inflation and unemployment both rise. Until the 1960's and 1970's, most economists thought there was an inverse correlation between inflation and unemployment that stopped them from both increasing. However, the 'Philips curve' theory that assumed this inverse correlation was disproved in the 1960's and 1970's when inflation and unemployment increased throughout Western economies.

Sub-prime lending: Financial lending to people who could not ordinarily afford to make a deposit on a mortgage. The sub-prime crisis was an important cause of the American economic recession that started in late 2007. The sub-prime crisis involved banks offering securitised mortgages to people who would not normally be able to afford them. Large investment banks and credit rating agencies were complicit in the sub-prime crisis and many, such as Lehman Brothers, were brought down by sub-prime lending liabilities.

Treaty of Versailles: The Treaty of Versailles was the peace treaty that concluded World War I between the Central Powers comprising Germany and the Austro-Hungarian Empire and the Triple Entente made up of Great Britain, France and Russia. The Versailles Treaty held Germany responsible for the war, forced her to pay war reparations to the British and French and redrew German borders to exclude the Rheinland and Saarland. The Versailles Treaty facilitated the rise of the German Nazi Party because of its harsh terms. John Maynard Keynes correctly predicted the Versailles Treaty would lead to another world war in *The Economic Consequences of the Peace*.

Tulip mania: Describes the tulip bubble mania in the Netherlands from 1635-7. The Dutch tulip mania is widely considered the first speculative bubble in the history of capitalism. The prices of tulip bulbs increased exponentially until they eventually collapsed. Along with the Mississippi and South Sea Bubbles, the Dutch tulip mania illustrates how frenzied speculation leads to giant bubbles and busts.

U.S. Federal Reserve: is America's central bank. The Fed was created by an act of Congress passed in 1913. The creation of the Federal Reserve ended the free bank era that had existed for most of American history since independence. Despite populist opposition to central banks in early U.S. history, the Fed has survived and is now a powerful force in the American economy. Ben Bernanke is the current head of the Federal Reserve.

WorkChoices: The name of the Howard government's industrial relations reforms that were introduced in 2006. The WorkChoices legislation was extremely divisive, with businesses supporting it and unions opposing it. WorkChoices gave more power to employers at the expense of employees and unions. WorkChoices' unpopularity with the Australian people is cited as a major cause of the Howard government's 2007 federal election defeat.

World Bank: is an international organisation that provides loans conditional on economic policy changes. The World Bank was established at the Bretton Woods Conference in 1944 and now has more than 180 members. World Bank loans require countries to improve their openness to the world economy by lowering tariffs, floating exchange rates and privatising state assets. By convention, the President of the World Bank is an American appointee.

Yuan: The Yuan, or Renminbi, is China's national currency. The Yuan is traded at a fixed exchange rate set by the Chinese government. The government has successfully set the Yuan at an artificially low level to give Chinese exports a key advantage in international trade. Calls are growing in the United States for the Chinese government to raise the Yuan's value or abandon the fixed exchange rate entirely.

Appendix on data

Bank Rate, UK, 1800 to 1914
Sir John Clapham, The Bank of England. A History, Volume II, 1797-1914, Cambridge, at the University Press, 1944, Reprinted 1958, Appendix B.

(Goods & Services) Inflation, Australia
Consumer price index, Australia, accumulated in PD Jonson private files.

(Goods & Services) Inflation, USA
Consumer price index, USA, accumulated in PD Jonson private files.

Unemployment, Australia
Rate of unemployment, Australia, accumulated in PD Jonson private files.

Unemployment, USA
Rate of unemployment, USA, accumulated in PD Jonson private files.

Australian dollar exchange rate, US/Australia
US/Australia exchange rate, accumulated in PD Jonson private files.

Share prices, Twentieth Century
- USA, Dow Jones Industrial Average
- USA, NASDAQ Composite Index
- Singapore, Straits Times Index
- Japan, Nikkei 225 Index
- Shanghai Composite Index

Data provided by author's broker. JK Galbraith in *The Great Crash 1929*, prefers The *New York Times* industrial average index, the 'arithmetical, unweighted' average of 25 'good, sound stocks with regular price changes and generally active markets'. (Galbraith, *The Great Crash 1929*, Footnote 8, p.7).

Share prices, USA, S&P 500, 1800 to 1914.
Global Financial Data, Inc, S&P 500, 1791-2010

Share prices, UK, FTSE All Share index, 1800 to 1914
Finfacts Ireland website
http://www.finfacts.com/Private/curency/ftseperformance.htm.

Index

Age of Aquarius, 6, 45-50, 162, 191, 194-195, 198, 204, 207, 211, 249, 283

Age of Innovation, 6, 34, 44-45, 76, 121, 123, 146, 222

Aggregate demand, 185, 231, 237

America. See United States

American Civil War, 43, 71, 74, 136-137

American isolationism, 271

Animal spirits, 26, 76, 182, 233. See also Keynesianism

Ashton, Thomas S., 98, 121-122

Association of Southeast Asian Nations (ASEAN), 216

Australian dollar, 12, 162-163, 197, 273

Australian Labor Party, 23, 155, 187

Authoritarian capitalism, 32, 248

Bank of England, 6, 14, 21, 28, 46, 101, 105-107, 109, 114, 121, 123, 128, 131-132, 135-137, 140, 142, 174, 188, 238, 240, 278

Bank for International Settlement, 280

Bank rate, 122-125, 131, 134-137, 140, 174, 216, 278

Bear Stearns, 19

Bernanke, Ben, 5, 25, 28, 169, 185, 239, 249, 253, 256

BHP Billiton, 11, 17

Blainey, Geoffrey, 1-2, 43-44, 65, 70, 75, 77, 88, 133, 144, 147, 149, 156-158, 182

Bolsheviks, 46, 67, 248

Bonaparte, Napoleon, 42, 64-65

British East India Company, 81

Bush, George W., 23, 27, 253

Business cycle, 11, 38, 43, 141

China, 7, 10, 12, 15, 17-18, 22-23, 27, 29, 35, 46, 54, 60-61, 69-70, 72-74, 102, 143, 165, 194-195, 198, 209, 211, 220-221, 235-237, 248, 257-258, 266-269, 271-272, 276, 278-279, 283-285

Churchill, Winston, 184, 236, 266

Clapham, John, 1, 132-137, 140, 270

Climate change, 23, 265, 279, 284

Commonwealth Bank, 187-188

Communism, 72-74, 167, 178, 248, 276

Comparative advantage, 33

Corn Laws, 130

Corporatism, 274

Costello, Peter, 164

Creative Destruction, 36

Deflation, 24, 43, 44, 51, 137, 141, 186, 204, 213, 236, 244, 246

Democractic capitalism, 32, 61

Democracy, 5, 9, 34, 36, 73-74, 76, 210, 225, 249, 269, 274-275, 285

Disequilibrium, 18, 86, 118, 235

Dow Jones Industrial Index, 16, 19

Drake, Francis, 58

Dutch East India Company, 41, 80, 99

Dutch Tulip Boom, 6, 79

Dutch West India Company, 62

Economist, The, 25, 131

Eureka Rebellion, 144

European Union (EU), 32, 61, 276

Externalities, 270

Federal Reserve, 5, 28, 169, 172-175, 178, 180, 188, 195, 197, 206, 240, 243

Ferguson, Niall, 1, 32, 42, 52, 76-77, 80-81, 185, 241, 243-245, 278

Fraser, Malcolm, 204

French Revolution, 42, 64, 132

Friedman, Milton, 1, 17, 185, 193, 196, 233-234, 237

Galbraith, John Kenneth, 1, 14, 28, 167-168, 170-177, 179-180, 182-186, 188-189, 240, 243

Garnaut, Ross, 2, 29, 162, 214, 284

Germany, 35, 45-47, 60, 66-68, 76, 83, 98, 137, 139-140, 181, 184, 198, 268

Glass-Steagall Act, 8, 13, 50, 175, 252

Global Financial Crisis (GFC), 5, 27, 29, 46, 52, 56, 90, 165, 166, 207, 214, 255, 258, 276, 281

Globalisation, 44-45, 52, 97, 105, 123, 264, 270, 275-276

Gold standard, 6, 8, 46, 48-49, 123, 130, 133, 141-142, 169, 185, 198, 198-199, 235-236, 238-239, 255, 257-258"

Goldman Sachs, 28, 165, 176

Great Depression, 5-6, 10-12, 21, 27, 39, 46-47, 55-56, 76, 150, 161, 167, 181, 183, 185, 187-188, 230, 233, 253-254, 260, 276

Great Society, 48, 194

Greenspan, Alan, 5, 13, 18, 25, 51-52, 86-87, 172, 188, 239, 249, 256

Hawke, R.J. (Bob), 2, 162, 164, 204

Hayek, Friedrich A., 1, 255

House of Lords, 107, 130

Howard, John, 2, 12, 164, 205

Hu, Jintao, 22

Hume, David, 1, 233

Imperfect information, 230

Inequality, 67, 168, 254, 279, 282

Inflation (asset), 10, 13, 16-20, 22-25, 236, 238, 258, 259

Inflation (general), 17, 43, 44, 50, 191-206, 244, 249, 250, 254, 264

Inflation (goods and services), 8, 10, 17, 18, 22-25, 236, 238, 258-259

International Monetary Fund (IMF), 21, 24, 216, 257-258, 280

Internet, 6, 73, 94, 222, 225, 227, 239, 269-270

Invisible hand, 29, 33, 128, 229, 245, 248, 270, 285

Islam, 61, 74, 266-267

Isolationism, USA, 74, 268, 271

Japan, 7, 19, 32, 50-51, 53, 55, 57, 60-61, 66, 68, 72, 76, 92-93, 161, 209-214, 216, 220-221, 242, 244, 268-269

Johnson, Lyndon B., 194

Keating, Paul, 2, 163-164, 197, 204-205

Kennedy, Paul, 60, 65-66

Keynes, John Maynard, 1, 26, 45-46, 58, 66-67, 122, 167-168, 182, 189, 228-231, 233, 242, 254, 258, 264

Keynesianism, 47, 49, 231, 242, 277

Kindelberger, Charles P., 41, 55, 98

Korean War, 48, 72, 145, 162

Laffer, Arthur, 232

Laissez-faire capitalism, 32-33, 132, 160, 276-277

Law, John, 41, 52, 80-81, 97-104, 108, 111-113, 119, 126, 141, 195, 238-239

Lehman Brothers, 14, 27-28, 91, 186, 253

Leverage, 15, 37, 41, 114, 154, 166, 176

Lincoln, Abraham, 136

Louisiana Purchase, 68

MacKay, Charles, 1, 5-6, 82-90, 100-102, 111, 113-114, 117, 119, 251

Main Street, 5, 109

Malthusian theory, 79

Marvellous Melbourne, 6, 124, 143, 146, 150, 166.

Marx, Karl, 10, 35, 54, 182

Mayne, Stephen, 225

McArthur, Stewart, 1

McGuinness, P.P., 1

Melbourne. See Marvellous Melbourne

Menzies, Robert, 204

Mercantilism, 32-33

Mill, John Stuart, 33

Minsky, Hyman, 1, 235-236, 239

Mississippi Bubble, 42, 53, 90, 97, 100

Monetary policy, 5, 7-8, 10, 18, 24, 26,

48-49, 52, 121, 137, 195, 197, 204, 236, 249, 256-259, 263-264, 278, 279-280, 283

Monopoly, 33, 35, 80, 102, 252, 274, 276

Moral Hazard, 5, 19, 232, 253-254, 281

Napoleonic Wars, 42-43, 64, 65, 126, 132

NASDAQ index, 223

Nathan Rothschild. See Rothschild family

National debt, 97, 99-100, 103, 107-108, 118. See also public debt

New York Stock Exchange (NYSE), 139

Nixon, Richard, 49, 195, 211, 238

Northern Rock, 14

Obama, Barack, 12, 23, 26

Oil, 20, 22, 24-26, 49-50, 55, 74, 92, 94, 162, 191, 194, 211, 217, 230, 237, 268-269, 271

Opium Wars, 69, 209

Organisation of the Petroleum Exporting Countries (OPEC), 49, 194

Paulson, Hank, 21

Phillips curve, 193-194, 237

Privatisation, 103, 164

Public debt, 80, 105

Quantitative easing, 11, 169, 189, 249, 283. See also inflation

Queen Elizabeth I, 58

Reagan, Ronald, 74, 197

Reserve Bank of Australia (RBA), 17-18, 20, 23-24, 27, 27, 49, 88, 153, 163-164, 197, 206, 240

Ricardo, David, 33

Roaring Twenties, 6, 36, 39, 52, 167-168, 171, 260

Roosevelt, Franklin D., 186, 188

Rothschild family, 9, 42, 127-128

Royal Bank of France, 102

Rudd, Kevin, 23

Say, Jean-Baptiste, 33

Schedvin, Boris, 2, 181, 187-188

Schumpeter, Joseph, 36, 98, 118, 141

Skidelsky, Robert, 1, 12, 26-28

Smith, Adam, 1, 33, 73, 122, 229

Smoot-Hawley tariff, 185

Socialist capitalism, 32

Soros, George, 37, 228

South Sea Bubble, 41, 53, 90, 94, 97, 104-105, 127

Standard and Poors Index (S&P), 36

Stevens, Glenn, 17, 24

Stiglitz, Joseph, 25

Sub-prime crisis, 12-14, 151, 156

Sub-prime mortgages, 19. See also sub-prime crisis

Suez Canal, 137, 148

Thatcher, Margaret, 196, 244

The Bank Act, 132, 137, 140

Tiger economies, 209, 215-216

Treaty of Versailles, 66-67

Tulipmania, 39, 41, 81-82, 85-86, 89-91, 94-95, 97, 118

Twin Bubbles of 1720,

Unemployment, 11, 23, 25, 44, 46, 136, 158, 181, 185, 187-189, 191, 191, 193-194, 196, 204-207, 237, 240, 243, 277

United Nations (UN), 284

United States of America, 57, 66, 68, 70-71, 73, 81, 101, 123, 135, 137, 139, 141, 147, 149, 167, 181, 185, 188, 206, 210, 227, 238, 252, 258-259

Victoria (colony and state of), 143-150, 152-156, 160-161, 253

Vietnam War, 72

Volcker, Paul, 8, 50, 54, 196-197, 205-206, 252

Wall Street, 5-6, 13, 15, 28, 37, 54, 93, 105, 110, 167, 170-171, 174, 176-177, 179-180, 184, 257

Wen, Jiabao, 285

Whitlam, Gough, 162, 195, 204-205

World Bank, 217

World War I, 43, 60, 67, 76, 124, 198, 236

World War II, 38, 51, 53, 55, 65, 68-69, 72, 76, 210, 245, 260

World Wide Web. See Internet

Zhou, Xiaochuan, 258

www.ingramcontent.com/pod-product-compliance
Lightning Source LLC
Chambersburg PA
CBHW021502210326
41599CB00012B/1100